A Critic's Notebook

BOOKS BY IRVING HOWE

Selected Writings, 1950–1990
The American Newness
Socialism and America
A Margin of Hope
Celebrations and Attacks
Leon Trotsky
World of Our Fathers
    (with the assistance of
    Kenneth Libo)
The Critical Point
Decline of the New
Steady Work: Essays in the Politics of
    Democratic Radicalism,
    1953–1966
Thomas Hardy: A Critical Study
A World More Attractive
The American Communist Party:
    A Critical History
    (with Lewis Coser)
Politics and the Novel
William Faulkner: A Critical Study
Sherwood Anderson: A Critical
    Biography
The U.A.W. and Walter Reuther
    (with B. J. Widick)

EDITED BY IRVING HOWE

The Penguin Book of Modern
    Yiddish Verse
    (with Ruth R. Wisse and Khone
    Shmeruk)
Short Shorts: An Anthology of the
    Shortest Stories
    (with Ilana Wiener Howe)
How We Lived
    (with Kenneth Libo)
The World of the Blue-Collar Worker
Essential Works of Socialism
The Seventies: Problems & Proposals
    (with Michael Harrington)
Jewish American Stories
Voices from the Yiddish
    (with Eliezer Greenberg)
A Treasury of Yiddish Poetry
    (with Eliezer Greenberg)
The Idea of the Modern
The Basic Writings of Trotsky
The Radical Imagination
Edith Wharton: A Critical Collection
The Radical Papers
A Treasury of Yiddish Stories
    (with Eliezer Greenberg)

IRVING HOWE

A Critic's Notebook

EDITED AND INTRODUCED BY
Nicholas Howe

A HARVEST BOOK
HARCOURT BRACE & COMPANY
SAN DIEGO   NEW YORK   LONDON

Library of Congress Cataloging-in-Publication Data
Howe, Irving.
A critic's notebook/Irving Howe; edited and introduced by
Nicholas Howe.—1st Harvest ed.
p.   cm—(A Harvest Book)
Originally published: New York: Harcourt Brace, c1994.
Includes index.
ISBN 0-15-600257-4
1. Criticism. 2. Literature—History and criticism.
I. Howe, Nicholas.   II. Title.
[PN81.H54   1995]
823.009—dc20   95-17560

Designed by Lori J. McThomas

Printed in the United States of America

First Harvest edition 1995
A B C D E

Contents

A Critic's Notebook

Introduction

DURING THE LAST five or six years of his life, my father wrote the essays on fiction gathered here as *A Critic's Notebook*. Though he had completed each of these pieces when he died in May 1993, he always imagined there would be another twelve or fifteen in this book. From the start, it was to be a mosaic of essays that would be diverse, even quirky, in content. In October 1992, he wrote to me: "Here's the list of titles so far. It's bewildering in its variety, I guess. Putting it in alphabetical order may make it seem less so." If his earlier criticism had been strictly focused by the choice of topic, as in *Politics and the Novel*, or by the shape of an author's career, as in his books on Anderson, Faulkner, and Hardy, this was to be a freer, more idiosyncratic project: a notebook of finished pieces rather than preliminary jottings. At first he called it "Selected Short Subjects," but rejected that as portentous. Among friends, he spoke of it as his *shtiklakh*, from the Yiddish for "little pieces" or "morsels," or, in his own idiom, for the turns of an accomplished performer. With a bemused irony no English title could summon, *shtiklakh* conveyed his pleasure in writing a more fragmentary criticism.

For there is something unexpected about these pieces when read as his work. Sometimes it is a matter of subject, as when he invents the category of "punitive fiction"; sometimes it is the choice of writers, as when late in his long career he turns to Tolstoy; sometimes it is a starkly luminous style that forgoes the virtuoso moves and polemical thrusts of his earlier work. As I edited these pieces, I kept hearing a passage from his 1979 essay on *Daniel Deronda* that traces the curve of a novelist's life:

> Toward the end of their careers, great writers are sometimes roused to a new energy by thoughts of risk. Some final stab at an area of human experience they had neglected or at a theme only recently become urgent: this excites their imaginations. They leave behind assured achievement, all they have done well and could still do better, and start clambering up the slopes of uncertainty and experiment. Watching them as they slide, slip, and start up again can be very moving—it can also make one very nervous.

He would have been embarrassed, even irritated, that I quote this passage to describe his last essays. He resisted the idea that one could talk about the ephemeral work of critics in the way he talks about the authors of *Persuasion*, *Our Mutual Friend*, and *Daniel Deronda*. I do so not to make a claim of greatness, for that is not a son's right, but to suggest that he knew the risks he ran in seeking a new form and voice late in his career.

During the last twenty years of his life, my father turned more and more in his books to his own past and the political milieu in which he grew up: *World of Our Fathers* (1976), *Leon Trotsky* (1978), *A Margin of Hope* (1982), *Socialism and America* (1985). He developed a voice in these books that made a shared melody of the public and the private, the analytic and the remembered. As he grew older, he found himself in a situation much like the one he ascribes to George Eliot: "Her work is torn between the modern passion for criticism, a criticism often grazing negation, and an intuitive love for the positive virtues, mostly nestling in memory." And as he gave himself over to memory in this precise and chastening way, he wrote relatively little criticism during those years, and that chiefly on fiction writers who caught his interest. Pieces on Leskov, J. M. Coetzee, and Raymond Carver come to mind. The anxiety that he might fall into repetition as a critic partly explains this particular silence in the 1970s and 1980s. His only extended literary work of this period, *The American Newness* (1986), was a long-contemplated engagement with writers like Emerson and Thoreau to whom, as both American and socialist, he had deeply ambivalent responses. By taking on these figures, he could avoid retreating into familiar writers and old themes. For the same reason, he decided not to write a sequel to *Politics and the Novel*. Much as he admired George Konrad, Milan Kundera, Gabriel García Márquez, Nadine Gordimer, J. M. Coetzee, and other contemporaries, he worried that he would pay too high a price for this form of self-repetition.

Yet his conversation during these years was full of talk about novels and the delight he found in them; he continued to give seminars on fiction at the Graduate Center of the City University of New York through the mid-1980s. Looking back, I think he knew he would return to criticism. I think he also knew this return would be worth making only if it yielded a different voice and style. Speaking at a memorial service for my father, Leon Wieseltier caught this change when he described the pieces from *A Critic's Notebook* that he had printed in *The New Republic*:

> They had the pellucid and re-invigorated qualities of late works: deceptive in their simplicity and determined in their clarity; contemptuous of all verbal and mental tricks; elementary in their themes and artisanal in their language. They were last words in a provisional tone—provisional last words, a contradiction in anyone else's hands, an achievement in Irving's hands.

From the start my father knew that the form he selected for *A Critic's Notebook* had its danger as well as its allure. The brief entry—ideally a piece of six or eight pages—would have a focused energy that a longer piece could not equal. He wanted to write only about what compelled him most joyously, and knew he no longer needed to argue as aggressively as he once had. By his life's work, he had earned the allusive, darting lucidity of *shtiklakh*, of bits and pieces that proved their value by freeing themselves from the essay's formal conventions.

Yet the danger was that the entries would grow into full essays because the subjects that most intrigued him were those least likely to fit the confines of a notebook entry. In early 1987, he wrote to me: "I'm starting to think and plan that book on fiction. One problem is that every item I think about seems likely to turn into a full-scale essay, which would violate the central idea of the book—you know, entries, etc. Let's talk about it?" Some of the topics did grow into long essays: "How Are Characters Created?" and "The Self in Literature" are the most obvious examples. But who, he would ask when we did talk about this problem, who can be brief on *these* topics? On others, he felt freer to sketch a topic or a writer without enforcing connections between his ideas. "Tolstoy: Five Comments" is exactly that, united only by a love for the late Tolstoy. So too with "Dickens: Three Notes" and, more amusingly because more audaciously, with the three entries devoted to the book's ostensible subject, "Criticism of Fiction." Such titles seem to say that there should be no last words on writers and subjects we love. A few *shtiklakh* will do.

Over his last years, my father felt an increasing sense that there were things he still wanted to say about fiction. Earlier, when he wrote long books, he might have dismissed the notebook form as incomplete, tentative, or, worst of all, self-indulgent. Faced with thoughts of mortality, though, he saw it as the form that could ease his fears and sustain his working life. These thoughts found expression in one of the last pieces he wrote for this book, the section on punitive fiction; its fascination with novels that offer no redemptive vision of human suffering followed from his own time in the hospital. In a letter of November 1992 to me, he described it knowingly as a "rather odd piece, which will not win universal acclaim but which I'm prepared to stand by." That might also have been his judgment of the book as a whole.

This sense of mortality explains why he wrote piece by piece, why he moved on to the next only after finishing the one at hand. He would have gone back, had he lived, to revise these pieces. After he reread *The Red and the Black* in the last year of his life, he said that he would have to rework "Farce and Fiction" because it had nothing about Stendhal. But these pieces were not early drafts to be polished in the fullness of time. Except for the section on style that I have gathered, each piece was completed and stored away so that it could be published without embarrassment. Most had on the first page a scribbled phrase or, more often, a check mark to signal that they were ready. This mark could also mean that he had revised a piece after it appeared in a magazine and planned to use the new version for *A Critic's Notebook*. I have followed these signals in establishing the text for this book. The only work that remained was checking quotations for accuracy; I have located many of these passages, but others have eluded me.

In the early spring of 1993, he told me that there were enough pieces for *A Critic's Notebook* to be published as it stood. The section I have called "Style and the Novel: Some Preliminary Paragraphs" was left on his desk when he died, though not in the form it appears here. He had begun at least four entries on style as a way of tackling a subject that he always spoke of as one of the most daunting. I do not know if he would have completed all or any of them, or if he would have combined them. These drafts are not ready for publication, but each has some sentences of finished quality which contain the insight that occasioned the piece and that would have been developed at length. In selecting these fragments I have violated his instruction that the book contain only finished pieces. I could not, however, exclude sentences of value from this critic's notebook simply because they were fragments of an unfinished *shtikl*.

The essays in this book reflect more than his other literary work my father's life as a teacher. I do not mean that they speak in a voice stiff with certainty, but, rather, that they are rich with the wonder that comes of reading and teaching novels across a lifetime. This book did not grow from a desire to correct the record or to reengage earlier arguments, but from a continual reading that opened and enlarged his thinking about fiction. His ideas came to ripeness when he had more time, after retirement, to think them through; they were the fruit of more than thirty years of talking about novels. The pieces in *A Critic's Notebook* concern some of the writers he taught regularly: Fielding, Sterne, Dickens, George Eliot, Gissing, Tolstoy, Kipling. Yet he puts these writers to uses not commonly found in surveys of the novel or thematic courses about fiction. There is a sense of ease in these pieces that makes itself felt less in the prose than in the choice of subjects.

Perhaps the most teacherly piece here is "On 'Gratuitous Details,' " those "unexpected pleasures . . . [that] strike us as moments of virtuosity, sometimes revelation." Dostoevsky is the master of the gratuitous detail because no writer better repays his virtuosity with revelation. The details that the critic notices—in Raskolnikov's dream it must be a *decrepit* carthorse that is beaten to death; in his remark that he likes streetsinging "on a cold, dark, damp autumn evening" he has to add "it must be damp"—are those that emerge from the novelist's imagination to "stay in memory" and thus to lead readers back to *Crime and Punishment*.

The detail that catches the critic's eye in a very different novel, *To the Lighthouse*, belongs because Virginia Woolf's characters cannot quite put into words what they wish to express. In a passage my father mentioned frequently in conversation, Woolf says of Mrs. Ramsay: "It was only that she never could say what she felt. Was there no crumb on his coat? Nothing she could do for him?" The detail of the crumb became for my father a measure of how people thought about fiction. If they understood why it had to be a crumb, why that detail conveyed a gesture of love beyond human articulation, then they were good readers. And that was the way he taught: not with the ideological rigor that one might expect of this political man, but with an attention to detail and language that conveyed his fascination with novelistic technique. "It's like the crumb" became his shorthand phrase to describe a successful "gratuitous detail" in novels or movies. At the end of the essay, he uses this matter of detail to describe what it means to live one's life as a reader: "Perhaps more than to the books in which they appear, it is to such moments, such 'gratuitous details' that we will return, as an index of memory."

As detail turns into story, it takes on the form of anecdote. In Sholom Aleichem's "A Yom Kippur Scandal," the anecdote tells of a local prodigy caught breaking the fast in the synagogue on the highest of holy days; the detail determines that the rabbi and congregation should, when they empty his pockets, discover "some well-gnawed chicken bones and a few dozen plum pits still moist from chewing." Not just a vague phrase, but chicken bones and plum pits, the remains of real food! The anecdote as form works best in writers like Leskov, Mark Twain, Sholom Aleichem, and Silone who belong neither to the tradition of the social novel nor to that of modernist experiment. This entry on the anecdote is the critic's homage to the traditional world of his fathers or, more truly, to the way in which he could hold to that world: "One of its attractions is that in times of dislocation, the anecdote holds out the possibility that human beings may still connect, perhaps only briefly, through memory and story."

The anecdote, as it edges toward becoming a parable, serves as a token of solidarity among those who have no other way to speak of their common plight. My father's favorite anecdote, one remembered in many of his books, comes from Silone. The novelist tells how his father chastised him because, as a young boy, he laughed at a man arrested by the police:

> "Never make fun of a man who's been arrested! Never!"
> "Why not?"
> "Because he can't defend himself. And because he may be innocent. In any case, because he's unhappy."

This sense of outrage at suffering inflicted on the poor and defenseless was the root of my father's politics. He told this anecdote because it acknowledged, to borrow again from Silone, his "choice of comrades." Nowhere, for that reason, does the anecdote take on a sharper edge in his writing than when he uses it to set his distance from Emerson in *The American Newness*:

> It would be unjust to think that Emerson would not have been touched by these stories [this anecdote from Silone and another from Rashi's *Commentaries*], or the ideas behind them, quite as much as we are. But it does seem fair to suggest that, with their evocation of such values as sociability and solidarity, these are not the kinds of stories he would have been likely to tell— one of his strange flaws is his indifference to stories in general.

This is why anecdotes matter and why the essay on anecdote, the first in *A Critic's Notebook*, should open: "You won't find much about the anecdote in studies of literary genre: it seems too humble a form to attract the eye of the theorist."

I could always tell my father was thinking about a new piece for this book when I answered the phone and heard, almost before his greeting, "Who's written something good on anecdotes? on the common reader? on tone in fiction?" Once in a while I could give him a suggestion, but more often I fell back on the resources of colleagues and friends, just as he did. When no one could suggest something on the topic he wanted, he would grumble with good-natured dismay: "How come nobody's written about anecdotes? All those books on theory and nobody has anything to say about anecdotes! Or the common reader! Why can't anyone tell me exactly what Dr. Johnson meant by that phrase?" When no one could give him a reference, he knew he'd hit on another *shtikl*. From these inquiries grew a network of friends and family; some who were part of it I know, others only he knew. He would have thanked each by name; I do so now collectively.

The most beautiful lament for my father came from Michael Walzer, who wrote in *Dissent* of his comrade and friend: "He was driven by a passion, not an ideology. He was politically committed like a man in love: attuned to the needs of the hour, to the actual experience of political life." These words are true, I think, of the man as a whole. For he read novels like a man in love: attuned to their form and style, to the experience of being unable to resist their pleasures. As a critic he was driven by his passions, not by fashions in literary practice or theory.

He was hard to classify as a critic, except perhaps by a phrase he made popular, "New York Intellectual." In the 1950s, when he began, he was often dismissed as a political or social critic by the reigning formalists, yet he was friendly with New Critics such as Allen Tate and Austin Warren. Later in his career he was judged insufficiently theoretical—he would have said, doctrinaire—for the reigning ideological critics, though the last review he wrote could mix real praise with sharp criticism of Edward Said's *Culture and Imperialism*. Throughout his career he mocked claims of methodological or theoretical purity that others rode to academic success and a coterie of disciples. He developed as a critic so that he was able late in life to write about authors he could not when young (Tolstoy, most obviously) but he was never predictable and he had throughout an endearing taste for unfashionable authors.

His productivity and versatility made him a hard writer to categorize, and it seemed easier for some in the months after his death to see only the political figure, the polemicist, the editor of *Dissent*, the man who did not stop worrying. His work as a literary critic sometimes passed without notice or was seen simply as respite from the struggle. At times it might have been so, as when he found great joy in editing Yiddish poetry during the 1960s. But to see the criticism as less fundamental to the man than the politics is a mistake no one who knew him would make. The ties between the political and the literary give his work its flavor and energy, but in ways that elude doctrinaire phrases or sectarian labels.

At a quick glance, *A Critic's Notebook* might seem the most literary of his books—it concerns itself with old-fashioned concepts of character and style, tone and genre—and thus seems distant from politics or its representation. Yet throughout this notebook there is the same imagination that animated his politics, that saw politics and literature not as ideology or theory but as lived experience bound by a sense of story. He had limits as a critic, but the "strange indifference to stories" he found in Emerson was not one of them. Stories were for him a way to think about the world.

There is a telling moment in "How Are Characters Conceived?" that gets at the unity of his work. Writing of Turgenev and the difficulties that many of his early readers, including his great friend Henry James, had with the political characters in *Fathers and Sons*, he observes:

> But readers brought up on Anglo-Saxon literature, with its bias
> in favor of a literature unalloyed with ideology, are not inclined
> to suppose that characters conceived through tendencies of pub-
> lic thought can have incisiveness of form or urgency of speech.

Someone once joked not unkindly that my father was the last nineteenth-century Russian writer. His intellectual style comes from a milieu where characters are incisive and urgent precisely because they live within these "tendencies of public thought." He knew the differences between literature and politics but he also knew that he worked best in the space where they overlap.

Many of the pieces here move between literature and politics. An essay will often open with a problem of literary interpretation: Who was the common reader in the eighteenth century? Why did Sir Walter Scott, once the most popular writer in the world, fall out of the canon? These might seem topics best left to literary historians until, surprisingly, the essay turns to engage historical and political circumstances.

This is the turn a writer might sketch in a notebook—state the theme, consider examples, plot an interpretation—in order to transform the terms of the question. The idea of the common reader or the problem of Scott is, finally, too interesting as a matter of cultural or ideological change to be left to the literary historian. The notebook form keeps the relation between literature and politics fluid.

In the essay on "The Common Reader," this move leads to the idea of a public democratic culture. After noting "the loss of faith, perhaps even interest, in the idea of the common reader" in contemporary culture, it surveys Dr. Johnson, Virginia Woolf, the New Critics, and the New York Critics—all familiar literary history. But the last stage of this chronicle, as it brings the New York Critics into the academic world, marks the crucial shift in the essay. It is also the story of my father's life. Perhaps for that reason, he releases a few barbs at the academic politics and "craft elitism" of deconstructionism and Marxism (which "has gone to the universities to die in comfort"). His impatience with the claims of theory came from an older sense of the responsibilities that literary figures owe their public. His hope for a democratic culture may seem dated or bourgeois to those in the academic vanguard but it has at its heart the liberating idea that there should be a public of readers "neither academic nor professionally literary, perhaps small, but providing writers with a flow of sentiment and response." To the end, he kept this utopian faith in the reader.

He prized clarity and loved it in literature when it yielded, even as it complicated and troubled our sense of things, some telling representation of experience. And if that were true of novelists, then it had also to be true of critics. They owed readers the respect of a direct and lucid prose. The spare style of these essays, what Leon Wieseltier calls their "artisanal" language, was meant as a political challenge to the obscurantist prose of academic criticism. If you announce the death of the common reader in jargon, he would have said, you've probably had a hand in the murder.

Among the very few working papers my father left on his death were notes for pieces he planned to write for *A Critic's Notebook*. There would have been, to judge from these notes, sections on Dickens's *Great Expectations*, Gissing's *The Odd Women*, and Frederic's *The Damnation of Theron Ware*. He also wrote a series of sentences about George Meredith that suggest the form his entry on that novelist would have taken:

> His opening chapters are almost impassable, like terribly bad overtures, which make you want immediately to leave the theater.
>
> His prose is insufferable because it is relentless, he doesn't stop, he piles one image on top of another, one *mot* on top of another, he has no sense of interval or rest, he wears one down and then out.
>
> Yet there is great intelligence in his work, not so much in the passages he expects to be quoted as in the situations, the figures: the man has a sense of human motivation.

And then the sentence that pulls these ideas into focus: "He is not so much brilliant as nervous."

Meredith appears in the notes for another entry, one on the ways poets might be read as story writers. Among them would have been George Crabbe, the Meredith of *Modern*

Love, and Edwin Arlington Robinson. My father once considered a short book on these three—along with such others as Thomas Hardy and Edward Thomas—as poets of everyday life. Their restrained style and stubborn wisdom moved him, and he thought they deserved better than what they had generally received from critics. The case he would have made for them in *A Critic's Notebook* is suggested by this paragraph:

> Robinson's *Isaac and Archibald* is the poem that one can most easily see as a good short story. The poem has the same "narrative time" as a short story, and its quiet tone could easily be imagined as that of a quiet story by . . . who? The psychological setting is almost Jamesian, except that James would not deal with this setting or such rural characters. Wharton? No; she is too harsh in "Summer" for this sort of pastoral psychology & elegiac tenderness. What would be lost in a prose version? Some lovely verse; but the story itself could easily be transferred.

When he goes on to say that *Modern Love* offers "a sequence of psychological insights & interpretations of a novel that is not there, or a story that is not there, but is glimpsed," we can glimpse his reason for this entry on poets. It would have let him think about how some writers tell their stories in shadow form and thus would have complemented entries on the dense narratives of Dickens and Tolstoy.

Less predictably, because nothing in my father's work prepared for it, there would also have been a portrait of Max Frisch. His interest in Frisch can be sensed from this note about the sort of novel he wrote: "[its] fundamental unit: the panel or vignette, a segment not so much of narrative as of portrayal. Best in showing a 'situation,' two figures entangled with one another." The fit between critic and novelist lies in this formal sense of panel or entry, but it extends to a vision of writing. He calls Frisch's *Gantenbein* the "most experimental of his novels" and notes its "segments/panels/vignettes." More intriguing, he quotes a passage from that novel—"A man has been through an experience, now he is looking for the story to go with it"—and adds, it is "a key to F[risch]'s work." The idea that a man should search for the story to go with his experience would have seemed compelling, even inevitable, to my father's sense of life.

Of the pieces sketched but never written, the most haunting is called "Picnics & Ponds." Of all the pieces he wrote or thought to write, this would have best fitted his vision of *A Critic's Notebook*. It centers on an event and a locale familiar to all readers but largely unnoticed by critics:

> In quiet novels, where "nothing" happens, it becomes convenient for the writer to gather together his/her characters in a sort of bunch or knot and force a confrontation of temperaments or needs. A convenient way of doing this is to arrange a picnic, since, after all, no one can question or undermine the verisimilitude of a picnic: it has a built-in probability. People come to a picnic with a certain mild expectation: they don't think they'll be swept off their feet, or knocked down, but "something" may happen.

The sketch for "Picnics & Ponds" moves first to *Emma*—"the greatest picnic in literature"—and then to *A Room with a View*. If Austen's depiction "is precise and clear: the limits of her world reveal its capacities," by contrast Forster's "limits are mostly aspirations, reachings, and the language is accordingly slippery, vague, amorphous." The picnic scene in Forster is "inferior" to that in Austen. "But the odd thing is that what is finally effective in EMF is often this 'poetry' of his, this fumbling rhetoric—it is this which forms his signature, just as the mordant irony forms Jane Austen's. Without this, EMF's books would be merely small." The notes for "Picnics & Ponds" end in these abruptly suggestive sentences: "And to reinforce, so to say, the picnic, EMF brings in the pond, with the bath & quasi-homosexual aspect, a little Lawrentian in touch, smallish scale. The pond, so to say, fulfills the picnic."

I am not entirely certain where this piece would have gone had my father lived to write it, but I sense it would have been somewhere he had never been before as a critic. Perhaps the best way to evoke that place, and thus to introduce this incomplete yet oddly finished notebook, is to quote the epigraph he offered to those novelists who sustained him throughout his life:

> Tolstoy once wrote that "the incompatibility of a man's position with his moral activity is the surest indication of his searching for truth," a remark that could stand as an epigraph for the work of Dickens and Stendhal, George Eliot and Dostoevsky, Flaubert and Hardy, Lawrence and Proust.

—NICHOLAS HOWE

Anecdote and Storyteller

YOU WON'T FIND much about the anecdote in studies of literary genre: it seems too humble a form to attract the eye of the theorist. Nor is the anecdote important in the kinds of nineteenth-century novels of society written by, say, Balzac and George Eliot. As for the twentieth-century modernists, they too find little, if any, use for the anecdote. But in certain kinds of fiction—what might be called the prenovelistic fiction of the age of the novel—it can play a major part, as a survival of the tradition of oral storytelling or at least as a canny simulation of it.

An anecdote is a brief, unelaborated, often humorous account of a single incident, taken to be piquant in its own right, and as such it may be found almost anywhere; but to matter in a larger work, to be more than decorative or incidental, it has to contain the germ of thematic and, occasionally, stylistic development. One of its attractions is that in times of dislocation, the anecdote holds out the possibility that human beings may still connect, perhaps only briefly, through memory and story.

Between anecdote and plot there is a tension or disparity. A tightly plotted novel may include anecdotes, but fundamentally it has no need for them. They are at best diversions, at worst distractions. But a prose fiction that follows the pattern of oral narrative, or that *seems* shrewdly to follow it, can accommodate the anecdote, since the rhythm of event in such a work is likely to be leisurely, with frequent occasions for introducing another voice. In such a fiction, the constraints of "the functional" (which often involves a confusion between discipline and mere tightness) can be avoided.

The anecdote is likely to flourish in fictions that deal with preurban societies—Leskov's provincial Russia, Mark Twain's Mississippi village, Sholom Aleichem's *shtetl*, Silone's Abruzzi. In such societies strong collective memories and myths can still be handed down from generation to generation. The narrative is loose and meandering, its tempo relaxed. Time isn't a problem, there's no place to hurry off to, another story is always welcome, things repeat themselves anyway. The narrator stands firmly at the center, claiming representative status as spokesman or at least as a dubious stepson of his culture.

In the written simulation of oral storytelling, which may entail some idealizing of its social function, there is, however, a curious combination of narrative expansiveness (the storyteller) and verbal compression (the anecdotes). Eager to test his powers, the narrator wants to hold and tease us into a charmed submission. In exchange he offers the lure of story and received wisdom. Maybe that wisdom is fading by now, and we can even wonder whether it hasn't been contrived a little—the sophisticated writer masquerading as folk voice—but often we are glad to be persuaded. Apart from occasional epics, traditional cultures hand down little stories embodying the crux of their experience.

Nikolai Leskov. Typical of this Russian master's work is the narrative sketch which Russian critics call the *skaz*, defined by Victor Erlich as "the mimicry of intonational, lexical, and phraseological mannerisms of a lowbrow narrator. . . . [The *skaz*] enacts and parodies the pattern of a bumbling, chatty oral narration." Plot is here reduced to a minimum or eliminated entirely, while verbal play and recurrent anecdotes come to the foreground.

Leskov's simulated oral narrative encourages a "bumbling" pace, with attractive digressions and remarks, yet the effect is often an unusual combination of speeds: adagio and allegro together. The narrator ambles, the narrative races. We seem—yes, it's odd—to be moving along two planes of velocity, with the narrator chattering away while the internal anecdotes are briskly dispatched.

What Leskov strives for in such brilliant short fictions as "The Robbery" and "The Sealed Angel" is an aura of complete assurance: this man who is talking to us, despite his apparent wanderings, knows his culture inside out, knows the provincial Russia of the first story and the culture of the Old Believers of the second. In some immediate sense—physical, cultural—he can be said to know the Russian countryside better than the Russian masters, and he takes over (or, in some instances, makes up?) its anecdotes with a wonderful ease. Everything moves smoothly, in a high-spirited celebration of the capacity of simple people to bring order to their lives. Leskov draws his readers into a compact that enables his fictional narrator to assume the air of congenial mastery which is the storyteller's privilege. He glides along without having to burden himself with moral dilemmas or other troubling notions. The man who knows the stories of his culture can brush everything else aside.

Mark Twain. He got his start by spinning yarns. "The Celebrated Jumping Frog" and "Jim Baker's Bluejay Yarn" are fragile anecdotes spun out a bit, told in deadpan style and related to the tall tale. They summon a gathering of Westerners around a stove or in a saloon, who listen to the narrator, an expert liar simultaneously able to get across his whoppers and share the audience's amusement at the fact that everyone knows he is fabricating. This sort of pre- or semiliterary storytelling links Twain to the popular entertainers of his time (Artemus Ward, for one), virtuosos of dialect and regional shrewdness, and also to the humor of "the old Southwest," written tales encased in respectable frames.

Anecdotes figure in most of Twain's work: tales of skill told by river pilots in "Old Times on the Mississippi," incidents of guile in *Tom Sawyer*, and the thread of narrative in *Huckleberry Finn*, most strongly through the voice of Nigger Jim, the book's moral center. As Huck and Jim float down the great river, savoring their freedom and companionship, they eat, sleep, and philosophize, exchanging anecdotes in a sort of muted ecstasy. The series of anecdotes told by Jim establishes his authority as a voice of kindness and truth, so that when we reach the anecdote about his deaf and dumb daughter we are prepared to accept the high poignancy of something that out of context might seem strained or sentimental. Here the miniature anecdote gradually opens into a central revelation.

Sholom Aleichem. This comic master, not a "folk writer" but a sophisticated artist close to folk sources, embodies the central values of East European Jewish culture. The deepest assumptions of a people, those gestures which undercut mere opinion and rest on the inflection of a phrase, the shrug of a shoulder, the timbre of laughter—all are brought to bear in Sholom Aleichem's use of folk anecdote.

"A Yom Kippur Scandal" is a little story in which a traveler recounts an experience: One Yom Kippur eve there arrives in Kasrilevke, Sholom Aleichem's mythical *shtetl*, a stranger from Lithuania (that is, a Litvak, a severe rationalist, maybe a wise guy). The visitor joins in the service. Toward the end he cries out that he had hidden 1800 rubles in his prayer stand and now they are gone—someone has stolen his money. A scandal, and on Yom Kippur eve! The Rabbi locks the synagogue and requires every worshiper to be searched. All submit except the local prodigy steeped in learning ("knew a thousand pages of *Talmud* by heart"). The men shake out his pockets and find some "well-gnawed chicken bones and a few dozen plum pits still moist from chewing." Everyone rocks with laughter, but for the poor Rabbi it's no joke. And the money? "What money?" answers the narrator, innocently. The 1800 rubles! Oh, "they were gone." Gone? "Gone forever."

Building upon a simple anecdote, "A Yom Kippur Scandal" moves into a culture's deep bias. There are two scandals: a guest in the synagogue is robbed on Yom Kippur (or pretends he is robbed), and a pious youth is discovered violating the fast. Both are serious matters, though in the eyes of the Rabbi, one of Sholom Aleichem's innocents, the first scandal is a sin against man and the second a sin against God. Which is greater?

Sholom Aleichem leaves the story up in the air—an anecdote floating on a film of metaphysics—so that we don't know what really happened to the stranger. But it doesn't matter, in light of the scandal with the chicken bones. In this one little anecdote Sholom Aleichem stakes out an entire morality: such is the blessing of compression.

Ignazio Silone. For this writer from the age of fascism, the anecdote serves as a token of moral resistance, the salvage achieved through peasant experience as it shoulders past ideological deceit. The anecdote is what remains undefiled in the life of the *cafoni*, the poorest peasants of the Abruzzi. The anecdote is the last defense of the downtrodden, the communal signal of the speechless. What intellectuals freeze into abstraction, the peasants thaw into miniature narrative. The thought behind their anecdotes, while often sly and sometimes profound, is seldom developed; it remains quick, intuitive, fixed on particulars. The anecdote ties things together, not by "raising" them to generality but by holding them close to the earth. And through it, Silone declares a stubborn, quizzical, but by no means romantic attachment to the folk.

In Silone's novels the anecdote brings bite and color, warding off that allegorical dryness which is one of his persistent weaknesses. The pessimistic humor of his main characters becomes Silone's closest approximation to something like—not exactly optimism, but—a style holding back pessimism. A peasant hears that many nations would be "prepared to pay to have [our leader, Mussolini] in their country," and with a neat bit of slyness, "as he disliked generalities," asks "exactly how much other nations would be willing to pay to acquire our leader." At another point a group of peasants is enjoying the "lovely fairy story" about wolves and lambs lying down together so that laws will no longer be necessary, and one of them says that as far as he's concerned, he would "replace all existing laws with one single law. . . . It would give every Italian the right to emigrate."

In Silone's wry voice, the anecdote becomes a shield against everything that is official and falsely pious. The anecdote speaks here for earth and air, bread and wine. It is inviolable.

Mr. Bennett and Mrs. Woolf

LITERARY POLEMICS COME and go, sparking a season of anger and gossip, and then turning to dust. A handful survive their moment: Dr. Johnson's demolition of Soame Jenyns, Hazlitt's attack on Coleridge. But few literary polemics can have been so damaging, or so lasting in consequences, as Virginia Woolf's 1924 essay "Mr. Bennett and Mrs. Brown," about the once widely read English novelists Arnold Bennett, H. G. Wells, and John Galsworthy.

For several literary generations now, Woolf's essay has been taken as the definitive word finishing off an old-fashioned school of fiction and thereby clearing the way for literary modernism. Writing with her glistening charm, and casting herself as the voice of the new (always a shrewd strategy in literary debate), Woolf quickly seized the high ground in her battle with Bennett. Against her needling thrusts, the old fellow never had a chance.

The debate has been nicely laid out by Samuel Hynes in his *Edwardian Occasions*, and I owe to him some of the following details. It all began in 1917 with Woolf's review of a collection of Bennett's literary pieces, a rather favorable review marred by the stylish snobbism that was becoming a trademark of the Bloomsbury circle. Bennett, wrote Woolf, had a materialistic view of the world, "he has been worrying himself to achieve infantile realisms." A catchy phrase, though exactly what "infantile realisms" meant Woolf did not trouble to say. During the next few years she kept returning to the attack, as if to prepare for "Mr. Bennett and Mrs. Brown." More than personal sensibilities or rivalries of status was involved here, though both were visible; Woolf was intent upon discrediting, if not simply dismissing, a group of literary predecessors who enjoyed a large readership.

In 1923 Bennett reviewed Woolf's novel *Jacob's Room*, praising its "originality" and "exquisite" prose, but concluding that "the characters do not vitally survive in the mind." For Bennett, this was a fatal flaw. And for his readers too—though not for the advanced literary public which by now was learning to suspect this kind of talk about "characters surviving" as a lazy apology for the shapeless and perhaps even mindless Victorian novel.

A year later Woolf published her famous essay, brilliantly sketching an imaginary old lady named Mrs. Brown whom she supplied with anecdotes and reflections as tokens of inner being. These released the sort of insights, suggested Woolf,

that would not occur to someone like Bennett, a writer obsessed with dull particulars of setting (weather, town, clothing,
furniture, etc.). Were Bennett to write about a Mrs. Brown,
he would describe her house in conscientious detail but never
penetrate her essential life, for—what a keen polemicist!—
"he is trying to hypnotize us into the belief that, because he
has made a house, there must be a person living there."* In a
quiet put-down of Bennett's novel *Hilda Lessways* (not one
of his best), Woolf gave a turn of the knife: "One line of
insight would have done more than all those lines of description. . . ."

From the suave but deadly attack of "Mr. Bennett and Mrs.
Brown," Bennett's literary reputation would never quite recover. He remained popular with the general public, but among
literary readers, the sort that would become the public for the
emerging modernists, the standard view has long been that he
was a middling, plodding sort of Edwardian novelist whose
work has been pushed aside by the revolutionary achievements
of Lawrence, Joyce and, to a smaller extent, Woolf herself.
When Bennett died in 1930, Woolf noted in her diary that "he
had some real understanding power, as well as a gigantic absorbing power [and] direct contact with life"—all attributes,
you might suppose, handy for a novelist but, for her, evidently
not sufficient. In saying this, remarks Hynes, Woolf gave Bennett, "perhaps, the 'reality gift' that [she] doubted in herself,
the gift that she despised and envied." Yes; in much of her

---

* Herself sensitive to the need for a room of her own, Woolf seemed indifferent to
what a house might mean for people who had risen somewhat in the world. For a
writer like Bennett, however, imagining a house was part of the way to locate "a
person living there."

fiction Woolf resembles Stevens' man with the blue guitar who "cannot bring a world quite round, / Although I patch it as I can."

Still, none of this kept Woolf from steadily sniping at Bennett's "shopkeeping view of literature." Bennett was a provincial from the Five Towns; Bennett was commercially successful; Bennett was an elder to be pulled down, as elders must always be pulled down even if they are also admired a little.

Through more than a decade of their guerrilla encounters, Bennett tried to parry Woolf's attacks, but as a polemicist he was sadly outclassed. (Hynes writes in a personal letter that Bennett was a poor polemicist "because he was simply too *nice*.") In 1920 Bennett made a fatal tactical blunder: he wrote in the *Evening Standard*, a London paper, that Woolf is "the queen of the high brows; and I am a low brow." Now this may have tickled his readers, but among the literary people who would be making and unmaking reputations, it was the equivalent of shooting himself in the foot. For one mark of the modern era has been a ready celebration of the high against the low brow—though Bennett wasn't really a low brow, he had been baited by Woolf into a truculent misrepresentation of himself. Years earlier he had already written in his journal that "we have absorbed from France that passion for artistic shapely presentation of truth, and that feeling for words as words, which animated Flaubert, the de Goncourts, and de Maupassant." Hardly the sentiments of a low brow. And in one or two of his novels Bennett would himself write in accord with the word "from France."

Feelings of class, always abrasive in England, also figured

in this dispute, and again Bennett was outmaneuvered. Woolf attacked from both sides, first as a patrician looking down a prominent nose at the grubby lower middle class of the provinces and then as a free spirit elegantly bohemian and contemptuous of shopkeeper mentality. Bennett couldn't even salvage for himself the doubtful advantage of claiming he was a sturdy proletarian—his father had been a solicitor in the Five Towns. And in the 1920s to be called a "shopkeeper's novelist" meant being thrust into philistine darkness.

Bennett and Woolf, writes Hynes, were "*not* antithetical in their views of their common art." After all, Bennett had shown respect for new writing, had praised Dostoevsky and Chekhov when the Russians were translated into English, had declared admiration for the "conscious art." What had actually happened, I think, was that Bennett had allowed feelings of class inferiority—they persisted despite his success, his yacht, his mistress—to shift to the arena of cultural judgment, and Woolf had been quick to take advantage of this confusion. Yet Hynes may be overstating the case a little when he sees nothing "antithetical in their views of their common art." There really was a serious clash regarding "their common art," and at one point in "Mr. Bennett and Mrs. Brown" Woolf made clear what the issue was. Older writers like Bennett and Wells were using one set of "conventions"—that's the key word—while younger writers found these to be "ruin . . . death." The "Edwardian tools," she said, "have laid an enormous stress on the fabric of things. They have given us a house in the hope that we may be able to deduce the human beings who live there." Or to put it in other words: the Edwardian novelists believed that human nature could be revealed by rendering conduct and circumstance—"from the outside," as some critics would say.*

In one of her objective moments, Woolf admitted that "the tools of one generation are useless for the next." What was consequently involved in her clash with Bennett was not the superiority of one set of fictional conventions over another— for it is very doubtful that such superiority can ever be demonstrated—but, rather, that two generations had reached a fundamental division over the kinds of novels to be written. Outside/inside, objective/subjective, social/psychological: let these stand as rough tokens of the division. Where Woolf gained a polemical advantage was in claiming, or at least arguing as if, there was something inherently better about the novel of sensibility as against the novel of circumstance. She didn't yet have to consider that in a while the new becomes old, giving way soon enough to the still newer new.

What I have just said is not, however, the most important point. True, Woolf was using her self-chosen role as advocate of the new in order to undermine Bennett, but she was also doing something else. She was writing in behalf of a great new cultural impulse, that of literary modernism. By 1924, if it had not yet entirely triumphed, this impulse was certainly well on the way to triumph, and in retrospect Woolf's essay seems less the outcry of a beleaguered minority than evidence that this minority was consolidating its cultural power. An attendant

---

* A memorable expression of this view is provided by a character in Henry James's *The Portrait of a Lady*. Madame Merle says, ". . . every human being has his shell. . . . By the shell I mean the whole envelope of circumstances. There is no such thing as an isolated man or woman. . . . What do you call one's self? Where does it begin? Where does it end? It overflows into everything that belongs to us—and then it flows back again."

irony is that while Woolf spoke for the new and had a certain right to do so, she was unfriendly to, indeed rather obtuse about, the great modernists: she found Joyce "indecent" and Eliot "obscure."

So Woolf won the battle, if not perhaps the argument. I remember several decades ago being informed by authoritative literary persons that Woolf, *once and for all*, had demolished Bennett. Growing older, I have come to recognize that "once and for all" often means no more than a few decades. By the end of our century, literary modernism has settled comfortably into the academy; there is no longer a need to defend it against detractors, and one might even look back upon it with a critical eye. The deeper issue, then, wasn't really, as both Woolf and Bennett said, which writer could create more persuasive characters; it was a clash over competing versions of the novel as a form. Such clashes are never fully settled; they keep recurring in new ways.

Matters become still more complicated if we glance at the novels Bennett and Woolf wrote. At least one of Woolf's novels is greatly to be admired, and that is *To the Lighthouse*, where in her own fragile and iridescent way she does command "the reality gift." But Woolf's reputation needs no defense these days; it has been inflated for reasons having little to do with her work as a novelist. What does need to be said is that Bennett still merits attention as a fine, largely traditional novelist in a few of his books (he wrote too many): *Anna of the Five Towns*, *The Old Wives' Tale*, *Clayhanger*, and *Riceyman Steps*. His prose is often slapdash and flavorless, quite without Woolf's felicity of phrasing; his psychology is intuitively bluff rather than precisely nuanced; and in technique he often stumbles.

Yet he had the true novelist's gift, what Woolf called "a gigantic absorbing power" or what the Russian critic M. Bakhtin meant when he wrote that "for the prose artist the world is full of the words of other people." Listening to those words, Bennett recorded through them the lives of ordinary people with what he once marvelously called a "crushed tenderness."

In his novels there is a strongly realized sense of place—those cramped dingy towns of provincial England, bristling with high aspirations, streaked with meanness of spirit. Place, not as a Hardyesque rising to spiritual transcendence, but confined, local, the narrow corner of a province. In *Clayhanger*, a modest classic in the subgenre of the *Bildungsroman*, Bennett faithfully charts the yearnings for emotional articulation of a printer's son in the Five Towns ("a new conception of himself"). He depicts the homely, almost speechless love of middle-aged, middle-class men and women with a stolid respect, if not the flair of a Woolf or the depth of a Lawrence. Bennett is a master of the middle range of life and literature, neither soarings of sublimity nor plunges into the soul. He is indeed the prosing poet of the shopkeepers (who may also deserve a poet of their own).

Riceyman Steps, published in 1923, late in Bennett's career, is something else again, a tour de force Flaubertian in its stringent organization but with moments of Balzacian power. In a style somewhat unnervingly detached, this short novel depicts the lives of shopkeepers trapped in miserliness, showing not only the predictable psychic costs but also how self-denial can become a twisted expression of the life-force. Here is the kind of passage that leads one to invoke Balzac; it describes a moment when the shopkeeper protagonist is at the height of his obsession:

He took a third drawer out of the safe, lifting it with both hands because of its weight, and put it on the table. It was full of gold sovereigns. Violet [his wife] had never seen this gold before nor suspected its existence. She was astounded, frightened, ravished. He must have kept it throughout the war, defying the government's appeal to patriots not to hoard. He was a superman, the most mysterious of supermen. And he was a fortress, impregnable.

Finally, however, even an admirer of Bennett must admit that there is something in his work—some strand of feeling or aspiration—that is thwarted, unfulfilled. In all his novels except *Riceyman Steps* the life of the narrative has a way of gradually draining out, as if creation were also a mode of exhaustion. A costive heaviness sets in. Why should this be? Perhaps because there is some truth in the idea that the kind of Victorian novel inherited by Bennett and the other Edwardians had reached a point of exhaustion, what might be called the routinization of realism. And Bennett, a latecomer in the development of the English novel, lacked those mad outpourings of energy which mark the greatest of the Victorians. At moments a touch of modern sadness seeps into his soul, some grim deprivation bred in provincial life.

Something like this may have been what D. H. Lawrence had in mind when he wrote: "I hate Bennett's resignation. Tragedy ought really to be a great kick at misery." Bennett himself seems occasionally to have had similar responses to his own work, though in a fine essay about George Gissing he provided a justification for its greyness of tone. Gissing, he said, "is . . . just, sober, calm, and proud against the gods;

he has seen, he knows, he is unmoved; he defeats fate by accepting it." Whether this quite disposes of Lawrence's criticism is a question, though I would venture the opinion that Lawrence's attack cut more deeply and painfully than Woolf's, even though it is Woolf's that has been remembered.

The years pass, and by now the dispute between Bennett and Woolf has settled into history. It may be time for a spot of justice for Arnold Bennett, not a great but at times a very good novelist. But I doubt that it will come, since it is a delusion to suppose that the passage of time is an aid to justice, and, in any case, there hovers over Bennett's work and reputation the shadow of the formidable Mrs. Brown, called into being by the silkily ferocious Mrs. Woolf.

Characters:
Are They Like People?

THE IDEA OF character, once taken to be central to the reading of novels, has recently come into critical disrepute. Literary theorists are eager to dismember the idea of character, one of them, Rawdon Wilson, writing for example that "the distinction between characters and people is an absolute one." Such theorists often assume a stern posture when writing about this matter, so that if you are caught discussing a fictional character in the way you might talk about a human being, you will probably be convicted of being "a naive reader." This scorn is extended, these days, to the innocent pleasures of responding in the usual moral and psychological terms to characters like Don Quixote and Pip, Julian Sorel and Odette, Hans Castorp and Leopold Bloom.

We are warned against supposing that characters in novels are real persons, though who, except the deranged, ever supposed they were, I cannot say. We are warned against supposing characters are even *like* actual persons. The theorist who wrote that the difference between characters and people is "absolute" (but what can that mean?) also argues that characters are "at most patterns of recurrence" (but of what if not traits similar to those we discern in human beings?). Another critic, something of a joker, writes that "Emma Woodhouse is not a woman nor need be described as if it were." A large gain in critical perception is evidently registered by calling Emma an "it." And the novelist-philosopher William Gass, shrugging off the lures of qualification, writes that "the so-called life one finds in novels, the worst and best of them, is nothing like actual life at all." *Nothing at all*: not Anna Karenina's passion, not Lucien de Rubempré's ambition, not Captain Ahab's obsession, not Gatsby's delusion? But if these are indeed not at all "like actual life," where then can we find the necessary descriptives when trying to evoke the clashing figures and interests of a novel?

We must repress the spontaneous impulse to describe the moral conduct and psychological motives of characters in the only language we have available and instead are to see them as elements or functions in the workings of narrative. Whether that makes them more accessible, to say nothing of more interesting, seems hardly to matter. And we are to repress our knowledge, or to judge it inconsequent, that the great novelists strove with all their powers to make characters who would indeed seem like actual persons. Taking that into account might be to share the ignorance of genius.

Some arguments of the new theorists have an ideological charge. The sophisticated if just barely readable French theorist

Hélène Cixous writes that a novel with mimetic characters turns into "a machine of repression," bourgeois repression of course, since it presents a historical given as if it were everlasting and thereby thwarts the hope of transcendence. Cixous's prose sputters fitfully but, insofar as I can make her out, she would seem to be saying something fairly close to what Roland Barthes has said. He believes, or once believed, that the very use of the preterite tense (like the notion of character?)

> is part of a security system . . . one of those numerous formal pacts made between the writer and society for the justification of the former and the serenity of the latter. [This is part of] a certain mythology of the universal typifying the bourgeois society of which the Novel is a characteristic product. . . . It is thanks to an expedient of the same kind that the triumphant bourgeoisie of the last century was able to look upon its values as universal. . . .

There is something bizarre in the notion that fictional characterization is an agency of repression or that the use of the preterite (or any other) tense is a justification of the status quo; this is to confuse narrative conventions with social categories. Where, in any case, have our strongest visions of possibility, as also our most telling social criticisms, come from if not the great novelists—it is they who have given imaginative substance to what the young Marx called "the human essence," and far better and more fully than any social theorists, Marx and Nietzsche included. Tolstoy once wrote that "the incompatibility of a man's position with his moral activity is the surest indication of his searching for truth," a remark that could stand as an epigraph for the work of Dickens and Stendhal, George

Eliot and Dostoevsky, Flaubert and Hardy, Lawrence and Proust. The ideological formulas of the social theorists have all too often been ripped apart by historical change, but the critical visions of the great novelists abide. If we can, in this somewhat dimmed moment, see beyond what Barthes calls "a certain mythology of the universal typifying the bourgeois society," that is largely because of the writings of novelists and poets who have lived in that society.

In what sense do characters "exist"? True, neither Anna Karenina nor Lily Bart is a real person as you and I are, though anyone who said these characters sometimes "seem more real than you and I" would quickly win nods of understanding. Why, then, should intelligent people choose to push against open doors? Perhaps because they have spent too many years teaching undergraduates that a distaste for Emma as a possible mate (or roommate) isn't exactly a fatal criticism of the novel in which she appears.

A fictional character emerges out of an arrangement of language which sets off in the reader's mind an imagined situation or "world": all-encompassing as in Tolstoy, miniature as in Austen, strange as in Kafka. Characters, as the neo-Aristotelian critic R. S. Crane puts it, are "concrete semblances of real men and women," with the term "concrete semblance" evoking the required tension between what is mimetic and what is constructed. How a novel is shaped, the arrangement and weighting of its parts, the authority through which its matter is established—such formal elements help to determine the nature of its characters. They do not come to us directly as people in a living room might; they are mediated, they must "fit" into the narrative—though in some novels they also spill across the limits of form, as if to suggest a surplus of vitality.

The novel is also a mimesis, an imitation drawing upon the writer's observations, intuitions, and imaginings—a mixture of his own experience and his relations to other writers dead or alive. To see the novel in this way has always troubled critics who would like to liberate it from gross contingencies. We may genuinely sympathize with this desire, but alas, it is in the nature of the very language such critics like to exalt that it should make for referential impurity. Words point, words evoke images and ideas, words betray. Words cannot be self-sufficient, as the stroke of the brush or sounds of an instrument may. Words impel us (I quote W. J. Harvey) to see a character as

> the sort of man who in such-and-such a situation would do so and so. . . . [The novelist] can frame the situation to justify the *would do such-and-such* in our reaction . . . he may also leave room enough for us to speculate and to frame other situations than those actually existing in the novel. . . . Such speculative activity may, in fact, compose a large part of the character's reality for us.

The moral-psychological traits that comprise a character are drawn from the writer's experience of the world. Where else? From past writers, some critics would say. That is true, but *somewhere* a writer must have engaged in direct observation on his own. Even the blind Homer must have "seen" something in the life about him. Literature cannot live off itself forever. Others will say, the writer draws upon his imagination. That is also true, yet we must ask: With what does the imagination do its work, where does it gather the materials it transfigures, if not from a perception of life? Imagination is not something apart and hermetic, not a way of leaving reality behind; it is a way of engaging reality. The imaginative work is what the writer does with and to reality: otherwise, why should the novel make such powerful claims upon us?

The novel thrives upon our interest in ourselves, our ways, our world. Lose or abandon that interest and it becomes a game we may indeed play with and gain pleasure from, but hardly "the bright book of life" D. H. Lawrence called it. "If the fascination of human types is an end in itself (and the novel generically reflects such an assumption)," writes Robert Alter, "the deepened experiential knowing of the imagined individual is a process that justifies itself." True, in a writer like Kafka that "imagined individual" becomes radically diminished, and in a writer like Samuel Beckett a dwindling in the "fascination of human types" becomes a central premise. But there is a thread of continuity with the past even in their break from the traditional novel, for the definition of the break would be impossible without the presence of the tradition.

Mirror and lamp: such is the doubled nature of the novel. Simply to serve as elements of narrative, characters have also to resemble, in one way or another, actual persons—which also means they must differ from them. (If we could even imagine a character utterly devoid of human traits, he or she, perhaps in this case "it," could not possibly be of any use to fictional narrative.) Every moderately sophisticated reader senses all this, just as every moderately sophisticated playgoer, even while shaken by Lear's fate, knows Lear to be a fiction, a semblance made for performance. Nor are the concepts of

mimesis and fictional construct to be seen as fixed and irrec-
oncilable opposites; they are categories of perception with
which to specify aspects of a work that, finally, we hope to
apprehend as a whole.

The great fictional characters, from Robinson Crusoe to
Flem Snopes, from Tess to Molly Bloom, cannot quite be
"fitted" into or regarded solely as functions of narrative. *Why
should we want to?* What but the delusions of system and total
grasp do we gain thereby? Such characters are too interesting,
too splendidly mysterious for mere functional placement.
(Who'd even look at Emma Woodhouse if she were just an
"it"?) Severe critics say that characters "exist only on the
page"—but why do critics want to be so severe? They are
wrong too: all that exists on the page are black marks. As
symbols for language, these marks stimulate impressions in our
minds which lead us to suppose—though we "know better"
—that characters exist in their own right, apart from the page.
They refuse to be banished. They will not be driven back
between covers.

Consider now the contrary view advanced by William Gass.
In his lucid essay "The Concept of Character in Fiction," he
offers as an example of a character, neither quite major nor
minor, Mr. Cashmore in Henry James's *The Awkward Age*.
Mr. Cashmore, writes William Gass, is "not a person." That
having been cleared up, Gass continues: "nothing whatever
that is appropriate to persons can be correctly said of him."
What then *is* Mr. Cashmore? "A verbal center."

Also: "1) a noise, 2) a proper name, 3) a complex system
of ideas, 4) a controlling conception, 5) an instrument of verbal

organization, 6) a pretended mode of referring, and 7) a source of verbal energy."

Well! Numbers 1, 2, and 7 (noise, name, and energy) can be attributed to actual persons, so these don't differentiate them sufficiently from fictional characters. Numbers 3 and 4 (complex system of ideas, controlling conception) help to specify the place of characters in novels, though it may be asked how we can speak, with regard to a fictional character, of either "a complex system of ideas" or "a controlling conception" except through some reference to imagined persons? For Mr. Cashmore is not per se greed or sexual squalor; he embodies these ideas and traits through images of individuality, which means that something "appropriate to persons" can indeed be said of him, with whatever complexities seem "appropriate."

We come back then to 6) "a pretended mode of referring." This seems perilously close to mimesis. Gass might reply that his key word is "pretended"—the novelist "pretends" to be representing real life while actually constructing an autonomous fiction. But if he wants that construct to be persuasive and consequential, he had better employ some materials incorporating his sense of actuality; otherwise he may not be able to endow his "pretending" with much force and point.

To prove how little Mr. Cashmore is conceived as mimesis, Gass has a lot of fun in showing that we actually know very little about him. Does Mr. Cashmore, he asks, even have a nose? Very likely; if he didn't, James would have been the first to notice. The real fun, however, resides in the name of Mr. Cashmore. Gass could hardly have chosen another character whose name points so insistently to "whatever is appropriate to persons." Who but a human being, real or simulated, wants

"more cash"? Is there another name in all literature, except
perhaps Bunyan's Badman, that brings us more urgently to the
precincts of common life? Cashmore and Badman, Investment
Counselors.

With his jolly vulgarity and slightly sinister air, Mr. Cashmore does his job admirably as a function of the narrative, but
he is also supremely *there* as an imagined figure. That he be
there is, indeed, a precondition for fulfilling his function in the
narrative.

Why should there be, in the academy, this humorless and
pleasure-denying attack upon the mimetic view of character?
At a time when the margin for authentic individuality keeps
shrinking, we might suppose that literary people would see the
value in such terms as self, individual, personality, character.
And if these prove to be somewhat frail defenses for a humane
or humanist view of things, that ought to make them still more
precious. To speak these days of a humanist view is perhaps
to risk embarrassment, since the phrase, like all the other val-
uable ones in our vocabulary, has been devalued through mis-
use and appropriation. But that hardly warrants dismissal, least
of all the scorn we hear for it as a sign of nostalgic liberalism.

I can see one further argument to be made for William
Gass's views, and it is a serious argument, glancingly anticipated in Meyer Schapiro's famous essay "On the Humanity
of Abstract Painting." Schapiro writes that "humanity in art
is . . . not confined to the image of man. Man shows himself
too in his relation to the surroundings, in his artifacts, and in
the expressive character of all the signs and marks he produces."
Correspondingly, it might be said that the formal arrange-

ments, the verbal patterns and sounds in a work of literature yield pleasure apart from any supposed relation between characters and persons. That is certainly true, but with two important points of complication. First, in referring to "the expressive character" of signs and marks Schapiro does not dismiss "the image of man" as a source of value and pleasure, he merely insists that this image is not the only evidence of "humanity in art." Second, there are crucial differences among the arts. When it comes to sensuous enticements, the written word can seldom compete with the sounds of a piano or the colors of a picture. Words have the inescapable property—call it, if you prefer, a fatality—of evoking imaginatively human figures and situations that seem to "exist" apart from the marks on the page. And thereby we gain an enduring companion of consciousness.

How Are Characters Conceived?

THE ONE TIME I met William Faulkner, I asked him how
he had come to imagine his truculent black character Lucas
Beauchamp. "I saw him," answered Faulkner, "walking across
my typewriter."

Faulkner intended to say, I suppose, that he had seen Lucas
Beauchamp whole and complete: the stubborn gait, the stiff
bearing that signals Lucas's rise above racial barriers and beyond racial rebellion. But this flash of perception must surely
have been a culmination of a lifetime of seeing. Words came
later.

Lucas strode across the typewriter in his vivid uniqueness,
but Faulkner could "see" him because he was drawing upon
traditional Southern notions about the sort of black man who
refused publicly to acknowledge white domination. Once,
however, Faulkner came to write *Intruder in the Dust*, the

novel in which Lucas has a major part, he had to modify the image of Lucas which he himself had formed in earlier fiction. He had to adapt the irascible Lucas of the earlier story, "The Fire and the Hearth," to the mystery-adventure plot of *Intruder in the Dust*, as also to its more substantial line of fable which casts Lucas as an unbending victim of bigotry. A too outspoken Lucas could have entailed an open racial conflict that neither Faulkner nor the plot of his novel was prepared to accommodate. So character had to bend a little, as it always must, to genre, plot, and theme.

But if the somewhat mechanical plot of *Intruder in the Dust* required that Faulkner "shrink" his character, there was a limit to what he could plausibly do. For by now Lucas had an "existence" of his own; he "lived" in the imaginations of both Faulkner and his readers; the character could be bent just so far and then the plot would have to give way. Lucas did not enter Faulkner's novel weightless. In bringing him back to his novel Faulkner was constrained quite as much as if he had modeled Lucas upon a well-known, actual person. Give a character a little space, and he has his rights.

All of which reinforces Elizabeth Bowen's point that "one cannot 'make' characters. . . . Characters pre-exist. They are *found*. They reveal themselves slowly to the novelist's perception"—on the streets, in books and graveyards, across the rim of a typewriter. One difficulty with Bowen's shrewd remark is that she may seem to be reducing the act of composition to mimetic passivity ("finding"—copying actual persons?). But Bowen quickly adds: "The novelist's perception of his characters takes place *in the course of the actual writing of the novel*." Very good; yet one wants perversely to ask:

Does this perception never occur *before* the actual writing?

Let's try a few distinctions. A character may be found during the writer's encounter with the world: the writer looks and surmises. But this act of "finding" soon narrows into a specific purpose, the writing of a book—which means that a sizable part of the "pre-existing" character will be discarded. Thereby the character, no longer quite "pre-existing," will become someone else, a figure newly created. Still, won't this transformed character also resemble "someone out there," or perhaps be formed out of a composite of partial and potential resemblances? This grazes the problem of imagination, about which I would merely say that imagination is not a self-subsistent faculty; it draws its substance from our interaction with the world. Or as I. A. Richards says, it is "the extrapolation of the known, in the interests of admiration." And if indeed there is reason for admiration, that is because the "extrapolation" has created something that is both new and entwined with what we already know. Imagination is a way of coping with common experience, not a way of dismissing it.

I hear an objection: Must all characterization be drawn from a stock of shared experience? Haven't some novelists "made up" radically new types of character that were previously unknown? Say, Dostoevsky's "underground man." Yes, the "underground man" constitutes a brilliantly novel perception, but he did not come out of thin air. Dostoevsky drew upon his knowledge of the St. Petersburg *déclassés*, semi-intellectuals adrift, and he borrowed from earlier works of literature, Chernyshevsky's *What Is to Be Done?* and perhaps Diderot's *Rameau's Nephew*. But, to be fair about it, he also added something new by developing his intimations of a future that was just starting to be visible but which he alone saw clearly. The materials that went into the imagining of the "underground man" were surely available to his contemporaries; but Dostoevsky gave them a visionary aspect, anticipating a whole strand of modern sensibility. So we can say that Dostoevsky "found" his "underground man" in the air, which must also mean within himself.

I hear another objection: Why should it be supposed that the act of literary representation always proceeds from common experience to individual text? Can't the imagination create a realm of its own? Doesn't life sometimes imitate art?

Goethe's Werther is a fictional character who became a model, a sort of culture hero, for young people in Europe, molding the feelings of an entire generation. Were there real-life figures upon whom the young Goethe drew? Or was the "finding" of Werther what first brought him into the light of day? We know about Sturm und Drang, the romantic sensibility of the moment in which the young Goethe wrote, but when you consult studies of German literature you find that they cite as major evidence for this sensibility . . . Goethe's Werther. Questions about causality lead to circular answers.

Where, then, did Werther come from? We know Goethe had been impressed by Rousseau's Saint-Preux; we suppose he glimpsed something in his milieu that enabled the creation of his character. Perhaps all he needed was within himself, and in his sublime self-assurance he assumed that whatever was within himself was worth "finding." Or—but really also—he "found" Werther in the very future he helped bring into being.

"Finding" a character is not only an act of mimesis, it can also be a kind of prophecy.

On an opening page of Balzac's novel *Ursule Mirouët* there is a lengthy description of the character Minoret-Levrault, one of those dismal provincial bourgeois who keep reappearing in *La Comédie humaine*. His face shows no "trace of a soul beneath the florid tints of gross, coarsening flesh." Hair, grey. Ears, "scarred at the edges by the eroding activity of a blood stream." Complexion, "purplish-blue." Eyes, "alert, sunken and hidden." Feet, "the size of an elephant." Belly, huge. And on and on.

Now this is not just conventional "background." We are meant to join in Balzac's persuasion, as set forth in another of his novels *Une Ténébreuse affaire* (*A Murky Affair*), that "the laws of physiognomy are precise, not only in their application to character, but also in relation to the destinies which govern human existence." Exactly what these "laws" are we do not quite learn, perhaps because Balzac supposes them to be common knowledge, confirmed by daily experience and nineteenth-century science. Nor is Balzac alone in this persuasion. The great English critic Hazlitt writes: "A man's look is the work of years, it is stamped on his countenance by the events of his whole life, nay, more, by the hand of nature, and it is not to be got rid of easily."

Few novelists would by now so boldly advance the notion that "laws of physiognomy" govern or at least "apply to" character, but a great many write as if physical appearance and psychological composition are intimately related. Perhaps they don't think of "laws" at all; perhaps they just use this supposed relation between appearance and character as a convention handed down from one generation of writers to another.

That a coarse-grained genius like Balzac should have relied on "the laws of physiognomy" is understandable; the mind of this "realist" was cluttered with fantasies and superstitions. But a writer as cultivated as Tolstoy, one of the three or four most powerful minds of the nineteenth century? Some decades ago the Russian critic D. S. Merezhkovsky shrewdly noted how frequently Tolstoy assigns a physical feature to his characters, as if it were an identity tag. "Rotundity," for example, is a favorite descriptive in *War and Peace*, applied to Kutuzov and Platon Karataev to suggest all that is natural and fulfilled in a human being. Merezhkovsky went so far as to elevate this device into an "insight into the body" (just a little short of "laws of physiognomy"), asserting that "by the motions of muscles or nerves we enter shortly and directly into the internal world of [Tolstoy's] characters, begin to live with them, and into them." Well, perhaps.

Something like this notion can be found in many other novelists. Fielding uses it in a rough-and-ready fashion, not always with complete seriousness. Sterne's Walter Shandy says "that a man of sense does not lay down his hat in coming into a room—or take it up in going out of it, but something escapes, which discovers him." Hardy transforms it into a sign of fatality. John O'Hara makes it into a behaviorist tic. The human body is assumed to mirror the soul, flesh the psyche, and then—a notable piece of literary legerdemain—this mirror transforms itself into a lamp illuminating essential being. This may indeed be a long-standing convention of fiction, but behind it there must be a deeper, perhaps unshakable folk belief: *Just looking at you I can tell . . .*

It is different in modern fiction. Writers of the past century have lost faith in the supposed correspondence between outer and inner, body and soul. To the modernist sensibility it's no longer clear that there are any discernible laws of being, whether in the cosmos or governing the psyche. Twentieth-century writers will usually content themselves with minute particulars, uneasily offered as evidence of the senses. About how many major characters in twentieth-century fiction can we say that we know very much about their appearance, their dress, their posture? Perhaps some of Faulkner's comic characters. But if we do retain an image of Joseph K. in *The Trial*, it is likely to derive less from the text itself than from a general sense of clerkship. Or we may recall that Michel, the protagonist of André Gide's *The Immoralist*, believes that "culture, born of life, [is] the destroyer of life," while about his body, his gait, his mannerisms we know almost nothing. This Michel hardly figures as a physical creature at all, since Gide, grown impatient with the paraphernalia of the traditional novel, regards him as no more than a transit for sentiments and thoughts. Whatever clues modernist writers may find between the outside and the inside of our being are likely to seem unsystematic, dubious, and tilted toward irony. When Balzac, with that amusing self-assurance of his, spoke about "the laws of physiognomy" he was expressing a general faith in the unity of things. Today novelists scamper about for ingenuity.

One of the most brilliant of these is Milan Kundera, in whom a pervasive skepticism and a liking for fiction as play have become inseparable. Yet even in the novels of this cleverest of contemporary writers, the old, seemingly worn-out and abandoned literary assumptions have a way of cropping up. In *The Unbearable Lightness of Being*, a work in which Kundera moves far away from the traditional novel, there is a passage about a woman who "perhaps . . . stood frequently in front of the mirror observing her body, trying to peer through it into her soul. . . . Surely, she, too, had harbored the blissful hope of using her body as a poster for her soul. But what a monstrous soul it would have to be if it reflected that body. . . ." Balzac would smile if he could read this passage and would offer to enlighten Kundera about "the laws of physiognomy"—a conversation I would love to overhear.

Whatever it may have been, perhaps a tenacious collective intuition, that led novelists to posit the notion that the body reflected the soul (or the soul the body), it is no longer an implicit convention in the drawing of fictional character. But neither does it pass away so readily. It persists even when it encounters disbelief, a "poster" without signs.

When we talk spontaneously about the nineteenth-century Russian masters, and not from the postures of criticism, we're likely to say that their work is "uniquely Russian." The tautology does not bother us; it has a point. In the work of these writers, great moral questions and social problems swarm across the pages, at once overwhelming and buoying the characters. Often these characters are defined, not simply as people of a certain age, gender, and temperament, but through the "positions" they take regarding the great Russian questions and problems. Among the major Russian novelists, it is only in the earlier Tolstoy and perhaps Gogol in some of his stories that character acquires an intrinsic value, to be exhibited quite for its own sake. Turgenev's Bazarov and his Lisa, Dostoevsky's Ivan Karamazov, Saltykov-Shchedrin's Yudishka, Lermontov's Pechorin: these are some of the most wonderful inventions in literature, yet they strike us not just as individual characters or even universal types, but still more, as figures who "stand for" something: a cultural position, a historical category, a generational attitude. And what they "stand for" is not a secondary attribute; it soon reveals itself as the very essence of their being. Purpose hovers over each of them, and really to grasp the novels in which they appear you must know a little about the cultural-political disputes of the time in which their creators wrote. As for the writers themselves, whatever their inclinations toward a pure art, they really have no choice but to entangle themselves with these disputes. They are Russians.

In a thick, suffocating society like that of czarist Russia, it becomes almost inevitable that the writer should regard the making of character as partly a public act signaling his world-outlook. Sometimes it works the other way round: the writer rejects his protagonist's world-outlook, as Turgenev rejected that of Bazarov and Dostoevsky that of Ivan Karamazov, yet so intensely does he register its gathering historical force that he dramatizes this world-outlook almost, indeed, as if it were his own. The rejection provides energy and need.

These characters of nineteenth-century Russian fiction come to us all of a piece, monolithic in design, creatures of opinion and ideology. They can be fully understood only when placed against the background of Russian culture. There is something awesome, even a little frightening about them, since, for all their vividness of being, what finally matters most about them is their destiny. They do not deviate from their ordained paths. Their ends are in their beginnings: to die young, to slide still more deeply into sloth, to exhaust themselves in behalf of a social idea or metaphysical obsession. And we respond to them not by close scrutiny of motive, but by yielding ourselves to the passion of their intent. For a few hours, but sometimes for a lifetime, we share their journeys of fatality. What need, then, is there to speculate about their "inner life" when a declared visible purpose quite defines them? It doesn't really quite define them; Bazarov and Ivan Karamazov succumb to the "smaller" human feelings, and that too is part of their drama.

To ask whether they are individuals or types is somehow to miss the point: they are both, and something more as well. They are representative men and women, sometimes of a stifling Russian way of life, sometimes of newly emerging groups that will shake the Russia of tomorrow. By no means are they "symbols," though they fully signify, bearing an aura of historical definition.

Readers who encountered *Fathers and Sons* soon after its publication recognized immediately that the book touched them vitally. The earliest response to Bazarov was less as a literary accomplishment than as a political-ideological conception: what did he stand for? whom did he stand with? This hurt Turgenev's feelings, but was surely an oblique testimony to Bazarov's "reality." After all, if you argue about his meaning, you take for granted his presence. Readers brought up on

Anglo-Saxon literature may find this strange or unattractive. They may suppose that characters in novels like *Fathers and Sons* must be "propagandistic," "tendentious," perhaps even "lifeless"—Turgenev's great friend Henry James never quite grasped what the Russian's work was all about, since he could not quite imagine what the condition of Russia was like. But readers brought up on Anglo-Saxon literature, with its bias in favor of a literature unalloyed with ideology, are not inclined to suppose that characters conceived through tendencies of public thought can have incisiveness of form or urgency of speech.

Pechorin, the hero of *A Hero of Our Time*, writes Lermontov, "will be characterized either by decisive inaction, or else by futile activity." For at least the readers of nineteenth-century Russia this was surely a sufficient clue. Pechorin's behavior is made to accord with a larger scheme of value, and only an innocent abroad will fail to summon a cluster of cultural tags while reading this remarkable work: Byronism, romantic irony, psychic division, nihilist perversities, etc. That such tags visit our minds while we are reading Lermontov's pages does not lessen our pleasure, since his laconic narrative is bringing a new kind of personality onto the historical stage. We need only have enough imagination to transport ourselves to Lermontov's moment, even as we also see it from our own.

Pechorin is the "superfluous man" turned upside down but still superfluous: active rather than passive, brilliant rather than dull, dashing rather than sluggish, witty rather than slow. Yet, at every turn, Pechorin finds himself unable to live by his finer impulses; some demon at his heart drives him to destruction and self-destruction—some demon, and an utter impatience with the triviality of circumstance. Pechorin is not a revolutionist, there isn't a hint of politics in the book, yet we quickly see why later generations of Russian revolutionists might find in him something of a kindred spirit. Whether the trouble lies in him or in the world hardly matters: all is division.

Lermontov's narrative moves from distant observation of the hero by his acquaintances to his own self-lacerations; but at the end, despite what seems like increasing inwardness of portrayal, we hardly know Pechorin better than at the beginning. Lermontov, a self-effacing writer before self-effacement became a literary fashion, offers no help. With each of the book's five sections we see a little more of Pechorin; the picture widens, the range deepens; but the difficulties in grasping him, in making him out, persist. They hardly matter, since what registers most strongly is that we have witnessed the entry of a new mode of human consciousness. Pechorin may reflect an emerging style and sensibility in Russian culture, or he may be initiating them, but only if intimately linked to that culture can his significance be grasped.

Later, with the distancing of time, the heroes and antiheroes of nineteenth-century Russian literature could gradually be perceived apart from their historical setting, as universal types or psychological models. This process of detaching characters from the circumstances of their creation recurs throughout literary history, perhaps as part of what we mean by the elevation of a text into a classic. But to retain the sharpness and the savor of the nineteenth-century Russian novel we must remember that its protagonists were mostly conceived in struggle, the children of debate. That too, at least in some cultures, can be a way of fictional creation.

The increasing subtlety of characterization in nineteenth-century fiction exacts a price: it delays or blocks the movement of narrative. You can see this in George Eliot's novels, where narrative chugs along while the scrutiny of character is quick, and later on, in the twentieth century, in the novels of Virginia Woolf and in Joyce's *Ulysses*, where narrative becomes distended and arhythmic, though often for attractive literary ends. The shift of world-outlook behind this move from narrative to character, cosmos to psyche, is familiar enough, and I propose here to discuss only a small fragment of it.

In the *roman fleuve*, the "flowing-like-a-river" sequence of novels popular in Europe during the early years of this century, writers like Roger Martin du Gard and Jules Romain expanded the novel into a vast historical chronicle, the spaciousness of which allowed every aspect of novelistic art to flourish. As a consequence, almost none did. Except for Martin du Gard's *The Thibaults*, these overambitious and gargantuan projects seem faded, rather pointless: take in everything and form ceases to exert its necessary pressures. It is when you turn to shorter kinds of fiction that a choice imposes itself between narrative and character. The form appropriate to one is ill-suited to the other.

Primary and imperious, narrative can simply "swallow up" the portrayal of character, sometimes making it seem a luxury of feeble composition. In a fleet and stringent narrative, the essentials of experience can be compressed into motions of behavior, interior into exterior. More properly, the distinction between inner and outer loses its meaning.

Whether Heinrich von Kleist had such thoughts in mind when composing his great novella *Michael Kohlhass* we do not know, but he might as well have. Though written at the crest of Romanticism, this novella is an example of the objectivist impulse taken to the extreme: Let the writer evoke with sufficient mastery the motions of conduct, gesture, situation, and setting, and nothing need remain unknown.

Michael Kohlhass spins out a sequence of sentences, windingly "legalistic" in their melody, which are set down with a studied dryness. Kleist has an "alienation effect" of his own: the terror of the objective. With a calm evenness, the narrative marches toward disaster. Michael Kohlhass, a horse dealer in mid-sixteenth-century Germany, suffers outrage at the hands of an arrogant nobleman. A self-confident bourgeois, but also a literalist of justice, Kohlhass becomes chief of a band of brigands after he fails to gain satisfaction from the aristocracy controlling the state. Mad for justice, maddened by its absence, he is prepared now to tear up everything. He engages in a series of quasi-revolutionary acts, issuing "manifestoes" in which he declares he owes "allegiance to none but God" and that he is speaking from "the Seat of Our Provisional World Government." Echoes of the French Revolution may linger in such phrases: Kleist had a keenly intuitive political sense in *Michael. Kohlhass*, even providing a brief moment when a semianarchic, semicriminal group breaks away from Kohlhass's band.

As Kohlhass tries to negotiate with the state, he is steadily tricked by its rulers and damaged by his own moralistic rigidity.

A prerevolutionary of the instincts, he ends on the gallows, vindicated in his claim to justice but destroyed for his acts of rebellion. There can be no other ending.

Kleist's novella comes to one hundred full pages, but at no point does he provide more than a few scraps of information about Kohlhass's state of mind. All we know about him are his actions, and as we race along with the narrative, it is really extraordinary how *sufficient* a masterly narrative can be. Nor is it precise to say, as I did earlier, that the narrative "swallows up" character. For in reading *Michael Kohlhass* we are rarely inclined to see character as an autonomous element to be considered apart from the action. Kohlhass simply does not emerge as a simulated person with an interior life, except for one brief moment when he weeps over his children (as another zealot, Captain Ahab, softens into speech with his first mate). In the main, Kohlhass is what he does, an idea given motion, an embodied passion.

What a gap there is, in thought and spirit, between Kleist—protomodernist though we may label him—and recent masters of fiction. One of the latter, Milan Kundera, writes: "Between the act and [man], a fissure opens. Man hopes to reveal his own image through his act, but that image bears no resemblance to him." This holds for many in our time and perhaps, at times, even for Kleist himself. But in *Michael Kohlhass* Kleist wrote out of the tacit premise that if you render a man's central actions, those by which he is prepared to stake his life and meet his death, that makes superfluous any effort to capture "his own image," the whole realm of intention and motive. Kleist's is a radical mode of narration, perhaps the most radical there can be: one in which character appears through disappearance. Yet there may be a certain loss too. The objectivist impulse in fiction, if carried far enough, ends with figures—they can hardly be called characters—that seem peculiarly abstract, mere reflexes of story. The gain, and this is what makes Kleist's novella so entrancing, is that such narrative permits a unity of experience which in almost every segment of our culture we know to have been lost.

BIOGRAPHY AND IDENTITY

From Fielding to Márquez, most efforts to provide histories of a character's life consist of brisk, often scrappy summary. A few sentences, an anecdote or two, and our disbelief melts away (if, that is, it ever does). The writer hurries off to wherever he proposes to stop, and it's only when he stops that the novel really gets under way.

A full-scale fictional biography is rare. Proust's Marcel? Mann's Buddenbrook? Dickens's Pip or David? Proust, Mann, Dickens contrive the impression of biography, but if we look closely, we may conclude that there are large gaps in the lives of their fictional heroes. There have to be. Fielding set a model with Tom Jones: detail for a few days, silence about many years. Dickens is especially artful in *Great Expectations*, making it seem that we accompany Pip step by step through his life; but of course we don't. Foreshortening, sudden leaps, dramatic focusing, all do their work. *David Copperfield* may look like a fictional life, but it breaks into two parts, the first a rich portrayal of childhood, the second a rather hurried finishing up. Mimicking biography, fiction wrenches it.

For the novelist is eager to get to the heart of the matter.

He knows his readers aren't going to extend him a blank check of attention. He has to keep busy preparing confrontations and climaxes—here literature is not at all like life—and he counts on his readers' willingness to cooperate by mentally filling in gaps in the character's story or, better yet, by recognizing that the gaps don't signify. What the writer needs most is to kidnap his readers' imagination: to place on an early page a crucial instance that will dissolve their cultivated skepticism. The neatly planted clue, the anticipatory sketch, sometimes no more than a well-turned phrase: let the writer provide these and we yield our credence. I offer a few quick examples.

Anna Karenina: The most famous and inevitable example, is alas, poor Karenin's ears. A writer keen enough to recognize that, with whatever shame, we find ourselves repelled by minor physical flaws that are beyond anyone's control—the gross thigh, the bulging nose, the protruding ears—is clearly a writer who will keep our attention. He has enough mischief in him to implicate us in disreputable feelings.

The Red and the Black: Madame de Renal notices Julien Sorel: "Very soon she began to laugh, with all a girl's irresponsible gaiety. She was laughing at herself, finding it impossible to comprehend the full extent of her happiness." A characteristic Stendhalian progression: from the acceptable first sentence to the fine opening clause of the second and then the concluding clause with its superb intimation of the vanity of pleasure. This writer will keep our attention.

The House by the Medlar Tree: A Sicilian peasant is conscripted into the army, he sends back a picture of himself—writes Giovanni Verga, master of Italian verismo—"looking like the Archangel in the flesh, with those feet planted in the carpet and that drapery above his head, just like the drapery of the Madonna of Ognina," so that his poor mother "couldn't stop gazing at the carpet and the drapery . . . and she thanked God and all the saints who had put her son among all those elegancies." Nothing is made explicit here, but what is so striking is Verga's use of conceptual feints ("the Archangel," "the Madonna") in order to get at the mother's true response, her adoration of objects: the carpet and the drapery. This is the art of the novel.

The Mayor of Casterbridge: The day laborer Michael Henchard, in a spasm of anger, is prepared to sell his wife to a stranger at a country fair. The pitiful, bedraggled wife, writes Hardy, keeps trying to stay "as close to his side as was possible without actual contact." It is a sensational—in more than one sense—opening, as it touches on the depths of an illicit male fantasy (*to be rid of the whole thing*) and, whether or not with Hardy's foreknowledge, as it is certain to rouse anger among female readers. The little detail about the wife's effort to keep close to Henchard's side but not touch him, is a bit of symbolic action through which Hardy dramatizes her feelings. With a shudder of guilty recognition or with a gesture of resentment, we read on.

All of these openings entangle us with fantasies and fears, touching on responses beneath consciousness or those which consciousness is ashamed of. Such "hooking" incidents seem to me largely a yield of intuition—you wonder whether they are planned or suddenly come to the writer. How can Karenin, poor devil, ever escape the destiny of ugly ears? Madame de Renal, how will she ever slip away from the charms of this boy who makes her laugh so delightedly? So it goes, quick encapsulations, symbolic moments, consisting of the merest bits of narrative or description—but they work only in retrospect, only if the rest of the novel works. In the satisfaction of the whole, we return to the enticing preparatory clue.

Let me cite one more instance where almost nothing is given of a major character's history. What do we know, in reading *Oliver Twist*, about Fagin's past, his inner life (supposing he has one), his psychic malformations? Nothing. Fagin is revealed in his essential being through glaring pictorial segments that supply whatever answers we might need about his identity. He exhausts the action allotted to him, so that here at least the frequent claim that character should be subordinate to plot is correct. We also know Fagin because Dickens draws upon a deeply imbedded folk myth about "the Jew" as money-grubbing criminal. While a moral embarrassment, this serves Dickens as a keen economy in the rendering of Fagin: he can count upon most readers to supply the darker mythology of Christianity. At one point, however, Dickens seems to be moving toward another—what might seem a more human—mode of presentation. Waiting in prison to be executed, Fagin cries out: "What right have they to butcher me?" I read this as a false move on Dickens's part: what right have we to know Fagin's outcry? Such sentimental distractions or nuances have no place when a mythic figure is acting out the gestures of his myth. Dickens has here provided just a little too much.

Except in multivolume works of fiction like those of Proust and Martin du Gard, the "biographies" of novelistic characters tend to be slippery, fragmented, mere sleight of hand. Most characters in novels are closer to "identities" (set configurations of traits) than to "histories" (chronological accounts of personal event). Or perhaps, more exactly, they are defined by a fixed role to which the writer, counting on his skill and our sophistication, attaches a semi- or pseudobiography. Good readers make much out of little.

CHARACTERS OUT OF CHARACTERS

Characters give birth, or give way, to other characters, some mere clones, a few mere sports, but others—the most satisfying variant—transformed into instances of potentiality and surprise. To ask whether novelists draw their characters from those of earlier writers or from their own observations is an idle though interesting question: idle because it cannot be answered, interesting because one wants to keep asking. Critics who stress continuity in literature find archetypes scattered through the ages: the fool, the miser, the ingenue, the rogue, the romantic hero, the sexy mistress, etc. There is also a continuity in human relationship, those configurations of friendship and antagonism that seem to survive all social changes and historical upheavals. Thinking about such enduring archetypes (some of them "humors" or obsessional type-figures) may even persuade us that beneath the agitations of history there is a more or less constant human nature.

A relationship frequent in literature is that between master and servant (or slave), signaling the continuous power of class in Western history and the occasional desire of writers to subvert that power. Almost always this relationship is used for comic effects—a temporary inversion of status, an unsettling of hierarchies strong enough to elicit a nervous frisson but not so severe as to endanger authority. The comic thrill of seeing a slave bossing or even beating his master, if only for a day, gives way to the soothing realization that, after all, it's only in play, a brief imagined loosening of bonds that will soon again be tightened. Only in secure societies can the "risk" of such an imagined reversal of roles become a subject of comedy. Were the risk strong, it would no longer be seen as comic.

Responses of this sort must have been at work in the comedies of Plautus, where the master-slave relationship becomes an occasion for bristling, superficial comedy. Erich Segal puts the matter nicely in *Roman Laughter*:

> Comedy has been described by the psychiatrist Ernst Kris as a "holiday for the superego" and Plautus, reflecting as he does the festive spirit, banishes Roman melancholy, turning everyday attitudes and everyday values completely upside down. To a society [like the Roman] with a fantastic compulsion for hierarchies, order, and obedience, he presents a saturnalian chaos.

But only for a day, and only as a festivity in which the relaxation of power confirms its persistence. The inversion of status brings the roguish slave an opportunity for some mischief (not rebellion), and we may imagine an audience of masters and would-be masters enjoying a spectacle about their "inferiors" (as American whites could enjoy plays about those rhythmic blacks), while at the same time basking in the knowledge that tomorrow the "natural" blessings of tyranny will be reinstated.

How does this literary pattern—master/servant, superior/subordinate—come down through the centuries, to turn up in the writings of dramatists and novelists? In some instances, as a direct influence, the handing down of premises, conventions, and stereotypes. More often, a configuration like that of the master-servant is "in the air," a set of notions writers absorb from the society they live in. And then too there seem to be some basic structures of human relationship that keep being enacted through a variety of social forms.

Roman New Comedy leads into plays by Ben Jonson and Molière, with the master-servant relationship projecting a morality through comic testing. The characters are put under just enough stress to pry open their obsessions and to disorder their conduct, though at the end, once a punishment has been exacted, the social order is reestablished, sometimes refined. This scheme acquires a deeper meaning in Cervantes, with the social relations between Don Quixote and Sancho Panza becoming the base, as it were, for a vision of conflicting possibilities in the human psyche.

Novelists repeatedly borrow the master-servant theme, especially in picaresque fictions where adventures along the road need to be differentiated between the gentlemanly and the vulgar and to be interspersed with amusing, occasionally wise conversations between the picaro and his servant-accomplice. In Smollett's *Roderick Random*, a fiction where the only significant energy lies in the prose, Roderick has as his servant (also foil and butt) a lively chap named Strap, who in a penultimate transformation becomes Monsieur d'Estrapes as a contrast to Roderick's fallen condition; at the end, of course, the appropriate social hierarchy is reestablished. In *Joseph Andrews* Fielding employs a subtler and more humane version of this scheme, with the subordinate figure, Dr. Adams, a moral teacher of the protagonist.

Perhaps the most charming instance of the master-servant

pattern in English fiction occurs in *Pickwick Papers*. Sam Weller never tries to rise above his place as servant, though he keeps it with a certain healthy assertiveness—and with a backup double, his father, Tony, who if less admirable is also even sturdier than Sam. The contrast between Pickwick and Sam is at first between innocence and worldliness, with the comedy turning on Sam's recurrent need to protect his master in the rough-and-tumble of the world. There then occurs a double learning: Pickwick learns something about the grimness of life, and Sam, enchanted with Pickwick's innocence, about the possibilities of humanity, so that the novel reaches, as it were, a fine sort of moral fusion. At no point, however, does Sam challenge the status quo: Dickens cast his book as an idyll, in which everyone is largely content with his place and affectionately respectful toward everyone else's. Even as the master-servant relationship is drawn with tender strokes, as a blossoming of friendship, its traditional pattern remains unshaken. Charmed as we are by the love between master and servant, it is by now hard not to see in the idyll of the youthful Dickens a willed refusal of realities.

Far more subversive, far more charged with social aggression, is Diderot's *Jacques the Fatalist*, in which the servant Jacques is a clearly individualized figure while the master, often a mere foil, does not even have a name. Like Figaro, Jacques is a proud, self-conscious plebeian, not at all reluctant to show his superiority to his master. Diderot, never hesitant to speak in his own voice, sees Jacques as an "original," remarking that "such characters would be more prevalent if first of all education, and then afterwards the ways of the world, did not wear men down like pieces of money which lose their definition in circulation." It is not exactly that Jacques is rebellious; it is that he behaves as if the claims of the lower orders had already been achieved, as if the conquests of the French Revolution, to occur in a few years, had already been won. And Jacques achieves equality not only as a character within an imagined setting but also as a voice within the narrative. It is he who tells the stories and indulges in the reflections that form the substance of the book. He speaks with what was once known as French lucidity, a plebeian who need take only a few more steps to become, like his creator, a *philosophe*. This scintillating book brings the master-servant relationship to an extreme point, almost indeed to the point of dissolution.

We might suppose there is not much more novelists could do with this subject, but there is one work, an American novel of the nineteenth century, which takes it beyond transformation and toward transcendence. In Mark Twain's *Huckleberry Finn* the role of master is taken by a white boy and the slave by a black man. As Huck and Jim float down the Mississippi, basking in a natural setting which severs them momentarily from the social oppressiveness of the shore, the relationship between the two is at first given a comic inversion, but then something wonderful occurs, something that can still surprise and exalt: the black slave becomes a kind of father, a mentor, while the white boy, without explicit awareness of the significance of his behavior, submits gladly to the wisdom of Jim. The master-slave relationship is dissolved into friendship, and for an exquisite moment something even better than formal equality—a fraternity of companions—is established. The writing modulates from comic to idyllic, but the idyll cannot last, of course, and in the somewhat dreary, if thematically appropriate, ending of the book Jim reverts, again mute, to the slave's mask. An undercurrent of sadness runs through the concluding pages, but one thing is clear: with the great scenes on the Mississippi, the master-servant relationship has come to a fitting end, a climax of self-dissolution.

THE USES OF OPACITY

In our responses to fictional character, there is often a deep fascination with the opaque. Struggling with the dark and difficult can link, even fuse our feelings about human existence with our notions about literary art. Serious readers, quite as an article of faith, give themselves to complexities of person and personality, rich obscurities of the psyche, all-but-insuperable barriers to "seeing" the other. This persuasion that whatever is difficult must be close to the truth draws upon a line of modern thought going back to Freud and Nietzsche; but it also has an esthetic dimension. We take pleasure in the struggle to make out a complex or obscure character: this constitutes part of the esthetics of form; it may also remind us of our experience in daily life. Modern sensibility favors open endings, incompleteness. We want an art upon which we can exercise interpretive skills, and indulge delusions of being quasi-artists too. We want to joust with alternative readings, perhaps even to relish our limitations as readers. The later James, Conrad, and Ford train us to become aware of those limitations. Such writers are great withholders, denying their readers the comforts of final knowledge and leaving them with a hunger for a meaning that is resolutely denied.

Taken together, the claims of experience and the claims of

art make a strong case for opacity in fictional character. A semiopaque character at the center of a novel transforms readers into novelists' apprentices burrowing for definition, and the lovely paradox of it all is that precisely this way of writing a novel, all artifice and high sophistication, can induce us to talk about characters—say, those of *Chance* or *The Good Soldier* —quite as if they were actual and therefore puzzling human beings. James took advantage of this temptation by incorporating it into *The Golden Bowl* as the recurrent buzz-buzz of the nosy Assinghams. Their buzz-buzz and our bewilderment.

The semiopaque protagonist must be placed at an optimum distance: in a realistic novel, nearly close up, so that the other characters can circle and dispute with him; and in a romance fiction, alluringly far away, so that the aura of mystery will not be dissipated. Soon enough, at whatever distance, we join the secondary characters in trying to figure things out. Or, and this seems especially to delight some critics, we gain a measure of satisfaction in coming to understand why the secondary characters have failed to understand.

Glance at a poised young Englishman, Vanderbank, in James's *The Awkward Age*, as he passes beyond the range of our full comprehension and partial sympathy. Yvor Winters provides a fine sketch: "Vanderbank is a creature through whose tranquil and pellucid character there arises at the slightest disturbance of his surface a fine cloud of silt, of ugly feeling far too subtle to be called suspicion, but darkening his entire nature." This takes us part of the way, locating symptoms but not causes. Nor does James really go further. He keeps a stringent discipline, refusing to break into his text as commentator, staying with a mode of representation that seems at first to resemble a well-made play but then offers far richer detail than any play could. We may, if we feel the need strongly enough, come to certain conclusions about Vanderbank, but only with much uncertainty, for the other characters are similarly, if in lesser degree, elusive. This novel resembles a field of variables each of which solicits definition from the other. James leaves us partly in the dark—not entirely, we do gain patches of comprehension—but what he finally creates is an interplay of light and dark, what we think we know and what we know we don't.

Tension, sadness, grief, these hover like a cloud across the frame of this novel, but their causes and consequences are problematic. As with our relations to actual persons, our knowledge remains fragmentary, uncertain, and sometimes it seems that our apparent access of insight is no more than a token of vanity. Yet this difficult but remarkable novel moves us, or at least some of us, and the question is: Why? Because James makes utterly persuasive the sufferings of the cultivated, somewhat decadent group of Londoners who are his main figures. What drives them, what misshapes them may never receive a final answer, but we know they bleed.

Melville also knew something about the uses of opacity. We first see Captain Ahab through a haze of awe. Nowhere in *Moby-Dick* does Melville pretend to explain Ahab or to penetrate his intentions: the grizzled old heretic remains apart, as if in the spaces of myth. That Ahab should remain largely opaque is a precondition for the submissiveness of the *Pequod*'s men: they obey because they do not understand. But the treatment of Ahab proceeds, as it were, from more general considerations. In a romance fiction like *Moby-Dick*, where the main antagonist is a totemic beast, the looming hero is rarely subjected to close-up; only once or twice is he even allowed the terms of ordinary humanity. He must seem "larger" than the other characters, and this requires a certain shrouding effect. Finally Captain Ahab is revealed as at least in part a false hero, but even a false hero has to be fixed into distance, grand in his freedom from familiar categories.

Faulkner also finds a use for opacity. *As I Lay Dying*, a work of great technical virtuosity, is organized as a cantata of voices, each passing the action along to the next. The characters are arranged on a scale of accessibility: first the totally and therefore comically lucid Cash and Anse Bundren, neither of whom casts any shadow; then Addie Bundren, hard to grasp but still reachable; and finally the sons, Jewel, Darl, and Vardaman, ranging into deepening layers of the opaque, sometimes falling into the merely incoherent. About this kind of novel, in which the author never appears in his own right, we cannot be certain that we gain its meaning fully—indeed, to elicit a response of doubt is one of its purposes. But I take it that Faulkner chose deliberately to show, first, how arid certain kinds of lucidity can be and, then, what might be called the richness of the dark, the garbled but genuine powers that can lie hidden in the opaque beings of Jewel, Darl, and even Vardaman. Sentimentality is a risk here, but Faulkner avoids it through a tone of comic grotesque. At times, however, it seems that the sheer ferocity of his conceptions has thrown up verbal blockages, into and beyond the opaque. This risk is inherent in modernist writing, with too great a yielding to the opaque verging on the devil's work.

GETTING OUT OF HAND

In talking about novels, we often say that a character has "gotten out of hand." What can we mean by that? At least two things: we may be expressing delight at the writer's fecundity or we may be noticing a breakdown in artistic control. It is a curiosity of language that the same phrase can simultaneously take on quite opposite meanings, a tacit recognition perhaps that polar statements display a certain symmetry.

If we speak with delight, it is usually in response to the resourcefulness of comic characters: Pecksniff, Chichikoff, Flem Snopes, Molly Bloom, the elder Karamazov (not entirely, but often, comic). Such a character bursts through the frame of the novel, grabbing more space and attention than the conception of the novel might warrant. In the happiest sense of the word, the character makes a *spectacle* of him- or herself—something most novelists seem to relish. This, of course, is a loose or metaphorical way of speaking, since on their own characters can't "do" anything. It is the writer who decides how much space to give them, whether to let them marry, and when to kill them off. Still, while quite aware of all this, we persist in taking pleasure in the notion that a character, fresh with energy, can overturn a writer's formative plan.

Thoughts such as these come freely when reading Dickens. It's as if there is a deeper Dickens, an ur-Dickens more anarchic and free, who thrusts his way past the Dickens who manufactures those tiresome plots. With an eloquent hiccup, Sarry Gamp stumbles past the contraptions of plot, to provide exalted entertainment; Pecksniff, sublime hypocrite, glows with the joy of performance; the Smallweeds grasp their turf, commanding attention through sheer grotesquerie. In such portions of Dickens's work we sense an abandonment to the demons of creation, as if the impulse to literary representation has overpowered theme, plot, and purpose. Or, when reading *The Brothers Karamazov*, we may find ourselves wishing that the elder Karamazov, that maestro of buffoonery, will hold center stage; we grow *impatient* for his antics, charmed by his readiness to disrupt whatever design Dostoevsky may have had in mind.

Such a response occurs most often with comic fiction because its formal demands need not be too stringent: it indulges a quantity of repetition improbable in other modes. But this can also occur with melodrama, as in those Balzac novels where Vautrin, theoretician of criminality, reduces everything, plot, scene, and characters, to miniature.

Why, in a serious novel like *The Brothers Karamazov*, doesn't the loquacity of the elder Karamazov, that incorrigible scene-stealer, annoy or irritate? Because the comic element forms a substructure in the book, opening up its rhythms, relieving metaphysics with farce. Because the book is organized like a series of overheated scenes in a badly made play, with the characters rushing in and out, confronting, scolding, adoring one another: a melee of assault and rhapsody that declines into exhaustion. The plot advances, when it does advance, like a sputter of recurrences rather than as a strict pattern of causality. Nor does it matter very much that the characters step out of, or throw off, their designated roles, since a main value of this novel is to indulge excess: excess of passion and of mind, modulated now and then by Alyosha's meekness. For portions of the novel, excess sweeps away Dostoevsky's design—well, not exactly sweeps away, but diverts, entangles, delays. In Dostoevsky's novels the major characters are always free to go the limit, with the limit an infiltration of the tragic into comic molds.

Dickens, Balzac, and to some extent Dostoevsky work out a kind of fiction that does not require stringency of form and tolerates carelessness of style; they seem to be waiting for the moment when the characters, or some of them, will "get out of hand"—as if that would prove to be a confirmation of their powers.

Balzac is excessive even in excess, the very idea of his fictional empire a kind of madness. Upon need he can turn out a compact little novel like *Ursule Mirouët*, but the true Balzacian note is struck in the big books, like *Lost Illusions*, and its sequel, in English, *A Harlot High and Low*. It is in this last, riotous work that Vautrin, "the Cromwell of the criminal settlements," comes to seem larger than life, one of Cain's "demonic progeny," summing up "all human energy . . . like those feverish animals of the wilderness whose form of life calls for the vast spaces they find there." What keeps Vautrin from shriveling into the sort of vapid monster often found in English gothic fiction is his social wit and a redeeming weakness of closet homosexuality. In him energy is indeed "eternal delight," amoral and fearless, superbly "out of hand"—a subversive vision best put forward in another novel, *A Murky Affair*, where Balzac writes about the "exceptional power" of generals, orators, and criminals (all pretty much the same to him) that "it seems as if some compelling influence is emitted from the brain . . . and that a man's will-power is pumped into others by his very gestures." This celebration of energy, superfluity, outpouring finds repeated expression in the great novelists of the nineteenth century: everything that has flourished after the French Revolution, from the exaltation of the individual to the ethos of romanticism, contributes to this style of exuberance, this love of human plenty. Critics have not, as a rule, been very friendly to this view of literature, perhaps because it makes them feel puny and unneeded.

Reading such novels as they shrug off prescriptions for austerity, we can take in a good amount of gratuitous material, big chunks of physical description, interludes of ill-connected representation. Something rather "primitive" happens here: the writer senses that a character, or a strand of action sustaining two or three characters, has come along, more "alive" than anything else he has done. A lucky break. And the writer then goes hell-bent with the characters who are straining to get out of his grip, while the novel's form must take the consequences.

We can understand why, after the subtleties and shrinkages of literary modernism, some twentieth-century writers should look back with hunger at the excesses of nineteenth-century fiction, as if to say: "Why can't my work also 'get out of hand' once in a while?" Wasn't it some such impulse that led Saul Bellow to turn from his constrained apprentice fiction to his simulation of an earlier abundance, that moment of innocence when literary representation was taken to have a value in its own right? If there is something a trifle willed in the picaresque energy of *The Adventures of Augie March* and its sequels, perhaps that is a price which has to be paid for a self-conscious return. And is worth paying.

"Excess" and "getting out of hand," I should say, are not quite the same. (I speak with some authority since these categories are my own.) Excess in a novel usually seems planned or at least indulged, while "getting out of hand" is something that happens, through a charge of unconscious energy.

Jay Gatsby is perfectly aligned with his role. Indeed, he *is* the role, so much so that he appears more as bearer of myth than character of a story. It would be hard to read *The Great Gatsby* without reflecting on its sense of American experience, and if there is any imperfection in this short novel, it is a danger of perfection gone lifeless—a danger Fitzgerald manages to escape mostly through the narrator's wry, deflating voice. By contrast, in *Tender Is the Night*, Dick Diver comes through only fitfully, in starts and gasps; he seems at times to "get out of hand," though never through excess. Yet for many readers this character evokes a strong emotional resonance; not only his flaws but perhaps even the flaws in Fitzgerald's presentation enhance our sensitivity to human frailty. Diver is not nearly so comfortable with his role as Gatsby with his, but we see Diver less in typicality than as a stricken individual who need not, though as his name suggests he may, symbolize something beyond his personal plight. What some may regard as an intermittent failure of control I take to be a satisfying relaxation of rigor, a small-scale instance of how "getting out of hand" can be a literary boon. And perhaps in creating the flawed Dick Diver, Fitzgerald had in mind the limitations of the perfect Jay Gatsby.

How, then, is the phrase "getting out of hand" used as a term of critical censure?

Surely we don't have in mind an unachieved character, about whom little can "get out of hand." We have in mind a disorder of intention or realization, the troubles that follow after a character, though sufficiently present, has not "behaved" as he or she was supposed to. The writer has lost control.

Such disorders may reflect illicit emotions the writer has invested in a character, some disabling identification that draws upon infantile or adolescent fantasy. Or there may break out a revolt of thwarted powers within the writer's psyche—angelic or demonic; who can be sure which? Or the character may be acting out a refusal to be boxed into a preordained or misconceived role ("No, no, that's not me," the character pleads with his creator), though we know of course that the refusal is actually taking place within the writer.

Hawthorne has a remarkable passage in his notebook:

> A person to be writing a tale, and to find that it shapes itself against his intentions; that the characters act otherwise than he thought; that unforeseen events occur; and a catastrophe which he strives in vain to avert. It might shadow forth his own fate —he having made himself one of the personages.

Hawthorne was here anticipating, I believe, what would later be called the return of the repressed, an eruption of feelings more difficult to contain, and therefore more dangerous, than those solicited by the writer's original intention. Especially keen is his concluding phrase—"he [the writer] having made himself one of the personages"—which points to confusions that may ensue when a writer, edging his way into his own work, can no longer distinguish between the world in which he lives and the world he makes up. (Cf. Melville's *Pierre*.)

What I have just been saying rests on the assumption that we can "know" with assurance what the structure of a novel requires from a character, that we can tell when Maggie Tulliver or Dorothea Brooke is doing the assigned job or is starting to act "otherwise than [George Eliot] thought." Such judgments are necessarily *post hoc*. In practice we do something like this: We construct an image of the novel's "ideal structure"—an image derived from our encounter with the novel in its flawed actuality—and then we decide how well the character has lived up to the part required by that "ideal structure." We imagine what the writer must have imagined the novel would be like.

Tacitly we accept the Jamesian precept that a character must be seen within "the whole envelope of circumstance." (Where else?) James's remark holds in a double sense. Insofar as we think of the character as a simulated person, he or she establishes an identity through participation in society, which provides "the envelope of circumstance." But insofar as we regard the character as one component in a literary structure, we can perceive him or her accurately only to the extent that we discern a relationship to other components (e.g., length or brevity, genre, narrative voice). Yet even while we may recognize the interdependence between character and other fictional components, we also see, or sense, that characters can partly escape from the constraints of fictional structure and assume a more or less independent being. No matter how many fingers of reproach formalist critics wag at us, we all do this—and they too, I suspect. Where do some fictional characters take on (what looks like or what we like to regard as) independent being? Precisely where they also exist as components of narrative: in the responses of readers. Only the dreariest of literalists would insist that Anna Karenina be seen merely as a cog in Tolstoy's apparatus.

A character "gets out of hand," in the negative sense, when

the writer fails to establish an appropriate distance between himself and the character. Some critics have written that George Eliot indulged in an excessive identification with Maggie Tulliver in *The Mill on the Floss* and Dorothea Brooke in *Middlemarch*, and that Henry James showed an excessive inclination to hover protectively over some of his heroines. This is a difficult call to make. If we do decide that George Eliot is damagingly involved with Maggie and Dorothea, one reason for proposing that judgment may be that in George Eliot's treatment of Gwendolyn Harleth in *Daniel Deronda* we see a brilliant contrasting instance of how a writer can present a heroine with both sympathy and criticism, warmth and objectivity. But can we be sure? Can we say with complete confidence (F. R. Leavis could) that what works so well in one novel is really an adequate measure for what seems to have gone wrong in another? Might it not be argued that the psychic temperature, the animating basis in feeling, of *The Mill on the Floss* is sharply different from that of *Daniel Deronda* and that it is therefore insensitive to use the work of George Eliot's later years as a stick with which to beat the work of her earlier years? Critics ought now and then to hesitate.

A more complex problem arises when a novelist creates a character who is "too interesting" for the part assigned. What can this mean? How can anything be "too interesting"? It means that, through sheer force of presence, the character "gets out of hand" by breaking up the intended scheme of the novel. Sometimes that happens because the character forms, in the writer's creative economy, an anticipatory sketch for something that will be developed only in a later work. Jane Fairfax of Austen's *Emma* seems out of place in the sedate little corner

of Highbury, where everything is filtered through minute ironies. At first, it is clear that Austen means Jane Fairfax to be
out of place: a familiar device for building narrative tension.
Jane Fairfax is shadowy, melancholy, reticent, and more refined than the buoyant Emma, and it's not at all hard to be
drawn to the romantic figure of Jane Fairfax even while wondering what Austen is doing with her. Is she setting up a com-
petition between two girls that is also a contrast in sensibilities?
Or does she have some unexamined need to allow a relatively
minor figure like Jane Fairfax to preempt our attention, at the
risk of radically upsetting the novel's balance? About two-
thirds of the way, as if realizing that Jane Fairfax has quite
fulfilled her role but meanwhile has emerged as an "interesting"
threat to her plan for the book, Austen manages to bring Jane
back to the margin where she belongs. We may sigh a little,
but must acknowledge the rightness of this move.

Perhaps, however, Austen is testing out the uses of a romantic heroine in preparation for Anne Elliot of *Persuasion*.
This may explain, if not justify, why Jane Fairfax looms as
large as, for a time, she does. And, what's more, the danger
that the neatly made structure of *Emma* will be damaged by
the romantic intrusion of Jane Fairfax adds a touch of excite-
ment, a kind of vicarious peril, to our reading of the book.
Will Austen recover in time? Will the novel be transformed
into something it was not supposed to be? And if that happens,
how can we be sure about what it was supposed to be? There
is still another, fairly remote possibility: that Austen was employing the literary convention according to which a comedy
brings everyone to a sunny conclusion—except for one character, Jane Fairfax. For even in comedic resolution there may

be (Malvolio in *Twelfth Night*) a character denied the general dispensation of happiness, as a nod from convention to reality.

These categories, "excess" and "getting out of hand," break down, I'm glad to say, when applied to a number of novels. (To be of use, categories should now and then break down.) A number of critics, including Edmund Wilson and Philip Toynbee, have, for example, argued that of the concluding three sections of Joyce's *Ulysses*—the coffee stall, the question-and-answers, and Molly's soliloquy—the first two are rhetorically overblown, the last a triumph. In some sense, Joyce's virtuosity overran his narrative. The novel finds its main narrative direction in the meeting and growing relation between Leopold Bloom and Stephen Dedalus, something that seems largely completed by the coffee-stall section, almost certainly exhausted by the question-and-answer section. Yet it would be very rash to speak of excess in any of the senses that I have done here, since Joyce is not only a novelist, but also *a writer* for whom the play of language has a value apart from the rhythm of the story. There is, I think, a clear letdown for inveterate novel readers when they reach the first two of the book's concluding three sections, but that may not be at all true for Joyce enthusiasts, who are not necessarily novel readers. With Joyce, nothing "gets out of hand"—it's hard even to imagine anything of the sort—and excess also seems an irrelevant category. What is happening in *Ulysses* is at once the fulfillment and the disintegration of the novel as a form. In Molly's soliloquy the onrushing force of her musings sweeps the book, if not the narrative, to completion, a triumph of genius over genre. But the problems for the novel that Joyce brought to absolute focus remain.

CHARACTER GOES, BUT ALSO REMAINS

The novel produces antinovels. From its glorious disintegration in the modernist period comes resurrected picaresque, essayistic fiction, dream stories for an age of nightmare. Only those over fifty and a few naive undergraduates, I suspect, still love the novel.

What most cultivated readers take to be satisfying characterization is likely to be culture-bound. Such people are hooked on the modes and premises of European fiction as written in the nineteenth and early twentieth centuries, even if they also take a stab at Robbe-Grillet, Gombrowicz, and Barthelme. The social novel, the *Bildungsroman*, the novel of manners—all place or locate their characters in a society palpable and populated, resembling (but how much and in what ways?) the actual world; all endow their characters with names such as actual persons might have (Buddenbrook, Vronsky, Hurstwood, Benjy, not Everyman, Christian, Joseph K.); and all treat the self as a precious reserve or fragile hypothesis of individuality, while acknowledging that it is also a social creation formed through our relations with others.

The farther away a prose fiction moves from the classical nineteenth-century novel, the less likely is it to contain "full" or "rounded" characters. Characters may be indispensable to novels; they are not to fictions. Neither Captain Ahab nor the white whale, Gregor Samsa nor the protagonist of Zamyatin's *We* could find a comfortable place in the traditional novel. Yet literary forms, like cultural styles, are slow to die, if they die at all; the very novels that father antinovels can occasionally still find in their ungrateful offspring an uncomfortable haven.

Ulysses is clearly not a novel in quite the way *Middlemarch* or *The Bostonians* is, though some parts of it are superbly novelistic. Still, the book contains notable characterization. It might of course be said that there is only one "full" character in *Ulysses*, and that is Leopold Bloom. The sections in which Bloom first makes his appearance, allying quasi-naturalistic narrative with interior monologue, are fairly close in their treatment of character to what we have come to expect in nineteenth-century novelists—or, at least, we can still see a connection between the two. Joyce may indeed be breaking away from, even breaking up, the traditional novel, but in the first third or so of *Ulysses* strong elements of it are still present. Only later, with the more experimental sections, in which the run of consciousness overwhelms portrayed event and style tends to smother plot, are the customary modes of treating character largely discarded. Joyce is moving toward something that is still fictional but not really novelistic. To abandon the conventions of the nineteenth-century novel he had, however, first to reinstate them with an all-but-unprecedented authority.

Novel and fiction: the relationship comes to a point of tension in Milan Kundera's *The Unbearable Lightness of Being*. Provocatively insistent upon his book's utter fictionality and steadily breaking the illusion of mimetic transparency, Kundera sets up a thematic contrast between "lightness" and "weight." Lightness: "the absolute absence of a burden," writes Kundera, "causes man to be lighter than air . . . his movements as free as they are insignificant." Lightness means a mode of existence content with the mere sequence of happenings and bearing within itself neither historical past nor moral consequence. Weight: "the heaviest of burdens," writes Kundera "is . . . an image of life's most intense fulfillment. The heavier the burden, the closer our lives come to the earth, the more real and truthful they become." Weight signifies the burden of repetition, or the repetition of burden, and elicits emotions beyond dismissal, such as guilt, jealousy, shame.

To represent "lightness" Kundera sketches a woman named Sabina, charming, sexy, intelligent, yet finally of slight consequence. Her only code is an esthetic one, the rejection of kitsch, but an esthetic by itself can never be adequate to man's condition. To represent "weight" Kundera sketches a woman named Tereza, fearful, jealous, neurotic, but living out the deepest intuitions of life and death. Sabina is an original, very much of our moment, the creature of Kundera's devilish eye. She releases Kundera's disdain for the kitsch of the Communist regime—that which draws upon collective sentimentalities— as well as for the kitsch of the West—that which falsely invokes the very intuitions by which Tereza lives. Sabina ends in the West, rich and footloose. A painter who paints paint, she sees through everything: that is her curse. Tereza, with whom the book's protagonist ends in a conventionally "warm" relationship, carries within her a bit of kitsch—but then, who doesn't? (For Kundera that's Original Sin: "No matter how we scorn it, kitsch is an integral part of the human condition.") She and her lover grow teary over the death of their dog, Karenin— the name no accident, invoking Tolstoy's character of unimaginative rectitude, the kind of man Sabina could not have tolerated for ten minutes. Sheer poison in its public forms, kitsch takes on, by the end of Kundera's book, a certain pastoral mistiness. The flinty brilliant Kundera, he too yields a little to kitsch.

Tereza submitting to ordinary life, Tereza contradicting Kundera's notions of what a character in one of his books should be like, Tereza is a transplant from the nineteenth-century novel: an old-fashioned creature, a character and not just a fictional convenience. She is the tribute Kundera pays to the literary traditions he would abandon. The old nestles in the new—how else could either be defined?

Five Instances of Characterization

Order is the ruling virtue of *Tom Jones*: the world ordered, our understanding of the world ordered, and our fictions ordered. It is not of course as if Fielding fails to recognize the vastness of disorder spread across the earth; he provides an abundance of catastrophe in his novels, more in each new one than in its predecessors, all grazing the edge of fear but then, except perhaps in his last one, *Amelia*, all calmed through the attentions of comedy. In Fielding's view of things, the surface of disorder must finally yield to an inner reality of order: that is an imperative of the universe, perhaps the design of the Almighty. In *Tom Jones* this idea of order firmly controls the narrative, through both ethical assertion and a hierarchical arrangement of character. Chaotic experience, and plenty of it, is available for depiction, but the depiction finally settles into a pattern of order.

And that is where our difficulties with this classic begin and end: we cannot, even if we might wish to, be assured disciples of order. Fielding seems too certain of his *Weltanschauung*, and modern readers are likely to be uncomfortable with a novel in which the author feels neither qualm nor hesitation about declaring a fixed ethical position. We suspect a writer who is so entirely in control of his assumptions; we suspect him more in a prose fiction than we might in a traditional epic, since the allowances we have learned to make for an epic are not yet available for a novel. That we use "didactic" as a pejorative rather than a neutral term tells the story, if not about Fielding, then about us. And the very order to which he is so strongly and, in the end, serenely committed can seem to us elusive. It is as if his words are familiar but his language is not—year by year, the book gradually slips away.

In his warm defense of Fielding, William Empson goes a bit too far when he writes that by the novel's end Tom Jones has become "a Gospel Christian"; poor Tom is never quite that worried in his morality, nor is Fielding. It may be enough to say that Tom has turned out to be a decent fellow. It may also be enough to observe that Fielding was advocating a mixture of judgment and tolerance, with the proportions unfixed; that he appreciated how difficult it is for human beings to live by the more stringent versions of Christianity; and that he turned a kindly eye upon those in whom principle is modulated by generosity, since they could be counted on to be quick with forgiveness, itself not the least of principles.

Now, while all of this seems admirable, the truth is, it does not engage modern readers very strongly. It does not seem sufficiently "dark" in its cognizance of evil; it lacks Kierkegaardian tumult; it seems too rationalistic and sensible. Empson suggests, a little wickedly, that "modern critics tend to assume . . . that the only high-minded doctrine to preach is despair and contempt for the world." Such critics prefer the burrowing, morbid psychology of a Richardson to the good spirit of a Fielding, perhaps because the former allows for greater bravura in criticism. Still, the things critics say are hardly the norms by which people live. Fielding's is a humane, if not especially profound, vision of life; it leads to neither the shedding of blood nor the shallows of decadence; it makes the ideal of a gentleman seem better than a mere sanction for privilege. And yet: not enough.

These problems of moral sensibility are but the other side of the problems we encounter when responding to Fielding's handling of character. Fielding, as R. S. Crane writes, was "able to invent or sustain characters . . . good *for the form*" (emphasis added) of the novel; good, that is, for the comic plot which guides the movement, often pleasurable in its own right, from phenomenal disorder to an essence of order.

Simply put, the characters of *Tom Jones* tend mainly to be "functional." As Robert Alter writes:

> There are, then, two kinds of knowledge of character which the novel form makes readily available—the empathic knowledge of imaginative identification and the evaluative knowledge of discriminating observation: characters in novels may be invitingly permeable or beautifully perspicuous. . . . Fielding is plainly a novelist wholly committed to perspicuity, not permeability, in the creation of character. . . . [His] refusal to render inner states is a conscious decision on his part. . . .

The characters of *Tom Jones* perform their roles admirably. That is how we are invited to see them, as figures that form a contrast in modes of conduct, representative figures who in a few instances come to resemble fleshed human beings. Through segments of action set in balanced contrast, the characters release the matter of the plot and thereby the theme as well. The hand of Fielding the judge and Fielding the pardoner is always felt: transparency of event or autonomy of character is rarely sought. A certain complex irony is present in the characterization of *Tom Jones*, felt not so much through the consciousness of individual figures (since, as Crane admits, not many of these are "intrinsically interesting") but through the interaction of roles, the dialectic of arrangement. They act, to borrow Fielding's phrase, in "this great theatre of Nature," and here both nouns signify: a "theatre" of expository narrative interspersed with diverting little "plays," and a fundamental "Nature," substance and source of universal order.

There's a lot to admire here. The characters "fit" their parts. Indeed, for the modern reader trained to view characters as semiautonomous beings who can be seen and thought about somewhat apart from the text, this is probably a major reason for not finding Fielding's characters "intrinsically interesting." We want at least the illusion of autonomy, characters that are a little opaque, not just see-through conveniences. Such desires Fielding satisfies rather little.

I am not saying that even when placed into a hierarchical arrangement all of his characters seem mere puppets. At least a few exist without the visible strings of his management: some, notably the choleric Squire Western and the compliant Jenny Jones, are allowed surprise, excess, a touch of "life" apart from the performance of role. Like people, they exist simply because they exist—and not just as components of a novelistic structure.

Now all of this ought to deepen our involvement as readers if only . . . if only we could fully engage with Fielding's moral scheme. Let the entirety of the book's conceptual system hold us fast, let us be able spontaneously to assent to its vision of order, and we will come to accept, grudgingly or freely, the subordination of characters to that system.

R. S. Crane, in his close study of the novel's mechanics, praises the characters as not only "good for the form" but also adds, though with some uneasiness, that several of them are "interesting in themselves, as the two Westerns and Partridge." The two Westerns yes, Partridge no. But what is striking here is that not even Fielding enthusiasts try to make out a case for the book's main characters—Tom, Sophia, Blifil, Allworthy —as "interesting in themselves." Even for a reader who respects the radically different expectations entertained for a novel two centuries ago—"interesting in themselves" might not then have been so strong a requirement—it is hard not to feel impatient when watching the resourceful mind of Fielding put the limited mind of Tom through its paces. This young tyro of beef and ale, so insistently good-natured and full-blooded, rushing from imbroglio to imbroglio, escaping by a hair's breadth the consequences of his impetuosity (and his frequent mindlessness too), and rarely stopping, even during his bouts of remorse, to examine himself or his motives: this Jones can seem as much a sign of English self-satisfaction as of moral perspicuity. We want now and again to whisper into Tom's ear, "a little less motion, a little more reflection."

But there Tom is, quite adequate to Fielding's pattern and a darling for all those unreconciled to the harsh ways of history, and there too are the other characters, all neatly going about their business, and with no great amount of texturing, since they do not need it. Besides, Fielding's own suave commentary provides a substitute. These characters are like dancers in choreography that rarely allows an interval for improvisation. They do not live beyond the pages of the book and they do not arouse much curiosity—who has ever wondered or worried about Tom's inner thoughts?

At least for those to whom traditional orders are not quite sacred, Fielding's genius for order keeps us at a certain remove, not quite acquiescing and not quite resisting. We can no longer be at ease with a novelist who seems so much at ease with (in D. H. Lawrence's phrase) his "certain moral scheme." We want novelists who create the illusion that their characters live in serious tension with *any* preconceived "moral scheme," characters who act out of autonomous natures, occasionally getting out of hand, even in rebellion against their creators. So it's not the formal mode of characterization in *Tom Jones* that is, in and of itself, the trouble for those of us who feel uneasy with this acknowledged classic. It's the world-view, the ontological comfort of Fielding, as it sets the hierarchy of the characters in place, which causes our discomfort when reading a novel the many virtues of which we take for granted.

Something has evidently been lost since Fielding wrote, something for which the word "order" is the merest shadow. And if we continue to read him, as of course we should, it is because we suspect that there is much to regret in this loss.

STERNE: DISORDERS OF CHARACTER

We do not read *Tristram Shandy* for a penetration of psychological depths or an assuaging coherence of character. Sterne does not allow that. He proceeds from a tacit denial that "depth" is a useful category in the presentation of character. He calls into question the premise of conventional fiction that character is an ascertainable structure or has a history open to synthesis. What he does, instead, is to lure us into the labyrinths of his own consciousness, more or less projected as that of his narrator, Tristram. These labyrinths, all on the surface, form a mixture of muddle and perversity. Sterne's purpose is to amuse through bafflement. A deeper purpose is to evoke a mocking helplessness before the self-enclosure of the mind. It is strongly implied in *Tristram Shandy* that the narrator's singular consciousness is to be seen as a version, or at least a fraction, of generic consciousness.

Tristram Shandy commits serious epistemological mischief: the unraveling of system—all systems, the very idea of system. Sterne undermines the notion that experience, even if conforming to a creator's legislation, is open to rational grasp. Along the way, he breaks down the structure of the syntactically ordered sentence. Assault one and you endanger the other. The world and the sentence, both crumble into fragments, to be reassembled by neither God nor man, but only (if at all) by the artist. Sterne anticipates the modern or Proustian feeling that art alone can yield the supreme ordering of the world's disorder, and thereby, perhaps, become a consolation for the bruises of disorder. He trains us, accordingly, to watch the play of artifice more than its product—indeed to see that the play of artifice *is* the product. We come to learn that the book's rich scatter of disorder is mostly a trick, part of the game of art, to gull both sophisticates and innocents, for Sterne knows perfectly well that the disorder of a text can be persuasively evoked only through devices of order. Even those fragments of the book that are clearly gratuitous, abandoning any pretense of focus upon the characters and bringing us directly to the author's mind, have their function. They force attention to the creative will, its refusal to be bound by the decorum of mere order, its stress upon the indeterminacy of evidence. Such juggling may have been what Sterne had in mind when writing that his object was to "baffle all criticism," surely one of the noblest projects ever conceived by a writer.

Sterne intends to trace the confusions of "what passes in a man's own mind." These may become manifest as obsessions due to external pressures upon consciousness: the weight of the world. Or they may derive from inner disarrangement of mind: the narrator's weight. In any case, there is little space or opportunity for that enlargement of moral faculties or that rich development of the psyche we will come to expect from nineteenth-century English fiction. In Sterne's book character is to be pressed in, rather than let out; it is to be abridged and locked up, rather than expanded and freed.

The notions of "My Father," Walter Shandy, about the shaping of character—its ultimate source in geniture, noses, and names—form a wild burlesque on theories of psychological determinism. (If the family romance, why not the configuration of the nose? If the early Freud, why not Walter Shandy?) But weaving through this burlesque runs a strand of acute observation: that our natures constantly fall prey to contingency.

Sterne is the poet of accident, the disobedience of nature. Accident he elevates to "law," the "law" of those absurd and humiliating little causes that yet determine psychic life. Quirks in our "association of ideas," erratic hoppings of the mind, became the materials for a stylized narrative. A casual linkage of the sex act and the striking of a clock comes for Tristram's mother to resemble fatality—repeat it often enough and it *is* fatality. The parody of Locke, or Locke unlocked, reduces to littleness both cause and consequence in human affairs.

Here is a hobbling instance of Sterne's view about the relation between "a man and his Hobby-Horse":

> there is a communication between them of some kind . . . and
> that by means of the heated parts of the rider, which come
> immediately into contact with the back of the Hobby-Horse.
> — By long journies and much friction, it so happens that the
> body of the rider is at length fill'd as full of HOBBY-HORSICAL
> matter as it can hold.

The image is comically literal, the idea acute. Uncle Toby, My Father, Corporal Trim: their characters are all shaped by their occupations and preoccupations, so that they become, as it were, functions of their functions, ridden saddle-sore by the hobbyhorse on which they ride.

The notion that characters should be "filled out" psychologically or probed into their hidden darkness, seems ridiculous to Sterne, or at best a mere literary convention to be shattered through the aggressions of play. What he sees on the surface is hopeless enough. In our later vocabulary we might say that he focuses upon personality rather than character, but if Sterne were to grasp the distinction, he would, I think, reject it, saying that personality is the mere noise and motion of character, or a belief in character the mere wisp of personality. What he does is to strip fictional character of its mimetic authority, partly through mock scholarship, partly through a strongly reductive psychology, and just as he makes war upon the sentence, breaking its unity through a guerrilla raid of dashes, so he breaks up the assumption that character is accessible to rational grasp. Traditional premises of correspondence between man and God, man and nature, which have long served to buoy our self-esteem, are parodied as Shandyan correspondence between psyche and tic. Character is a dark surface, evoked in arrhythmic gestures and stammering phrases. At one point, exasperated with Uncle Toby's innocent obtuseness,

> —My father thrust back his chair, — rose up, — put on his hat, — took four long strides to the door, — jerked it open, — thrust his head half way out, — shut the door again, — took no notice of the bad hinge, — returned to the table, — pluck'd my mother's thread-paper out of *Slawkenbergius's* book, — went hastily to his bureau, — walk'd slowly back, twisting my mother's thread-paper about his thumb, — unbutton'd his waistcoat, — threw my mother's thread-paper into the fire, — bit her sattin pin-cushion in two, fill'd his mouth with bran, — confounded it; — but mark! — the oath of confusion was levell'd at my uncle *Toby's* brain, which was e'en confused enough already, — the curse came charged only with the bran, the bran, may it please your honours, — was no more than powder to the ball.

This passage, so like a slow burn, brings together acute phenomenological detail, sly touches of wit, and punctuation as obbligato. We see My Father's temper stiffening into gestures of helplessness. Voice and body stammer together.

In the Shandyan universe there are indeed laws of being, but these manifest themselves through puny actions and unflattering motions. Sterne's characters are fixed through private ritual, obscure posture, compulsive gesture, the psychopathology of everyday life. Comparing ourselves to the gods we have created out of vanity and need, we like to think of human beings as autonomous agents, but this view of things is demoted in *Tristram Shandy* to a mere consoling fiction. We are, in the Shandyan view, our own fragments. Uncle Toby and My Father are put together from an assortment of tics and obsessions. The tics signal the obsessions, the obsessions trigger the tics. Accept these as the substance of character—or, what for *Tristram Shandy* comes to the same thing, as Sterne's surrogate notations—and they can be a source of humor and charm, with reason laughed into a corner and nothing to be done with disbelief except suspend it.

Uncle Toby reduces everything to a ritual game of his toy fortifications; My Father enlarges everything to grand hypotheses. Finally, however, there is little difference between reduction and expansion. Neither Uncle Toby nor My Father can reach ease of feeling or behavior, a goal Sterne regards as quite utopian. When his characters set out to reason, they cap the comedy of miscommunication; little goes right in this world of isolates. The slipperiness of words contributes to the waywardness of thought. In proper philosophical style, "before I venture to make use of the word *Nose* a second time," Tristram sets out "to define, with all possible exactness," a nose. At the end, "I declare, by that word I mean a Nose, and nothing more or less." Sterne's characters are locked in a cell of language and the most they can do is to shake the bars. Uncle Toby doesn't bother to try.

Sterne's character-sketching is abrupt, rapid, in curves of outline. A play of wit circles the trapped, indeed, the tragic incapacities of his characters' minds. What remains for Sterne are touches of sentiment, sometimes a little damp. Or as Sydney Greenstreet once remarked in a memorably wicked film role, what the world needs "is a little more kindness." Uncle Toby offers it and Tristram approves, grinning, sometimes leering.

Tristram Shandy, in all its artful chaos, invites at least some readers, usually those raised on realism, to "reconstruct" the book as a conventional narrative. The chronology is there, if only you trouble to straighten it out. But if you allow this rebuilt "shadow" novel to obliterate the ordered jumble which is the actual book, you lose its wit and point. For to reassemble the book into a conventional novel is to validate Sterne's refusal of standard conventions. The claim here is that artifice brings us as close to reality as ordinary verisimilitude—at least in Sterne's hands.

Finally Sterne's hobbled mode of characterization, for all its brilliant innovation, leads to a sense of the human lot that is not radically different from that advanced in realistic fiction. The difference is one of avenue, not destination. The obsessed and bewildered creatures of *Tristram Shandy*, emerging through Sterne's devices but also seeming to exist a little apart from them, are entirely familiar. They live in our bodies and our homes; we recognize them quite as readily as we do the subtle figures of Henry James or the morally active ones of Tolstoy. Talking about Sterne's book, Coleridge nicely remarked on the "continuity of the characters"—not only with one another but also with almost everyone. Think of Proust's Charlus in a novel about as different from Sterne's as it could be, yet Charlus and My Father are about equally trapped in habits and obsessions. We are all prisoners.

When Sterne wrote *Tristram Shandy* the tradition of realistic character-drawing was still at an early stage. But even before the norms of realism came to full development, Sterne had already created the "deviation." Putting it this way would not of course be acceptable to either Sterne or to many modern critics, who refuse to give realism any privilege in the life of the novel. Well, we all proceed, bumpily, upon our own hobbyhorses.

GEORGE ELIOT: CONSCIOUSNESS AND CHARACTER

In her late novels George Eliot does for her characters what she has become convinced God can no longer do for men and women: she offers shelter. Like God, she hands down commandments, and like God, she imposes a strict obligation to duty. But she also engages with the moral life from the standpoint of a frail humanity, as if to support Saint Augustine's plaint to deity: "Thou hast counselled a better course than thou hast permitted."

From Feuerbach's anthropology, George Eliot learned that our reigning norms, even when ascribed to deity, are the creations of men and women. What she also saw was how readily these norms can break their creators, and here, though we can hardly imagine her being sympathetic to Freud's more radical ideas, she does anticipate somewhat the Freud of *Civilization and Its Discontents*. Her work is torn between the modern passion for criticism, a criticism often grazing negation, and an intuitive love for the positive virtues, mostly nestling in memory. Mankind, she felt, had entered a phase in which the gods have withdrawn, a condition Octavio Paz calls "universal orphanhood," and now the orphans must band together if they are to survive heaven's indifferent blue. In a sentence that anyone talking about George Eliot must quote, she writes that we have to endure pain "without opium," which is to say, without myth or faith, and that this lucid stoicism should form our "highest 'calling and election.' " The agnostic falls back on the terms of Christianity: we are nourished by what we abandon.

In the judgments that control George Eliot's treatment of character, she can be extremely severe. The recurrent danger of her work is a received, even punitive moralism, and against this she has to mobilize all her resources of feeling and intelligence. Irony saves her; irony and the sense of shared weakness. None of her characters, not even the heroines over whom she hovers protectively, escapes the lash of irony, but by the same token, the irony seldom turns into a gesture of exclusion. Whichever of her characters shows a trace of conscience or good faith she stays with, undeluded yet protective. In an indifferent universe, the struggle for moral responsiveness is a staggering, even "unfair" burden. And so she gathers in her characters, even while caustic in exposing their vanities. She must be caustic; there is no other judge at hand.

A steady theme in George Eliot's work is that only consciousness—which means a constant struggle within and against the self—keeps us from slipping into the abyss of egotism and its nihilist reduction. In her novels consciousness is seen not just as the site of reflection or as a faculty of being: it becomes a high enterprise and sometimes, as she writes about Lydgate in *Middlemarch*, an "intellectual passion." Character is consequently seen as a history, not a genetic fixity, and in few other English novelists is the experience of change— growth, decline, self-realization, self-destruction—so crucial. There is something quite terrifying in this invocation to consciousness: how frail a support it seems for the making of a significant life, how inadequate, even treacherous as a moral resource! Precisely because she is aware that the self-subsistent life is so fragile, George Eliot makes her novels into muted gestures of solidarity with both characters and readers. Not in any flaunting way, not through high declaration, but with a reflective murmur. She hopes to "mitigate the harshness of all fatalities," and it is this sentiment that keeps her work from stiffening into a mere secularized Puritanism.

Characters such as Dorothea Brooke, Lydgate, Casaubon, and Bulstrode, all in *Middlemarch*, serve as centers of consciousness, and also, in consequence, as its victims. Almost all her characters give way to that low clamor of self which, by a turn of mischief, can also appear as a favorite of consciousness. For the most that consciousness can promise, though at times George Eliot seems to expect more from it, is a relentless search for self-knowledge. With even a limited freedom implying a fall, dependence on consciousness necessarily makes possible, perhaps unavoidable, a variety of self-deceptions. Still, most of George Eliot's characters, even the dried-out Casaubon and the righteous Bulstrode, wrest a few moments of understanding and thereby a little grasp of their inner feelings—or what is more painful, their inner feelings press hard upon them, causing disquiet and guilt. In George Eliot's later fiction, the major characters think and, thinking, suffer.

For a novelist to place so large a burden upon consciousness means that her characters will come to us through, and as, mixed states of feeling and belief. They cannot be declared by blunt categorical statements, but must be shown, through small eddyings of mood and will, as they struggle with the moral vocation. Many of the usual devices of characterization are still available to George Eliot, but what gives her fiction its distinctive and still-fresh qualities is an almost intolerable demand upon the inner life, the self wracked by its inescapable turbulence.

In her final novel, *Daniel Deronda*, George Eliot submits her matured vision to a stringent criticism, so much so that we may wonder whether her "religion of humanity" can survive it. Her earlier stress upon consciousness, for all its realistic cautions and discounts, had implied, I think, at least a partial attribution of positive moral value. After all, how could she not have slipped into the assumption, so tempting to the secular mind, that a history of consciousness would yield signs of progress? Perhaps it does, but in *Daniel Deronda*, with only occasional flinching, she faced up to the possibility of a complete separation between consciousness and value, a possibility that threatened her entire world-view.

Through the character of Grandcourt, the supercilious aristocrat in whom she embodied a *system* of dehumanized relations, George Eliot invoked the barbarism steadily shadowing civilization as a kind of double—and in this respect her last novel, for all its numerous flaws, represents an advance in perceptual power over even the great *Middlemarch*. Monster that he is, Grandcourt cannot be said to lack consciousness. Not only is he indifferent to the usual prescripts of morality, he takes a peculiar pleasure in enlisting his intelligence in a sustained violation of morality. Consciousness becomes a pleased witness of the very ends it would supposedly resist, as Grandcourt's lust for power, his marital sadism and suave pathology are all put at the service of a "principled" masterdom.

The sign that Grandcourt may finally have been too much for George Eliot is that she could dispose of him only through a dubious or at least an ambiguous accident. Evidently the character had grown too powerful for the role to which the fiction assigns him. Finally George Eliot has trouble—as does everyone else—in accounting for the existence of Grandcourt, which may be why she keeps so severe a distance from his inner life, depicting him solely through behavioral notation. In creating this civilized monster, or, more accurately, this monster of civilization, George Eliot the novelist achieved a triumph, but George Eliot the ethicist took a hard blow, being left all but helpless with her earlier world-view.

There is one passage in which she does make a stab at comprehending Grandcourt. She observes, brilliantly, the way his perversity can be defined, or at least brought to light, by class feeling:

> If this white-handed man with the perpendicular profile had been sent to govern a difficult colony, he might have won reputation among his contemporaries. He had certainly ability, would have understood that it was safer to exterminate than to cajole superseded proprietors, and would not have flinched from making things safe in that way.

Here George Eliot has to acknowledge social power as something more decisive than and perhaps not reducible to the distortions and perversities of individual character. She has to acknowledge that people exert and often enjoy exerting domination over others, and that before this fact consciousness may either be ineffectual or rendered complicit. This surely represents a darkening of moral tone, a deep gash in that "religion of humanity" which had been George Eliot's organizing creed through the years of her creative work; and very likely it also represents a loss of confidence in the ameliorative liberalism to which she had been committed. The cost of artistic triumph is often discomfort of belief.

In George Eliot's previous novels consciousness serves as an ultimate touchstone, not only crowding out some of the matter of traditional plot but also becoming the very matrix of characterization. Formally, her characters seem designed as figures of unity, but actually they tend to break into fragmented beings, partial selves burdened with moral expectations they must acknowledge but can seldom realize. This is a consequence of her reliance upon consciousness as the central element of fiction, and in *Middlemarch* it becomes a kind of program, a vision of lucidity.

It may by now be clear why in her novels George Eliot so often speaks in her own right. Critics who used to sneer at her "didacticism" later deplored her "intrusions," but while strains of righteousness do now and then mar her commentary—the sibyl resorts to a pointer—most of what she says in her own right has great intellectual weight. Quentin Anderson is right in saying that admirers of *Middlemarch* "are far more tempted to invest themselves with [George Eliot's] sensibility than they

are to identify themselves with that of any of her characters."
For the passages in which she speaks directly are not only
distinguished, but become inseparable from the dramatic texture of the work and soon seem quite as vital as story, characters, and dialogue.

So commanding is the Eliot voice that we can readily
suppose that the consciousness of her characters is imbedded
in the consciousness of their creator. The characters maintain
their own existence, filled out through dramatic scene and narrative summary, but when one reaches the finest parts of
Middlemarch—Dorothea waiting for her stricken husband to
come down from the study, Lydgate slowly recognizing how
hopeless his marriage has become—we grow aware of the
looming presence of George Eliot, that grave intelligence en-
veloping these figures in both judgment and compassion, the
two fused in her calm scrutiny. The authorial voice comes, as
it were, to be the soil of her characters' existence, and for a
moment we can toy with the fancy that the deity George Eliot
denied has been replaced by her sheltering spirit. Author and
characters come together, binding all in a solidarity of fate.

GISSING: TECHNIQUE AND SENSIBILITY

George Gissing wrote his novels—too many of them—at a
difficult moment: the beefy Victorian novel had pretty much
come to a point of exhaustion, the "new novel" of experi-
mentation and personal sensibility had barely begun. He was
not an innovator in technique, yet thematically and in their
controlling outlook, his novels seem to call for such innovation.
It is a rather poignant dilemma: a very serious writer, notable

for integrity, torn between a conservative temperament and insights prodding him toward modernism.

In Gissing's best novel, the distinguished *New Grub Street*, all the elements of technique are derived from the Victorian writers. The book moves at a stately, even sluggish pace; there are long patches of strung-out dialogue; the foreshortenings of plot and rapid dramatic leaps, such as seem necessary, seldom appear; and the novel's events are registered through an omniscient narrator standing at a stiff remove. So too with characterization: there is a lack of authorial flexibility, lightness of foot, in varying his distance from the characters. Gissing enables us to infer the inner lives of his figures—and they do, we are earnestly persuaded, have rich, painful inner lives—from what can be seen and heard of them. He rarely moves into their psyches, and at best provides brief, low-charged summaries of what they think and feel. The characters are treated as if they were fixed and synthetic entities, even when shown as open to shifts of impulse and mood; the effort to dramatize inner being through psychological notation and/or "stream of consciousness" is not yet at work in Gissing's novels.

New Grub Street remains, then, a Victorian novel in structure, diction, and treatment of character; yet Gissing in both his choice of subjects and the vision that informs his work is really post-Victorian. A deep split between technique and sensibility runs through almost all of his books. The recurrent theme of his fiction—the torments of a civilized man in a coarse, inhospitable world, the ordeals of a writer with moderate talents and small energies—might lead one to expect that he would be turning toward more unconventional, elliptical, and "subjective" modes of characterization. The experience of the leading figures in books like *New Grub Street*—sensitive men trapped in their sensitivity, learning to observe themselves as if they were "outside" themselves—would seem to require an invasion of the characters' "innerness," a penetration of isolated consciousness. But this does not happen. Perhaps because his poverty kept forcing him to churn out the standard three-volume fictions, perhaps because of his growing intellectual irritability and temperamental conservatism, Gissing kept plodding along in the old, familiar ways—by now too well worn. In 1885 he noticed a little sadly, however, that "Thackeray and Dickens wrote at enormous length, and with profusion of detail. . . . Far more artistic, I think, is the later method of merely suggesting: of dealing with episodes, instead of writing biographies. . . ."

Yet *New Grub Street* is a very fine novel, and a few of Gissing's other books—*Born to Exile, The Odd Women, Eve's Ransom*—have interesting, sometimes notable segments. Blocked out in the heavy old-fashioned manner, with introductory physical descriptions, occasional supporting biographical sketches, large chunks of steady narrative, the central characters of *New Grub Street*—Edwin Reardon, Marian Yule, Jasper Milvain—settle into our imaginations as permanent figures. If we believe in the modern notion that technique and sensibility are finally inseparable, how can this be?

I think the answer is that there is no necessary or ineluctable correlation between technique and sensibility. The serious writer can achieve serious work even if he sticks to a technique that, by the time he comes to use it, may be regarded as outmoded, worn, even inappropriate. A certain dogged, last-ditch sort of artistic and moral integrity—these two really are inseparable—can make up for a good many lacks in sophistication and inventiveness. Henry James did not believe this, but experience, our actual reading of works of fiction, must be given precedence over theory.

In *New Grub Street*, and to a lesser extent in the other novels I have named, Gissing succeeded through steadiness, repetition, a firm grasp of his subject, and an incorrigible honesty. There was strength in this thin-skinned writer. The prose drags a little, but we keep on, convinced that we are in the hands of a man who cares more for the truth than anything else. We see how the characters could have been presented more cleverly, more sharply, but in their solid, often rather stolid ways they live. Technique lags behind sensibility: oh, why doesn't he take an occasional leap, turn out an occasional sparkling sentence, risk an occasional psychological speculation? And yet, we are fixed in a world, and we believe in its happenings, especially its losses.

Technique may almost be, but it is not, everything.

LAWRENCE: ANOTHER LANGUAGE ALMOST

D. H. Lawrence invites us to respond to his characters as Ursula, a heroine of *The Rainbow*, responds to the life about her: "She could not understand, but she seemed to feel far-off things." These "far-off things" are not only of absolutes and immensities, what Lawrence calls "the infinite world, eternal, unchanging," nor are they only what he calls "a want [Ursula] could put no name to," though that "want" might seem like the familiar yearnings for moments of grace. No, Lawrence's "far-off things" are close within us, deep down, untapped. He wishes, in Hamlet's words, to "set you up a glass / Where you may see the inmost part of you." Or nearly so, for Lawrence had a dread of reaching the very "inmost part." Something should be left untouched.

Only seldom does Lawrence try to explain his work, since he had the same difficulty as critics have: how to put insights verging on the ineffable into a language of rational discourse. The closest he came to explanation is probably his famous remark that he wished to drop "the old stable ego" and reach "a stratum [of being] deeper than I think anyone has ever gone in the novel." This helps, but mostly as a negative: it affirms his desire to shake off the earlier premise that a fictional character should be presented as a coherent and definable entity— a premise that has since come to seem a time-bound convention rather than a necessity of our nature.

In *The Rainbow* Lawrence wishes to locate and then to represent states of being which his characters know to be powerful but find hard to name or describe. "There is another seat of consciousness than the brain and the nervous system," wrote Lawrence to Bertrand Russell, "there is the blood-consciousness, with the sexual connection holding the same relation as the eye, in seeing, to the mental consciousness. . . . This is one half of life, belonging to the darkness."

Through analogy and metaphor, since he could not find a denotative vocabulary for this "deeper stratum," Lawrence means to explore the "other seat of consciousness." Is this what's commonly called the unconscious? In the nature of things, the distinction between "blood-consciousness" and the unconscious must be vague; if we could speak about these matters with ordinary clarity, there would be no need to speak about them. But I think a distinction can be made between the two, first, because Lawrence himself spoke of a variant of consciousness and, second, because this "deeper stratum," unlike the unconscious, is something his characters can at least fitfully be in touch with, now and then reaching it on their own.

Through long, loping alternations of submission and resistance to this state of being, some of the Brangwens "know" it, or at least feel themselves to be in its grip. Acutely or drowsily, they sense that within nether layers of consciousness there swirl great supplies of energy, and that this energy is not to be controlled entirely by intelligence or will; on the contrary, their fulfillment can come only through yielding to the force and authority of these deep-seated rhythms as they move toward union with another person and then withdrawal back into the self. Lawrence's characters strive for at least some accord with the powers they feel to be within themselves. They submit to their thrust and pull; sometimes they throw up barriers of resistance; but except for Ursula, they do not propose, or even think it possible, to name them.

Naming things, identifying the deepest surges of instinctual life, becomes a possibility only for the third generation of Brangwens, that of Ursula, though by the second generation, that of Will Brangwen, there is a certain groping for meanings that elude words. This wish to describe the inner actions of psychic life coincides with and may even be a consequence of a yearning to move "upward" spiritually, a yearning that can be felt even when Lawrence's characters are still in a sensual drowse. Naming things is a capacity Will Brangwen would like to have, though his inarticulateness—it is a strength also—keeps him from even saying what he would like to be able to name. Only his daughter Ursula, in the sequel to *The Rainbow*, may succeed in doing this.

Naming things, an act of mental consciousness, appears as a culmination of that sequence of generations which provides the story of *The Rainbow*. It is also something about which Lawrence feels sharp inner conflict. He sees it as a striving after "higher" values ("How should they [Will and Anna] learn the entry into the finer, more vivid circle of life?"), but also as a sign of what he regards as the sickness of an overrationalized consciousness. Lawrence may admire those who live in "another seat of consciousness than the brain and the nervous system," he may even make them into the exemplars of his fiction; but he is himself a creature of "the brain and nervous system" and writes most familiarly about characters that have in fact entered "the finer, more vivid circle of life." Only the latter are capable of doing so much as imagining "another seat of consciousness"—those who are there do not know or need to know it.

The three generations of Brangwens, segmented into narrative groups, act out a sequence of relationship that may be called dialectical. The oldest generation, that of the farmer Tom Brangwen and his foreign-born wife, Lydia, is still untouched by modern nervousness. As Lawrence writes about Tom, "he did not like to have things dragged into consciousness." For him, the ways of tradition—earth, habit, shared mores—suffice for the passage of life. Tom's portion of the novel embodies a life beneath our life, a life releasing and molding, though sometimes also thwarting, our common life of "day-to-dayness." The states of being Lawrence strives to evoke are intervals in long swings of psychic-emotional energy, deep into "the darkness" and then back to the outer air. Mostly the characters are unaware of these states of being, though at some instinctual level they submit to them; and then, suddenly, for brief moments, they feel themselves acutely in touch with their "blood-consciousness." There is a bruised solitary apartness, the stuff out of which a self is made, and then there are mergings with others, sometimes ecstatic, as if to break into the very marrow of existence, and sometimes sullen, as if fearful of yielding individuality.

These swings of attraction and repulsion seem largely apart from the workings of the will. Gathering and starting up at the base of consciousness, they largely determine how Lawrence's characters—he would have said the same about actual persons—behave across stretches of time, listening to their "blood." Lawrence wrote out of the belief that what largely shapes our experience are these strong undertows of psychic energy, moving within us yet also, somehow, apart from us, manifested through sexuality yet also deeper than sexuality. It is through these rhythms that Lawrence seeks to validate his characters, stressing not their individualities but their inner motions of being. When Middleton Murry reviewed *The Rainbow* he complained that the characters are insufficiently differentiated; I think he was both right and wrong, for what Lawrence has done in this great novel is both to show his characters in their distinctness and then in that state where they sink beneath mere individuality. Yet in a backhanded way,

Murry was on to something, namely, that Lawrence was presenting character in a radically new way. Perhaps a few anticipations can be found in George Eliot and Hardy, but seen in terms of the history of the novel, Lawrence's treatment was revolutionary. It still is.

In the first third of the novel Tom and Lydia barely trouble to articulate—they have neither gift nor need for it—their feelings about those shifts of condition that pull them now into union, now into apartness. They accept the commands of their "innerness" quite as they accept the physical commands of their bodies. Of the several life patterns set forth in *The Rainbow* theirs is the least troubled, the most fulfilled. It subsists within itself, blind to the world and thought (with both of which, however, Lawrence himself is hopelessly entangled). The portraiture of Tom and Lydia is done through slabs of behavioral notation, rudimentary bursts of anger and passion, for in this new mode of characterization there is little need to portray specific moments of this day or that night, there is mostly a need to chart the larger movement of relationship, back and forth, between husband and wife. The first generation of Brangwens often seems more a force of energy than a group of demarcated persons. Lawrence's repeated images of flame, dread, hawk, and assault contribute to this impression. "What does it matter who they were, whether they knew each other or not?" Enough to live in the common grip.

The Tom-Lydia relationship resembles a myth, with the two characters, as is appropriate to myth, seeming both more and less than human: they are the agents, the carriers, almost impersonal, of "blood-consciousness." In the second segment, that of Will and Anna, the love-struggle always on the verge of clarity, the intermittent sensual immersions and then the flaring up and burning out of articulate aggressions, is shown in a brighter, clearer lighting. What this couple experience is less magnificent but surely more familiar than what we are shown of Tom and Lydia. The second generation is represented through a mixture of conventional and Lawrentian characterization, as the novel keeps edging toward individuated consciousness. Will and Anna are transitional figures, from blood to brain, sharing in both, but uneasily. With Ursula, the self-conscious center of the third generation—she who would like to retrieve the life-force of the earlier Brangwens while moving into high intellectuality—Lawrence seems less successful. Her piercing troubles seem too close to Lawrence's own, and at one point when Lawrence starts ranting about Jesus, the pretense that he is reporting Ursula's feelings simply collapses. The Ursula of *The Rainbow* does reach a certain credibility, more perhaps as a type-figure than an individual, since the reader who is experienced in the ways of Lawrence is prepared for her struggles. We provide Ursula with the sustaining context of *Bildungsroman*, to which Lawrence contributes occasional sharply realistic detail.

But for what is most original in *The Rainbow* there is no ready language. Lawrence must turn to a murky diction of clash, flow, dynamic, resolution—all of these abstract terms of interior action. Somewhat as George Eliot's intellectual consciousness forms the element in which the characters of *Middlemarch* exist, so it is with Lawrence through matted ribbons of language that approach "blood-consciousness." In the main, it is Lawrence's voice that we hear, as if his characters were aspects of himself. To be sure, the Brangwens "exist" in their own right, now and then quite similar to characters in traditional fictions; but mostly they come to us through Lawrence's outpouring. In his major works you must trust the teller, who rules the tale.

The Common Reader

FEW ASPECTS OF recent literary life seem more important than the loss of faith, perhaps even interest, in the idea of the common reader. Most literary people now live and work in universities, and not many of these still write for the common reader. It sometimes seems almost as if that figure has been banished, at least in the academic literary world, as an irritant or intruder, the kind of obsolete person who still enjoys stories as stories and still supposes that characters bear some resemblance to human beings.

"I rejoice," wrote Dr. Johnson in his life of Gray, "to concur with the common reader; for by the common sense of readers uncorrupted with literary prejudices, after all the refinements of subtlety and the dogmatism of learning, must be finally decided all claims to poetical honors." As tantalizing as it is famous, this remark has occasioned an abundance of schol-

arly investigation, much of it illuminating, almost all of it scrupulously inconclusive. Did Dr. Johnson really know who this
common reader was? Did he have in mind a distinct social
group, or did the common reader serve as an emblem, a shorthand convenience, for the Augustan belief that the culture of
England was still bound by shared understandings? Or was the
common reader simply a mask behind which Dr. Johnson
could deliver his authoritative judgments?

Eighteenth-century scholars can locate with fair accuracy,
if not through quantitative weightings, the publics for which
Dr. Johnson wrote in his own and other periodicals. There
was evidently a small remnant of the aristocracy and the gentry
with cultivated tastes; there were prosperous members of the
commercial classes, part of a new reading public reaching
out for breadth of cultivation; and there were literary people
of indeterminate social standing. Especially noteworthy, remarked Dr. Johnson, was the growing number of women readers. But it seems clear that he did not see, indeed could not
see, the common reader as we might.

James Basker, a scholar of eighteenth-century English literature, has written that Dr. Johnson's common reader should
not be seen as "a single entity. . . . [Dr. Johnson] imagined
many different kinds of readers. . . . Within a given work he
would vary his rhetorical register to address now one group,
now another, at moments perhaps all together." This varying
of the "rhetorical register" is, of course, a common practice
among journalists; and Dr. Johnson was, among other things,
a journalist. Another scholar, Clarence Tracy, believes that
what Dr. Johnson saw in the common reader was "the basic
man," that generic figure "who was so much the preoccupation

of seventeenth- and eighteenth-century thinkers," though in practice Dr. Johnson "seems often to have thought of [the common reader] as belonging to the lower middle class, to the vulgar, a word that he defined in the *Dictionary* as 'the common people.' " And in the eyes of still other scholars, Dr. Johnson's common reader simply referred to someone who read for pleasure, without a friend to boost or a cause to promote.

What can we conclude from this pleasant haze? That what mattered most to Dr. Johnson was a negative trait: the common reader was not a professional, not a university man, and usually had no Latin. Perhaps also the common reader was partly a creature of desire, a postulated figure made to represent some widely shared sentiments of a culture.

By the time Virginia Woolf picked up the term, the common reader had acquired a more precise social physiognomy. Woolf had in mind a community of literate persons who were not, in the narrow or professional sense, literary. They were drawn to, and held by, literature, but they did not stand within literary life. The common reader had also begun to suggest ambitious young plebeians eager to claim their portion of the cultural heritage: real-life versions, say, of Jude Fawley or Leonard Bast, the sort of people Woolf would have met at the evening educational institutes for working people at which she occasionally (and uneasily) lectured.

Woolf was not without a touch of condescension toward the very reader whom she placed in the forefront of her audience. He "differs from the critic and the scholar. He reads for his own pleasure rather than to impart knowledge or correct the opinions of others." By the time Woolf was saying these things, she and her Bloomsbury friends may have begun to suspect that the common reader was slipping out of sight, just as the parallel figure of the man of letters was. Neither of these could withstand the increasing professionalization of literary life that began around the First World War.

From the more advanced literary circles of the time, there emerged the verdict that the common reader and the man of letters had sealed a pact in behalf of a genteel amateurism, the decline of literary criticism into impressionist chatter. Pound and Eliot were among the outstanding figures who wrote as if the premise of the common reader had been pretty securely overturned. Was not this figure, or the notion behind this figure, a barrier in the way of the new, the revolutionary innovations of literary modernism? Modernist literature, by its very nature, could attract only a specialized readership, and a readership narrowing into those who steadily "worked" on it—this last, of course, an exaggeration, but not a pointless one. (The common reader could hardly be expected to devote a lifetime to the study of Joyce's fiction in order to satisfy the demand that Joyce made for such attention.)

Still, in the United States as late as the 1950s, many of the leading critics, both New and New York, continued to take seriously the idea of the common reader. Meanwhile this protean, elusive figure had undergone a change. For the *Partisan Review* and *Kenyon Review* critics, the common reader now signified a small audience of nonspecialist people: say, university teachers in the social sciences and humanities, scientists interested in culture, left-wing politicals of some cultivation, students hoping to become writers, and so on. These critics wrote as if they still had readers other than other critics, as if there still were people who turned to critics for illumination while keeping an optimal distance from those noisy disputes in which critics seem fated to indulge.

Such readers of the 1940s and 1950s were likely to follow Clement Greenberg on the new painting, Eric Bentley on theater, James Agee on film, Randall Jarrell on poetry, Edmund Wilson, Philip Rahv, and Lionel Trilling on the novel, as well as reviewers like Robert Fitzgerald, Marius Bewley, and Dwight Macdonald. These readers had, by now, probably read Eliot's poems and essays, which had gained academic respectability and were being taught in the colleges, and they were also reading Hemingway and Faulkner, among American writers, and Joyce, Proust, and Mann, among European. But they were decidedly not interested in the writings of the Chicago neo-Aristotelians, or in the "heresies" and "fallacies" unearthed by some New Critics.

Just as Dr. Johnson had shifted his "rhetorical register" because he knew (or sensed) that he wrote for a variegated public, so the contributors to the major quarterlies of the time were prepared, no matter which "school" they adhered to or kept apart from, to accept a division between topics that mattered to their small but crucial public (really *un*common common readers) and topics best left to graduate seminars. As I recall, there was certainly a touch of antiacademic prejudice in these literary circles, but it was neither pervasive nor inescapable.

The more clever among the critics, aware that there was no single kind of common reader, that the category actually covered a span of figures and interests, tried to direct their work to both outsiders and insiders, amateurs and professionals, sometimes in alternation and, when really ambitious, simultaneously. I doubt that many common readers kept turning eagerly to John Crowe Ransom's *Kenyon Review*, with its few thousand readers forming a public no larger, proportionately, than the five hundred of Dr. Johnson's *Rambler*. But at least some of Ransom's contributors, though writing for and quarreling with one another, also shared a desire to reach some portion of the publics we designate as common readers. I recall conversations among admirers of R. P. Blackmur's criticism who were distressed at the increasing opacity of his later work: Who but themselves (and even then . . .) would try to make it out? Difficulty was accepted as necessary at times, but obscurity not. Almost every critic would have agreed with Allen Tate's remark that "critical style ought to be as plain as the nose on one's face."

If the quarterlies could at times also put off many common readers with their internal debates and mandarin styles, there were still the book pages of the political weeklies in which the New York critics appeared. A few of the New Critics did also, very occasionally; but some of those I knew wanted to, and regretted their seeming inability to write in a way that would be at once serious and accessible. It was then generally assumed that the line of great English critics, from Dr. Johnson and Hazlitt to Arnold and Eliot, had cultivated, as a matter of course, a certain journalistic bent (critics often *had* to be journalists) and that the migration of critics to the universities that began in the early 1950s, while a practical advantage, was still a somewhat uncomfortable development. Surely in the history of American literary life, this was a major turning point. The new circumstances of our economy made it close to impossible for a free-lance man (or woman) of letters to survive. And this change must be one of the major reasons for the shift in attitudes toward the idea of the common reader.

Let me propose the hypothesis—it could be tested adequately only in a comprehensive cultural history—that in the years between the two world wars there occurred a fracturing or proliferation of literary publics. There were now perhaps more kinds of common readers than ever before, ranging from the few who saw themselves as devotees of the literary quarterlies to those who read magazines like *Harper's* and the dreary *Saturday Review*. And somewhere in between was *The New Yorker*, with at least a portion of its readers interested in cultural criticism.

After the Second World War, as gifted writers like Edmund Wilson, W. H. Auden, Dwight Macdonald, and Mary McCarthy began to appear in *The New Yorker*, it became harder still to make clear or sharp distinctions among common readers. Perhaps one distinction that still holds is that the literary quarterlies and political weeklies involved their readers in intellectual exchange and debate, or at least opened their pages to such exchange and debate, while *The New Yorker* presented the work of its contributors as finished products, not as something open to scrutiny through question or polemic within a community of letters. The kind of common reader who took *The New Yorker* was, in that capacity, a consumer. The kind who read *Partisan Review, The Nation, The New Republic*, and later *The New York Review of Books* was now and again a participant in an ongoing life of cultural exchange. This distinction is not an absolute one, since it seems probable that at least some readers of the quarterlies and weeklies took on the role of passive consumer quite as the readers of *The New*

Yorker did. But the point to be stressed here is that radically different views of the life of culture were reflected in the divergent attitudes toward controversy between the quarterlies and weeklies, on the one hand, and *The New Yorker*, on the other. Even when *The New Yorker* printed something as deeply controversial as Hannah Arendt's work on Eichmann, it would not print any refutations or commentaries.

It is possible, of course, that the idea of the common reader, from the time of Dr. Johnson to our present moment, was mostly an enabling hypothesis that enticed critics into exegesis and lucidity. But it must have been more too: there were people I knew in the American socialist milieu who, often somewhat shyly, immersed themselves in Proust, Kafka, and Eliot. Especially in recent decades, when the great works of literary modernism were still fresh, and it had not yet become the dubious custom to minimize their difficulty, even learned and sophisticated people, some of whom rather foolishly looked down on critics like Edmund Wilson, could profit from the kind of exegesis and lucidity he exemplified.

Thus, even if the common reader was a contrivance of critics to satisfy their desire for an audience other than fellow critics (and I don't think it really was such a contrivance), the *idea* of the common reader served a useful purpose. At least during the first decade or two after the Second World War, there were critics who kept one eye on the reader outside the classroom. All of them, while naturally concerned with the responses of their colleagues, still wanted to reach someone "out there," one kind of common reader or another.

But things have changed radically in the last decades. There now flourishes an academic community of younger, accomplished, and, as it appears, self-assured professors of literature for whom the idea of the common reader seems to be of small interest. Such professors are likely to regard the common reader as an indulgence of an earlier generation of litterateurs that resulted mostly in ephemeral journalism. Today most of the ambitious and talented young people within the literary academy publish only in journals read by their colleagues, and they seem to find this an acceptable, indeed a normal, condition.

I was just about to use an unfriendly phrase, "within the narrow confines of the literary academy"; but that would no longer be quite accurate. Those "confines" are no longer narrow. The American university system has expanded so rapidly that it is possible for aspiring professors to feel that their colleagues *do* form a sufficient audience. And in a way, they do: an audience that is attentive, self-absorbed, and with a vocabulary of its own. Give a paper at the Modern Language Association on Heidegger or de Man and you will probably enjoy a larger and more responsive audience than if you write about Ashbery's poems or Naipaul's novels in a literary magazine.

Why are literary academics so keenly drawn to purely "theoretical" theory? It is a question that could take us far afield, but since it has a bearing on my topic, I offer a few quick speculations. There has been a growing tendency toward internal specialization in all academic fields, and this holds true for the literary academy as well. Each guild, or guild of guilds, lives absorbed in its own rituals, norms, disputes. There has been a general decay of strong beliefs, if not ideologies, among the intellectual classes; and the sophisticated skepticism, sometimes slipping into nihilism, that now dominates literary theory seems made to order for the mood of the moment. And then, to be fair, there are some powerful minds at work in literary theory who naturally win over younger people (who, decades before, might have been converts to earlier theories, earlier schools).

What results is a conviction that the literary theorist, rid of the grubby tasks of practical criticism and not obliged to pay very much attention to literature itself, can find satisfying expression by remaining within the academy, speaking to fellow theorists, and not having to worry about that nuisance, real or imagined, known as the common reader. The freewheeling literary intellectual of an earlier day, reaching several audiences and coping with a number of subjects, is all but gone. Our literary academics stay academic to the last, or to the last theory. And they find it good.

To avoid misunderstanding, I should say that it seems entirely appropriate for scholars to publish mainly in scholarly journals. So it has been, so it should remain. But when it comes to literary people who teach in universities and are not exactly or primarily scholars, the tendency to turn inward is disheartening. It means that the teaching of literature falls increasingly into the hands of people who lack a vital relation to, or strong feeling for, the writing of the moment, into the hands of professors for whom Hélène Cixous is more interesting than Nadine Gordimer, and Jean Baudrillard more important than Milan Kundera. It means that literary academics, or at least some of them, are inclined to a mild—and not always mild—condescension toward those critics who still find it desirable to review novels and books of poetry. And what is quite as disturbing: a snobbish disdain for students who prefer to read novels and poems.

One reason for the inward turn of literary academics may be that recent American writing has not been especially "great." But "great" is a loaded word, and writers to whom it can be applied do not appear every day. There *are* interesting American writers, some talented and many serious, perhaps no fewer than at other times; and it is hard to envision a vigorous culture in which some of the most influential and the most talented literary people pay little attention to living writers. True, the academics of the 1920s and 1930s, when the United States could boast of a major literature, were not greatly concerned with living writers, either; but in those days it hardly mattered, since good critics flourished outside the academy, grouping themselves around such magazines as *The Dial* and *Hound and Horn*.

The very idea of a literary culture, one that would encompass the literary academy but not be confined to it, has now come into question. Which brings me to another, perhaps central, question: What happens to the idea of a democratic culture, advanced by almost every major American critic since Emerson and Whitman, if the increasingly powerful and self-assured literary academy, barely challenged by critics outside its walls, remains aloof from the larger culture, remains content to live and work within its own space?

To hope for a democratic culture, we need not cherish earlier populist or Marxist notions about the masses. The vision of a public spiritedly and independently engaged with literature has always been a precarious, if also a precious, one. Whoever thinks back to the vulgarities and the buffooneries of the 1988 presidential campaign knows it would be foolish to indulge in high rhetoric about the prospects for a democratic culture (perhaps even for a democratic politics). Clearly the decline in the public of informed, discriminating, yet nonspecialized readers—or, more likely, the decline of concern with that public among academic literary people—has not been caused by recent trends within the academy, though it may have been hastened by them. The spreading blight of television, the slippage of the magazines, the disasters of our school system, the native tradition of anti-intellectualism, the cultivation of ignorance by portions of the counterculture, the breakdown of coherent political and cultural publics, the loss of firm convictions within the educated classes—these, in merest summary, are among the reasons for the decline in both the presence and the idea of the common reader.

And yet the idea of a democratic culture, which must mean a culture that extends beyond the academy, is one that we cannot afford to surrender, not if we remain attached to the idea of a democratic politics. Indeed, it is hardly within our power to abandon such ideas, so deeply rooted are they in the traditions of this country. Emerson asked for "confidence in the unsearched might of man. . . . The literature of the poor, the feelings of the child, the philosophy of the street, the meaning of household life, are the topics of the time." Whitman spoke for those "within whose thought rages the battle . . . between democracy's convictions, aspirations, and the people's crudeness, vice, caprices." Toward the end of this wretched century it is hard to summon the buoyant tones of Emerson and Whitman; but we remain, with whatever modulations, their cultural offspring, whether we acknowledge it or not.

The inward turn among literary academics has not been accompanied by a large-scale or explicitly reactionary politics,

‑/

such as several decades ago was being advanced by Eliot and
Pound. What flourishes in the academy now is a craft elitism,
expressed at times as a readiness to look on the large society
as incorrigibly debased, or to dismiss it as inconsequential. The
academy, it seems, is enough.

Sometimes this self-satisfied acquiescence even comes with
assertions of radicalism. A number of those drawn to decon-
structionist theory, for example, feel that their writings have
political implications, though that does not lead them, so far
as I can tell, to any visible politics available in the United States.
A small academic group describes itself as Marxist, but that
strikes me as a bit comic: whatever Marxism may have been,
it always saw itself attached to, or in search of, a mass movement of the working class. It was not merely a "method" for
literary criticism. But Marxism has gone to the universities to
die in comfort.

It is true that the idea of a democratic culture remains,
historically, a novelty not fully tested, and may even turn out
to be no more than an attractive yearning. It may refer to several
aspects of literature or the literary life. We may have in mind
the dominant voices or ideas of a literature, so that we can
speak of a democratic culture even with regard to writing (some
of Melville, some of Henry James) that has little popular appeal, is alienated in spirit, and sets itself up as an adversary to
the society's dominant values. In that somewhat restricted
sense, we have had a democratic literature since the days of
Emerson, and probably into, or close to, our own time.

But the idea of a democratic culture may also refer to something more ambitious and difficult: to the relations between
writers and an active, autonomous public, neither academic

nor professionally literary, perhaps small, but providing writers with a flow of sentiment and response. The odds against maintaining a vital link between a literary community and a literary public are pretty high these days. If we cannot locate the common reader, however, we must try to help him/her/them reappear. Critics might learn once more to speak to the common reader, as if he still matters, as if she will soon respond; and to speak in English, a language that for some time served criticism well.

Criticism of Fiction

WHAT CAN WE DO WITH CHEKHOV?

I want to take a look at one of Chekhov's late stories, "In the
Cart" (1897), a mere eight pages long and seldom noticed by
his critics. It is a modest piece, with a frail action and lacking
so much as a single striking phrase; there are, at least in translation, no images to trace or entwine; and I can find few of
the complexities that mark such major Chekhov stories as "In
the Ravine" or "Ward No. 6." Nothing more, it might seem,
has to be said—except that the story is a small masterpiece and
that, precisely in its transparency, its lack of complicating devices, it constitutes a challenge to modern criticism. What can
a critic "do" with it?

Here is a quick description of its matter:

The setting is spring, when "the sleepy trees . . . basked
in the breath" of renewal. But spring in a Russian village,
muddy and forlorn. The narrative line is lucid and unadorned.

Marya, for thirteen years a village schoolmistress, is being driven to town by an old peasant in order to collect her salary and buy food. It is a journey she has taken many times: "all she ever wanted was to get it over with."

On the road Marya meets Squire Khanov, a landowner, handsome and pleasant, but a heavy drinker. She fantasizes about him: "kind, gentle, innocent." But we know nothing about him directly, only what we can see through her yearning. Even while detecting "a hint . . . of a feeble, poisoned creature," she feels that "if she was his wife or sister she would very likely give her whole life to saving him."

As she muses upon the deprivations of her life, Marya arrives in town, experiences some humiliating moments with drunks at the local inn, and sets off again for the village. Her grouchy peasant driver chooses to ford a river instead of taking a nearby bridge, Marya gets soaked, her provisions are spoiled. The cart reaches a railroad track, and Marya imagines that she has caught a glimpse of her mother in a passing train. This forms the first slight elevation of tone in the story:

> Vividly, with striking clarity, for the first time in thirteen years, she pictured her mother and father, her brother, their Moscow flat, the fish-tank and goldfish—all down to the last detail. Suddenly she heard a piano playing, heard her father's voice and felt as she had felt then, young, pretty, well-dressed in a warm, light room. . . . In a sudden surge of joy and happiness she clasped her head rapturously in her hands.

But as suddenly as it came so does the rapture leave her, giving way to tears—"at which moment Khanov drove up with his coach and four. Seeing him, she imagined such happiness as has never been on earth"—and she greets him as "her friend and equal." All of her life seems like a bad dream, now that "she had woken up." But then "it all vanished," this fantasy of joy and hope, as the cart brings her back to the wretched village.

The diction of this story is plain. One or two sentences seem to come from Chekhov or his surrogate narrator, e.g., "She imagined such happiness as has never been on earth." A bit earlier Chekhov inserts an exchange between Marya and the peasant driver about an official in town who "helped some Germans in Moscow kill Mayor Alekseyev"—why this seeming irrelevance? Perhaps to show the distance between the village and events "out there," in the world. The rest is narrative.

I will assume that the reader is as deeply or almost as deeply moved by this story (not of course by my bare summary) as I am. Otherwise, there is no point in asking: What has Chekhov done to make this fairly commonplace narrative, hardly more than an anecdote, into a miniature work of art?

Many of the gambits available to criticism are of little use here. There is no ideological material to elucidate, as with Dostoevsky; there are no allusions to clarify, as with Joyce; there is no complex symbolism to unravel, as with Melville. Some things criticism can do here, and I will start where perhaps I should end: that Chekhov as the author predisposes us to a warm receptivity. I may be violating any number of critical theories in saying this, but I adduce it as an incontrovertible fact. Chekhov's name invokes a complex of expectations: we know that almost anything written in his mature years will dispense with tricks of plot, will brush past the formulas of literary psychology, will persuade or train us to confront a human situation in its bareness. Chekhov's signature prepares us for a work of moral lucidity and dispassionate sympathy; indeed, for the Chekhov devotee, starting one of his stories can resemble the preliminaries of a religious ceremony. Am I saying, then, that a reader unfamiliar with Chekhov is likely to be less affected by the story than one who has read him over the years? I think so.

Criticism can do more. It can point to the convenience of Chekhov's structural arrangement (village-town-village); to the steadiness with which narrative point of view is kept going; to the implicit harmony between theme or motivating concern and the direct, referential style. And it is worth pointing to some fine details: When Marya fantasizes about the squire, she tells herself she could be "his wife or sister," but we suppose ourselves to know which of these she prefers, and at the end, after her illusory moment of happiness, she feels herself to be his "friend and equal," though all that follows must cause us to doubt that she can sustain that feeling for very long.

There is a sophisticated critical notion which urges that all fictions must employ formal conventions and that the apparent "naturalness" of "In the Cart" is also a sort of convention, dependent on a contrast with other, more familiar kinds. Agreed. But the "naturalness," the disarming simplicity of the story remains—a miniature of our delusions and frustrations.

Criticism has often assumed that the acceptance of simplicity as a literary value should be regarded with suspicion. Modern criticism especially thrives on the idea of complexity, and it steadily employs the gambit of demonstrating that what appears to be simple is "really" (with the critic's help) complex. But may there not be in literature a simplicity that is neither to be reduced to something else nor compounded into something else, a simplicity sufficing as an emblem of at least part of our experience?

Let us return to the story. Its effect is not tragic; the characters, only one of them at all glimpsed, are quite ordinary, perhaps even mediocre people, small in reach and hope, though it is one of Chekhov's deepest perceptions that such people can suffer quite as much as the brilliant and the profound. Chekhov's tone here is a sort of dry pathos, that which remains after a reckoning of common deprivation. (Does Chekhov ever reach the tragic? Only, I think, in some of his comic plays.) Nor can we say that "In the Cart" is a story which like, say, "Bartleby" or "A Hunger Artist" or "The Death of Ivan Ilych" has a universal resonance; it would be foolish to claim for Chekhov, except in a few of his writings, the scope of the very greatest writers.

Chekhov's simplicity in this story is of a very special kind. It is not the mannered or studied simplicity of the late Tolstoy, such as tries to ensare us in a web of ideology. What seems so admirable about "In the Cart" is that Chekhov submits entirely to his imagined situation, he is completely loyal to it. By loyal I mean a kind of good faith in the perception of what his figures are, a refusal to lower or elevate them, to add a scintilla of comfort or (what in our own time may be still more treacherous) a scintilla of anguish. There is a steadfastness of vision which lifts the small bits and pieces of observation into truth, so that the fiction, in its essentials, becomes a sort of muted fable. Technique enters into such an achievement, and technique may indeed be the only thing we can really point to with any sort of assurance; but there is also something else—every sensitive reader feels this—there is the writer's spirit. A vague and portentous word "spirit" may be, but we lose something precious if we refuse it entirely. And it is Chekhov's spirit— an honesty rendering transcendence superfluous—that makes this story so lovely. We can point to it, but hardly do more.

Well, let us suppose a critic more gifted than I will examine "In the Cart." Let us suppose it is the most brilliant critic of our century, for which honor I nominate William Empson. He would find points of technique and subtleties I have missed. But would he thereby "capture" the story? "capture" it any more than I have? Is the "spirit" of a work of art no more than the sum of its technical elements?

The question is hardly new. Tzvetan Todorov writes that "there is an *untheorizable* element in literature . . . if theory presupposes scientific language. One function of literature is the subversion of this very language." I would prefer "undecipherable" or, perhaps better, "ungraspable"; but let that be. We are groping toward the same perception: that no matter how many things criticism can tell us about a work of literature—a good many—it may finally be unable to explain its essential quality. If this is so, you might say that it should apply to all works of literature. No doubt; but it becomes especially clear with those works, like "In the Cart," where there is almost nothing to talk about except their essential quality.

The problem for critics is that between what they can show about the elements of a story like "In the Cart" and "the story itself" there is an enormous gap. Some critics will say, of course, that there is no such thing as "the story itself," there are only its constituent elements. For them, there is no problem (but perhaps also no literature). But I think there is a gap and that it is good to suppose there is a gap, for it encourages a certain humility before the work of art in its mysterious glory.

GOGOL'S OVERCOAT, EICHENBAUM'S STITCHING

Boris Eichenbaum's 1919 essay "How Gogol's 'Overcoat' Is Made" is a classic of modern criticism, a tour de force in the formalist vein. What makes it so fine a piece of work is in part its lack of fixed preconceptions as to "method" (once having excluded the "material," or, as we might say, the content of fiction from their consideration, the Russian formalists were quite prepared to be flexible in their approach to a text). Eichenbaum stays very close to the movement of Gogol's story, responding with a sensory richness to its details. Alert to every sound of Gogol's mimicry, this critic has eyes, nose, above all, ears.

Since I wish to note some limitations in this admirable piece of work, let me put down the bare outline of Eichenbaum's essay, while necessarily omitting his vivid linguistic citations:

1) He starts with quoted passages from Gogol's contemporaries who recall how brilliantly the writer would read his own stories: rapid shifts of intonation, sudden comic turns of sonority. "The Overcoat" is "made up of live spoken performances . . . a special role is played by articulation, mimicry, sound gestures. . . . The sound 'envelope' of a word, its acoustical characteristic becomes meaningful in Gogol's speech independently of its logical meaning or material referent." Gogol is here using what Russian critics call the *skaz*, defined by Victor Erlich as "the mimicry of intonational, lexical, and

phraseological mannerisms of a lowbrow narrator. . . ." In the simulation of oral narrative that constitutes the *skaz*, continues Eichenbaum, "plot has only an external significance. . . . The real dynamic . . . lies in the construction of the *skaz*, the play of language." In "The Overcoat" "a purely comic *skaz* . . . is united with a declamation full of pathos, forming, as it were, a second stratum." This declamation of pathos, dwelling on the poor clerk who has deprived himself of subsistence in order to buy a new overcoat, which is stolen the first night he wears it, was taken by "progressive" nineteenth-century Russian critics like Belinsky to be the theme or "message" of the story. How mistaken they were Eichenbaum will show.

2) Now comes the heart of Eichenbaum's analysis: Gogol's use of puns, "the device of taking things to absurdity or to illogical word combinations," the use of "meaningless" words for "an original semantics of sounds," the elaborate play with names (rather Dickensian), the stylization of careless chatter, the use of quasi-rhymes, rhythmic accretion, etc. all in order to create "a grotesque in which the mimicry of laughter alternates with the mimicry of sorrow, and both the one and the other have the appearance of a game, with a controlled alternation of gestures and intonations."

Here is an example from the story's opening paragraph which describes the protagonist, Akaky Akakievich, a name with scatological associations in Russian:

And so, in a certain department served a certain clerk, a clerk one couldn't call very remarkable: of short stature, a little bit pocky [*ryabovat*], a little bit ruddy [*ryzhevat*], even, to look at, a little bit squinty [*podslepovat*], with a small bald spot on top, with wrinkles along both sides of his cheeks and with a complexion that is called hemorrhoidal. . . . [Russian provided by translator].

In Russian, according to Eichenbaum, the language here is "contrived" and "acoustical," and it ends with "the grandiosely resonant and almost meaningless word, 'hemorrhoidal.' " But stop; for the first time we must pull back a little. "Hemorrhoidal" is by no means "almost meaningless." Eichenbaum is forcing his analysis in behalf of formalist hermeticism, the story as a "closed space." If anything, the word is heavily loaded with associations as to pain, color, sedentary airlessness, smell, occupation (a clerk's fate). Eichenbaum is here denying the strong referentiality of Gogol's language, and it will not do.

3) Eichenbaum next describes the alternation, within the limits of the *skaz*, between "the mimicry of laughter" and "the mimicry of sorrow." The intent now is openly polemical, against "naive" critics who take a "sentimentally melodramatic digression" of humane feeling about Akaky Akakievich as if it represents Gogol's own feelings inserted into the text. Eichenbaum argues:

> Given the basic proposition that in a work of art not a single sentence can be in itself a simple "reflection" of the personal feelings of the author, but is always a construction and a performance, *we cannot and have no right* to see in such an excerpt anything other than a definite artistic device. . . . The artist's soul, like that of a man *experiencing* various moods, always remains and must remain outside the limits of his creation. . . . *There neither is nor can there be* a place in it for the reflection of the empiricism of the soul.

I would, by contrast, argue that while the "humanitarian" passage in "The Overcoat" may indeed be integral to Gogol's structure, it also, in whole or in part, reflects his personal feelings. "Performance" and "the empiricism of the soul" are not utter contraries. From a strictly internal reading of the story we may never quite be sure to what extent an isolated passage is a simple "reflection" of the author's feelings; but we need not confine ourselves to such internal readings as if they were decreed from on high. The passages of comment in the novels of Tolstoy, Proust, and George Eliot can also, perhaps with a bit of stretching, be seen as integral to their narratives, yet it would take an act of the will, it would constitute a rigid ideological bias to fail to read these as wholly or in part the sentiments of their authors.

One may wonder at the either/or character of Eichenbaum's assertion on this score, departing as it does from his close critical scrutiny of the text to expound theoretical premises insufficiently argued. The relation of the "purely anecdotal" *skaz* to the "melodramatic and solemn declamation" of Gogol's "humane" passage may indeed be determined by the dominating form of the grotesque; the end of all this may also be "*a play with reality*, [the] breaking up and freely displacing [of] its elements." But to say that in such a story "the artist is at liberty to exaggerate details and upset the usual proportions of the world" is tacitly to acknowledge the story's mimetic character, no matter how oblique that mimesis may be. Gogol may indeed be "freely" displacing "the elements of reality," but that compositional act is not arbitrary or unbounded; it is in the service of a certain vision of reality.

Eichenbaum concludes with a keen analysis of Gogol's ending, the way Akaky Akakievich's ghost haunts his tormenters, though it turns out that, as in his life, his ghost has been dispossessed by the robber who had taken the overcoat. "The initial, purely comic *skaz* returns . . . dissolving in laughter." Our critic remains faithful to his chosen limits.

I have already made one or two critical remarks about Eichenbaum's approach. What else remains to be said?

Eichenbaum's essay is detached not only from history in the usual sense but also from literary history. There is not the slightest indication here—indeed, we detect a strict refusal to notice—that "The Overcoat" should be seen as, among other things, an instance of the emergence in the nineteenth century of a literature of the city, with some kinships to fiction by Melville and Dickens. Such a placement endows the story with certain (tacit, convoluted, implicit) orientations and thematic concerns which can be avoided only by decision. The point has been anticipated by Philip Rahv:

> It is true, of course, that Gogol never deliberately set out to describe his social environment; but the fact is that his subjective method of exaggeration, of caricature and farce, produced an imagery of sloth, ugliness and self-satisfied inferiority which, if not directly reflective, is none the less fully expressive of the realities of life in Czarist Russia. [The "dynamic plebeianism of Gogol's genius"] enabled him to make a radically new selection of material. . . .

Eichenbaum's description of "The Overcoat"—first-rate as far as it goes and seriously damaging the Belinsky approach—is deficient in one crucial respect: *it all but eliminates the overcoat itself as object or symbol*, and it largely eliminates the overcoat's owner as well. But the overcoat is not mere neutral "material" (to use one of the favorite terms of the Russian formalists), nor is it a mere "sound gesture." The overcoat is the dominating presence of the story, and it is rich with experiential and historical associations, no more to be removed from the reader's responses than the verbal associations set off by the name of Gogol's clerk. The overcoat speaks to everyone who has ever been cold—and that must include Russian formalists. It speaks for the self-denial that it cost the poor clerk, it speaks for the pitifulness of aspiration which prevails among the lowly (surely one of Gogol's themes), it speaks for the cruelty of fate suffered by . . . by all those who have ever needed an overcoat.

The recognition that there is a streak of cruelty, even sadism, in Gogol's treatment of Akaky Akakievich—what Victor Erlich calls his "not quite human strain"—does not necessarily destroy the reading of the story, one among others, as social or moral critique. If, in Erlich's words, we can no longer say that the story's import is that "petty clerks are human too," but with an "existential sigh" must say "how embarrassingly petty are so many human pursuits, involvements, aspirations," there still remains the powerful social import which derives directly from Eichenbaum's reading of the story as grotesque. The "embarrassing pettiness" of Akaky Akakievich's aspirations cannot be detached from, though they are clearly not confined to, his clerkship. They are the marks, the psychic stigmata, of a "humbleness" terrible in its passivity and self-laceration, somewhat like that of Bontsha Schweig in the famous Yiddish story by I. L. Peretz.

Precisely in our acceptance of Eichenbaum's analysis do

we have the ground for seeing the story as a mordant social critique. And nowhere is this more evident than at the story's end, where Akaky Akakievich's ghost is displaced by the thief who stole his overcoat. Eichenbaum sees this as "a return to laughter"—yes, but the laughter of bitterness which is heard in heaven when Bontsha reveals the paltriness of his desire. I see the ending as Gogol's masterstroke: that in another life, the life of ghosts, there will be no more justice for the wretched Akaky Akakievich than there is in this life.

ON "GRATUITOUS DETAILS"

Structure is probably the analytic category to which modern criticism grants most respect. It is also one of the more mysterious terms in the critical vocabulary. A recent handbook of literature reports that structure is "the planned framework of a piece of literature"—which is marvelously unhelpful—and that it is "generally regarded as the most reliable as well as the most revealing key to the meaning of the work"—which is either a truism or an overstatement.

An authoritative literary scholar, M. H. Abrams, writes that many critics use the term "structure" to signify "an equilibrium or an interaction, or an ironic and paradoxical tension, of diverse words and images in a stable totality of 'meanings.'" This is at least a usable definition, though, somewhat irreverently, I retain an image of a suspension bridge in which the parts support one another, and the result is a system at once efficient and self-contained—above all, a system unified. Most critics live for unity: mechanical or organic, manifest or deep-breathing. Unity makes the whole critical enterprise seem more

manageable. Critics seldom join with William James in rejecting "the love of unity at any cost."

There are, of course, works that satisfy the desire for structural unity, but many others, especially novels, bulge and
splutter with improvisation, false starts, dead ends, inspired
digressions. Novels suffer, but sometimes profit, from an in-
congruent relation between theme and plot—when the stitch-
ing isn't neat, verisimilitude may creep through. Novels rarely
attain a single level of voice. Novels are often long, which
means they cannot avoid stretches of boredom, patches of bad-
land. Novels cannot be read at a single sitting, so that in memory their organization of event often succumbs to the deceit
of selection.

In the actual experience of reading, considerations of
structure—such as the relations among parts, the disposition
of stresses, the jibing of segments and the whole—do not play
nearly so great a part as they do in the formal discourse of
many modern critics. We tend, in our reading, to take novels
in portions, and to be roused by them at unexpected moments,
intermittently. Our sense of the novel's unity comes out of an
act of remembrance, a recollected coherence, a settling of memory and stiffening of impression. When we speak about the
unity of a novel, we often have in mind a perception gained
only after a stretch of time, through mental and emotional
struggle. And often enough novels have parts left over or missing; they rarely end as well as they start; they can even hold
us through strategies of incompleteness.

In a fine essay, "The Irrelevant Detail and the Emergence
of Form," Martin Price writes about "irrelevant" details in

novels which, upon consideration, turn out to be quite relevant. Such details serve in "sustaining the virtual [imagined?] world" of the novel and thereby reinforce the total significance of the work. We are required, says Price, to observe about the detail "only so much particularity . . . as is consonant with that conceptual force the detail acquires in the large structure." Good; but I propose a further step. There are details with so strong or intense a "particularity" that they resist being absorbed entirely into "the large structure." They have, it strikes the reader, a "conceptual force" greater than their presumed function requires. Only later, if we are the sort of readers (or, more likely, critics) who share the need for unity above all else, do we find a way of placing such details within "the large structure." And anyone inclined to think about such matters is likely to be ingenious enough to do this.

About some details we may say that not only do they serve as moments or incidents crystallizing the thematic intention of the work. They seem also to grip us in their own right, they seem even to possess or claim a miniature "unity" of their own, with a significance beyond their role in the narrative. They stand out. In some ultimate sense, no doubt, such details come to be seen as functional, with their representative power at least partly related to the workings of "the large structure." But, strictly speaking, they do not seem to be mandated by the work's "large structure." They succeed, as nubs of suggestion, on their own, without any plausible ascription of function in the novel as a whole.

I prefer the term "gratuitous" to Martin Price's "irrelevant," because "gratuitous" suggests something pleasing, an extra benefit. Encountering gratuitous details, we feel grateful, as upon the arrival of unexpected pleasures. These details strike us as moments of virtuosity, sometimes revelation.

The master of the gratuitous detail is Dostoevsky. No writer can match him in the ability to transform a digression into a crux of perception, even one that may overtake and undermine the idea with which he had begun a novel. And still more remarkable, Dostoevsky has a way of inducing us to not be *too* attentive to niceties or comeliness of form; indeed, to follow him into byways of narrative with the expectation that they will, in their own right, prove to be central.

At one point before Raskolnikov in *Crime and Punishment* has killed the old moneylender but after he has cajoled himself into planning the murder, he has a dream, somewhat realistic in character. He is "a child again," passing a tavern on the way to the cemetery, where he wishes to visit his grandmother's grave. At the tavern there is "some special festivity going on . . . peasants and all kinds of rabble . . . all drunk and bawling out songs." Nearby stands a huge cart drawn not by the usual "great cart-horses" but by a "small, lean, decrepit old dun-colored horse." The peasants pile into the cart; they shower blows on the wretched horse; the little boy cries out in pity for the animal; the peasant who owns the horse shouts, "She's mine, isn't she? I can do what I like with my own"; the horse tries feebly to rebel but finally perishes from the beatings.

Now there are at least two ways of approaching this bit of narrative, both of them legitimate. One would see the dream as an anticipatory cue for what Raskolnikov will do to the old lady; let us call this the functional approach. The other, toward which I incline, would accept the understanding of the first view but would be so strongly gripped by the power of this "gratuitous detail" as to make of it something like an autonomous or self-sufficient narrative event. The dream incident would, so to say, take on a life of its own.

Once Raskolnikov has killed the moneylender, he is walking in the Haymarket, where a young man grinds out "a sentimental ballad on a barrel-organ" and a fifteen-year-old girl sings along with him. In an unexplained spasm of generosity Raskolnikov gives them a large coin, whereupon they break off and leave. Raskolnikov then turns to a bystander to say how much he enjoys street-singing "on a cold, dark, damp autumn evening—it must be damp—when the faces of all the passersby look greenish and sickly. . . ." Alarmed, the man stares at Raskolnikov and hurries away.

This cryptic anecdote can also be connected with the novel's theme: it reveals the growing isolation of Raskolnikov as a criminal, his need to talk with almost anyone about almost anything. But is that all? Doesn't this detail come to seem self-sufficient, or almost so? And that astonishing clause, "it must be damp," how is that to be subordinated to the main theme? Doesn't it, with the power of a great invention, stay in memory quite apart from Raskolnikov's situation?

Let me turn to a few other examples:

In George Gissing's *New Grub Street*, the central character, Edwin Reardon, is a minor novelist too sensitive for the milieu of popular fiction in which he has to work. Slipping into poverty, he is soon abandoned by his wife. After she leaves, he stumbles about mechanically, in a daze. Gissing, with his phlegmatic insight, continues:

As it was a very cold day, he lit a fire. Whilst it burned up he sat reading a torn portion of a newspaper, and became quite interested in the report of a commercial meeting in the City, a thing he would never have glanced at under ordinary circumstances. The fragment fell at length from his hands; his head drooped. . . .

In Faulkner's *Sanctuary*, Popeye, whose soul is said to resemble the texture of "stamped tin," waits to be electrocuted for his crime. A moment before the execution he whispers to the sheriff, as if to make his last minimal demand upon life: "Pssst! . . . Fix my hair, Jack."

At the end of the first part of Virginia Woolf's *To the Lighthouse*, in which the Ramsay family has been portrayed with some fullness, we come to recognize the depths of love in the profoundly uneasy relation of Mr. and Mrs. Ramsay. Mr. Ramsay, the almost-great scholar, is restless, needy, wanting from his wife a word of reassurance beyond her (perhaps anyone's) power to give:

He found talking so much easier than she did. He could say things—she never could. So naturally it was always he that said the things, and then for some reason he would mind this suddenly. . . . A heartless woman he called her; she never told him that she loved him. But it was not so—it was not so. It was only that she never could say what she felt. Was there no crumb on his coat? Nothing she could do for him?

Robinson Crusoe, long confined to his island, discovers "one day about noon . . . the print of a man's naked foot on the shore." In one of the most dazzling inventions in all prose fiction, Defoe proceeds to describe Crusoe:

> I stood like one thunder-struck, or as if I had seen an apparition; I listen'd, I look'd round me, I could hear nothing, nor see any thing; I went up to a rising ground to look farther; I went up the shore and down the shore, but it was all one, I could see no other impression but that one. I went to it again to see if there were any more, and to observe if it might not be my fancy; but there was no room for that, for there was exactly the very print of a foot, toes, heel, and every part of a foot. . . .

In Hardy's *Return of the Native* there comes a moment when the marriage of Clym and Eustacia must be dissolved. As she decides to leave him,

> At last all her things were on. Her little hands quivered so violently as she held them to her chin to fasten her bonnet that she could not tie the strings and after a few moments she relinquished the attempt. Seeing this he moved forward and said, 'Let me tie them.'

Now, what do all these details have in common? A contextualist critic intent upon affirming structural unities will say that each of these little incidents forms an organic part of the novels' structures, serving to ratify, to clinch, to illuminate their actions. Thereby the details fit into the novels' "planned frameworks." Perhaps. Yet all of them could easily have been omitted from the novels in which they appear and their structures would have remained quite the same, if less vividly or tellingly so. Readers would not miss these details, since for us to miss them there must first be the genius—the improvisatory genius—of the writer to provide them, or, perhaps I should say, to come upon them. If you or I had written *Robinson Crusoe* we would surely not have "seen" that left footprint, forever present in its unresolved eeriness, its virtual independence of the plot. In that one little shape lies the difference between Defoe and just about everyone else.

The detail in Gissing—a stricken man poring over a newspaper report—does indeed serve as a confirming incident; but it is more. It forces us to a generalized reflection upon human behavior, it prods us to go a little beyond the confines of the story—ah, this is how people behave. We may even imagine that, in some rather obscure sense, the sequence of action in Gissing's novel is there to confirm the detail rather than the other way round, for the detail may well live in memory after the novel itself has faded.

With Faulkner and Woolf we move farther away from Martin Price's detail in the service of "the large structure." Popeye's need to straighten his hair a moment before death is a last gesture of definition, while the iridescent crumb which Mrs. Ramsay cannot find speaks of the immensity of her love. But these incidents are doing more than enabling "the large structure." They almost seem *imposed* upon action and character in order to serve as symbolic versions of human possibility. We feel Mrs. Ramsay's moment to be archetypal, virtually detached from the novel called *To the Lighthouse*, raised to a magnitude of vision that leaves behind any question of its role or function. So too with Crusoe's footprint, the terror of which is an essential terror of unmediated existence. What does that footprint really have to do with the structure, such as it is, of *Robinson Crusoe*?

And so too with the bit from *Return of the Native*: Clym tying Eustacia's bonnet at the moment of separation. This strikes me as a bit of transcendent revelation, revealing the force of habit in marriage even at the point of its dissolution. True, for their full impact such details need the context of the entire work, but soon they seem to leave the context behind. Only a great writer can invent such details, for at such moments the novelist works not only through but also *upon* his action, raising it to an inclusive generality. Perhaps more than to the books in which they appear, it is to such moments, such "gratuitous details" that we will return, as an index of memory.

Dickens: Three Notes

ABSOLUTE GOODNESS AND THE LIMITS OF FICTION

It is a truism frequently acknowledged that few things are more difficult for the novelist than to portray an absolutely good person—indeed, the greater the goodness, the greater the difficulty. I see no reason to challenge this judgment, but propose here to glance at a few instances that may yield attractive complications.

Let's start with the approximation that unalloyed goodness may take the form of a ready submission of selfhood to the needs, even the desires of others. Such behavior can excite our admiration almost as much as it may violate our sense of probability. The truly good person, whether we seek him in ourselves or in others, seems mostly a figment of hope. And this persuasion as to how things really are, this moral realism—it need not be engraved as a dogma of original sin—serves as a powerful controlling presence in our responses to works of fiction, including those written in nonrealistic modes.

The effort to portray, even the ability to imagine, a state of absolute goodness takes the mind into realms—misty, speculative, transcendent—which the novel as a genre finds hard to accommodate. Grubbing along in the low vistas of actuality, or at least simulated versions of actuality, the novel is not usually hospitable to elves, fairies, ghosts, angels, devils, and gods. Many novels show God as a figure keenly desired, but only rarely does He make an appearance, whether as voice or sheet of flame; and as for devils, they have the decency, when they do make an occasional entry, to dress as gentlemen. Now it is true that such hypothetical beings are not unconditionally excluded from novels, since of all modern genres the novel is best able to put up with alien matter; but God and the angels, especially the unfallen ones, are clearly not as comfortable with Balzac as with Milton.

When we think about the problem of rendering goodness in fiction, we are likely to turn, first of all, to Don Quixote. It's not at all clear, however, that "goodness" is the most accurate description of the Knight of the Mournful Countenance. He lives by a chivalric code of good works, he sees himself as a man of action, and when in the grip of his mania, which is throughout the richest parts of the book, he is completely serious about his intention to bring justice to earth: "I am the valorous Don Quixote de la Mancha, righter of wrongs and injustices," he says. And "What are we to do? Favor and aid the weak and needy." Precisely his exalted aims, bringing him to the threshold of grace, are what unhinge the poor fellow, as each act in quest of justice leads to an absurd pratfall.

We are not invited by Cervantes to disparage Don Quixote's intentions, but we cannot avoid recognizing that, more often than not, he either does unwitting harm or turns out to be ineffectual. An insatiable hunger for *purpose*, for a goal beyond the mere exercise or gratification of ego, drives him into recurrent states of agitation—and this, while surely admirable, is rather different from a pure goodness. Once "the idealism of [Don Quixote's] idée fixe takes hold of him," remarks Erich Auerbach, "everything he does in that state is completely senseless and so incompatible with the existing world that it produces only comic confusion there." It also produces intense pathos, though the confusion and the pathos must both be distinguished from the visible presence of goodness.

Don Quixote wishes to release an *active* principle in the workings of the world, which is one reason he must always be on the move. His behavior, sometimes heroism and sometimes a parody of heroism, seems to confirm or shadow the idea, similar perhaps to the quietist element in Christianity, that action, as it locks into the fallen world, carries within itself the seeds of destruction. Between actor and act there is a chasm not to be bridged—not, at least, in this world. Only when Don Quixote turns his back on the windmills, the giants and other phantasms of his sublime delusion, only when he ceases to be Don Quixote can he revert—we are now at the end of Cervantes's book—to his decent, flawed, commonplace self, Alonso el Bueno, Alonso the Good. This return to familiar sanity and alloyed goodness is purchased at the price of spiritual and, soon enough, physical death, so that the book may be read as implying—or is this a modernist misreading prompted by the ethic of striving?—that the return to sanity should be taken as a kind of fall. Throughout most of the book Don Quixote is too exalted or too deluded—he is always too busy—to live by the norms of absolute goodness, whatever those might be, indeed, to live by any norms but the chivalry of madness.

Dostoevsky, struggling with *The Idiot*, wrote a letter to his niece in 1868 speculating on the problem of positive goodness in fiction:

> The chief idea of the novel [the one he is writing] is to portray the positively good man. There is nothing in the world more difficult to do, and especially now. All writers, and not only ours, but even all Europeans who have tried to portray the *positively* good man have always failed. . . . There is only one positively good man in the world—Christ (so that the appearance of this immeasurably, infinitely good person is, of course, an infinite miracle in itself). . . . Of the good figures in Christian literature, the most perfect is Don Quixote. But he is good only because at the same time he is ridiculous [comic]. Dickens' Pickwick (an infinitely weaker conception than Don Quixote, but nevertheless immense) is also ridiculous [comic] and succeeds only by virtue of that fact. Compassion appears toward the good that is mocked and does not know its own value. . . .*

---

* There are problems of translation here. I have used the version in Ernest Simmons's biography of Dostoevsky, since it seems the clearest, but in the English translation of Konstantin Mochulsky's study of Dostoevsky, the key phrase is rendered as "a positively beautiful individual." I think it all but certain that, given Dostoevsky's cast of mind, he would have been referring to moral qualities. Simmons translates Dostoevsky's description of Don Quixote and Pickwick as "ridiculous"; the translator of Mochulsky prefers "comic." Both convey Dostoevsky's point, but for my purposes "comic" seems preferable.

Why does Dostoevsky believe "positive goodness" to be credible, or more credible, when presented as "comic" or "ridiculous"? Because our compassion is stirred when we see a virtue "that does not know its own value," a virtue neither proud nor self-conscious that is being mocked. (This, by the way, may echo Turgenev's remark in his 1860 lecture "Don Quixote and Hamlet": "we are ready to love someone whom we have laughed at.") It is, then, the innocence or naivete of the good person, the refusal to take affront at the world's mockery, that wins our love.

Let me suggest another reason for thinking that goodness is credible, or more credible, when presented through the lens of the comic. Goodness so regarded tends to shrink to something life-size or smaller than life; it does not disconcert us or fill us with a despairing awe as might a "positive goodness" of large scope.

Mulling over this matter in his notebooks for *The Idiot*, Dostoevsky writes about Prince Myshkin, the character he hoped to establish as an exemplar of "positive goodness": "How to make the hero's character sympathetic to readers? If Don Quixote and Pickwick, as virtuous types, are sympathetic to the reader . . . it is because they are comic."

But in *The Idiot*, Dostoevsky instructs himself, he will try for something much more difficult. "The hero of the novel, if not comical, then possesses another sympathetic trait—*he is innocent*." Rather than gain the effect of innocence through the oblique devices of comedy, as Cervantes and Dickens did, Dostoevsky would now try to represent innocence directly, full-face, without comic aids or embellishments.

But is this what he actually did in *The Idiot*? I think not, and, what's more, I think he could not. His intention has been shrewdly inferred by Harold Rosenberg: "Myshkin's function is not to alter the course of the action but to disseminate the aura of a new state of being, let events occur as they will." Yes; but simply because it *is* a novel and not an idyll or allegory, the book Dostoevsky wrote demonstrates that despite Myshkin's marvelous qualities he cannot long remain a figure emanating "a new state of being." Very quickly he is drawn into the Dostoevskian chaos, the typical ambience of this writer (some might add, of the world), and there Myshkin must, alas, become a force of disorder, altering events in ways he had not anticipated, perhaps even in ways Dostoevsky had not planned. Myshkin has no choice. In his own lovable way he turns out to be almost as destructive as the worldly and malevolent figures Dostoevsky sets off against him. A searcher who cannot remain at rest, Myshkin strains, a little like Don Quixote, to negotiate radical transformations of consciousness and thereby reach a universal state of goodness. But for this, in the Russia within which he must act, he has little capacity and less time. It seems to be a "rule" in fictions devoted to such characters that they cannot be granted long stretches of time—a keen intuition shared by greatly different writers about both the nature of reality and the limits of fiction.

Myshkin is a deeply affecting creature, at times even magnificent, but he is hardly innocent. Good Dostoevskian character that he is, Myshkin admits that "it is terribly difficult to fight against these *double* thoughts. I've tried. Goodness only knows how they come and how they arise." They sound, these "double thoughts," very much like the afflictions suffered by the rest of humanity, and perhaps to make certain that even

the slowest reader will get the point, Dostoevsky makes Myshkin into an epileptic, a sufficiently gross sign of imperfection.

One of Dostoevsky's notebooks contains this remarkable
sentence: *"Meekness is the most powerful force that exists in
the world."* If this remark helps explain the power of goodness
in Christ and Buddha, it may also explain the power of destruction in Christ and Buddha. "What is so destructive in
[Myshkin]," writes Murray Krieger, "is the sense others must
get from his infinite meekness that they are being judged. Of
course, Myshkin knows the sin of pride that is involved in
judging and so carefully refrains, condemning himself instead.
But this very inversion of the process constitutes a form of
judgment too for the guilty. . . ." Aglaya, the acute young
woman with whom Myshkin becomes involved, says to him:
"You have no tenderness, nothing but the truth, and so you
judge unjustly." A remark at once astonishing and profound
—and worth remembering with regard to Melville's Captain
Vere. I see it as clear evidence that Dostoevsky knew that,
whatever else, he had not succeeded in his stated intention
regarding Myshkin.

What he did succeed in doing was to write a wonderful
novel, in good part because he moved past his stated intention.
He complicated the portrayal of goodness with mental im-
broglios, murderous attacks, epileptic seizures, and sexual disasters. The road to great fiction is strewn with the collapse of
high intentions.

From Prince Myshkin to Milly Theale, the fragile heroine of
Henry James's *Wings of the Dove*, there is an enormous distance, but there is also one crucial similarity: neither character

can find a place in common life; the very distinction of each constitutes a sentence of doom. Each displays loveliness of soul, but both Dostoevsky and James refuse to grant them, perhaps because they cannot locate, the ground for a sustained exercise of goodness. Myshkin, suffering from a surplus of consciousness, cannot manage the circumstances of the Russia into which he is thrust; Milly, radiating generosity of spirit, cannot deal with the ways of London society.

Exquisite, dove-like, Milly Theale rises, as the novel continues, to heights of the angelic. Forgiving all who have betrayed her and casting the shadow of her luminous wings over their lives, Milly suggests something of the cold purity, but also the sheer terror, of angelic being. The more she seems to rise above the comfortably human, the more she is unable to gain the small pleasures and fulfillments of the human—and, as if in recognition that this does not permit of any sustained representation, James sees that he must rapidly withdraw his angelic creature from the shabby milieu into which, as a novelist, he felt obliged to put her. Milly's loveliness is signaled by her fatality: at least on earth, the angelic has no prospect of duration. So Milly barely lingers with the actualities of goodness: she passes beyond these, into a tremor of sublimity, now hovering, as the mildest of rebukes, over the mortals who survive her.

Dickens, in a few of his novels, also struggles with the problem of rendering absolute goodness. He succeeds with Pickwick, though on a smaller scale than Cervantes with Don Quixote, because he does not strain to make Pickwick into an archetype. A good-hearted, sweet-souled petty bourgeois, Pickwick serves as a "local deity" of Olde England, created to lull readers into a persuasion that benevolence can smooth away the difficulties of life. Pickwick does not try to rise above his class position; he realizes himself through limited social definition and inherited bias, occasionally stretching but never breaking these. He is always on the move, but never moves very far. He cannot be imagined as existing anywhere but in stagecoach England, indeed, anywhere but in his own neighborhood, as an ornament of the provincial imagination. Precisely this historical specificity makes him so greatly loved by the English reading public, and sometimes bewildering to those who know him only through translation. For a moment, with Pickwick and his bumbling troupe, the clock of history stands still: that is the pleasure of it.

Everyone knows how numerous are the tests of goodness that would be beyond Pickwick, and everyone feels glad that Dickens has shielded him from them. Brought low through comic plotting, Pickwick finds himself briefly in prison, from which Dickens contrives through some appropriately silly business to rescue him. It is a traditional strategy of the comic to glance just a little beyond its limits, into stretches of experience that comedy is ill-equipped to cope with. Pickwick's goodness, insofar as we agree to suspend disbelief for a while, can thrive only in the spaces of a comedy that history has made irretrievable.

A deeper conception informs Dickens's treatment of Little Dorrit. Mild, unassertive, and selfless, she neither represents the virtues of local custom, like Pickwick, nor strains toward universality of value, like Myshkin. She is a figure at rest, in a setting where everything else is turbulent and false; she is sufficient unto herself, harmonious in nature, unqualifiedly responsive to others. She has no need to think about, nor in responding to her do we feel obliged to invoke, the categorical imperative or any universalization of Christian values. Her goodness is a quality of being without any pressure to invoke whatever might be "higher" than or "beyond" goodness. The imaginative realization of this figure is so pure and lucid, mere ideas fade away.

Little Dorrit is not innocent and rarely, if ever, sentimental. No one who has grown up in the Marshalsea prison could be innocent; no one who has had to put up with all those wretched Dorrits could long be sentimental. She knows quite enough about the varieties of selfishness; that is why Dickens has provided her with the family she has, to educate her in the ways of the world. And though she exists entirely within the world, she has no designs upon it, neither to transform nor transcend it. She has no designs of any kind; she is simply a possibility, very rare, of our existence.

What seems to have inspired the creation of Little Dorrit was Dickens's residual sentiment of Christianity, a sense or memory of a faith unalloyed by dogma, aggression, or institution. This is a "religion," if religion at all, of affection, or an ethic without prescription or formula. Dickens himself, as he knew quite well, was far from embodying anything of the sort, but his imagination cherished the possibility, arousing in him the sort of upwelling emotions that the vision of Billy Budd must have aroused in Melville. The religious experience had largely been lost to

Dickens, except insofar as it might leave a sediment of purity.

Little Dorrit is not at all a "Christ figure." She does not ask anyone to abandon the world's goods and follow her; she could not drive the money changers from the temple; nor can one imagine her on a cross, though she might be among those mourning near it. Nothing even requires that we see her as a distinctively Christian figure, though nothing prevents us either. The great demand upon the reader of *Little Dorrit*—it can bring on a virtual moral crisis—is to see her quite as she is, unhaloed, not at all "symbolic," perhaps sublime but in no way transcendent. She makes no demands upon anyone, nor does she try to distinguish herself in any respect. Her behavior is geared entirely to the needs and feelings of those who are near her. She is a great comforter, which may be all that goodness can be in this world. No one could possibly say of Little Dorrit, as Aglaya says of Prince Myshkin, that she lacks tenderness and "has nothing but the truth." What can truth be to her, who lives by the grace of daily obligation?

Little Dorrit is an astonishing conception, perhaps the sole entirely persuasive figure of "positive goodness" in modern fiction. (The only possible rival is the grandmother in Proust's great novel.) As against Dostoevsky's prescription, she is drawn neither in the comic mode nor as an innocent. For modern readers she constitutes a severe problem. Some dismiss her as insipid, others find it difficult to credit her reality and perhaps difficult to live with that reality if they do credit it. Finally, as with all literary judgments, we reach a point where exegesis, persuasion, and eloquence break down, and fundamental differences of perception have to be acknowledged. I myself feel that a failure to respond to the shy magnificence of what Dickens has done here signifies a depletion of life.

How does he manage it? I wish there were some great clinching formula but do not believe there is—a part of critical wisdom is to recognize the limits of critical reach. Part of the answer, a fairly small part, may be due to what some critics have seen as Dickens's limitation: his inability to conceptualize in a style persuasive to modern readers, or, still more to the point, his lack of interest in trying to conceptualize. Dickens makes no claim for Little Dorrit, he fits her into no theological or theoretical system, he cares little if at all about her symbolic resonance. He simply *sees* her, a gleam of imagination. He trusts to the sufficiency of his depiction, a feat of discipline by a writer not always disciplined.

Quite deliberately Dickens shrinks Little Dorrit in size, voice, will, and gesture. Though clearly an adult, she seems almost childlike. She loves Arthur Clennam, the thoughtful, melancholy man worn down by failure. They marry, not in a rush of sensuality but as a pact of "making do," two people bruised into tenderness. Other writers seeking to validate goodness have fixed upon their characters' revealing flaws in order to retain some plausibility. Dickens, however, presents goodness not through the persuasiveness of a flaw but through the realism of a price. The price of Little Dorrit's goodness, as of her marriage to Clennam, is a sadly reduced sexuality—an equivalent perhaps to Billy Budd's stammer. It is as if Dickens had an unspoken belief that a precondition for goodness is the removal of that aggression which may well be intrinsic to the sexual life.

IMPRESARIO OF MINOR CHARACTERS

The picaresque novel sets in motion a line of episodes, which in principle is open to indefinite extension, the sole limitations being the protagonist's energy and the reader's patience. The picaro moves from adventure to adventure, and each cluster of incidents brings him into relation with a new set of minor characters whose task it is to speed the action and then fade away (also to entertain a bit). Within the picaro (assuming he has a "within"), nothing much happens: he simply moves along to the next episode. What counts here is not experience but energy—which may explain why a mode of fiction in which the central figure keeps rushing through events comes finally to seem quite static. It is a little like running in place.

Dickens, in his last great novels, takes the picaresque line of action and bends it into a sphere or circle enclosing the modern city. The picaro's seemingly endless dash through linear space now becomes a claustral repetitiveness of set pieces, with each cluster of incidents bringing back an ensemble of minor characters. But now, especially in *Bleak House*, the most original of Dickens's formal innovations, the "minor characters" come to occupy or to appropriate the forefront of the action. In Dickens's hands, the novel draws upon a large number of interlocking and juxtaposed social groups, in their sum constituting what has been called a polyphonic structure. Simultaneously, the novel appears to acquire a voice of its own, the collective voice of the city, for which Dickens's virtuoso rhetoric serves as stand-in. In this atmosphere of bewildering appearances and shifting phantasms, the city comes to seem an enormous, spreading, and threatening creature, a fearsome

Other apart from the men and women inhabiting it. London, by the time Dickens wrote his last complete novel, *Our Mutual Friend*, struck him as a hopeless city "where the whole metropolis was a heap of vapour charged with muffled sounds of wheels, and enfolding a gigantic catarrh." This sense of the city will spread through large parts of European literature, from Döblin to Céline, Beckett to Kafka. If by now it seems familiar, an effort of the historical imagination can recapture its revolutionary character.

Revolutionary too is Dickens's treatment of minor characters in the late novels, especially *Bleak House* and *Little Dorrit*. In Smollett's picaresque fictions, obviously an important influence on the early Dickens, it barely matters whether his figures are reasonable facsimiles of human beings, let alone whether they have finely demarcated selves. Like the physicist Laplace dismissing God as an unneeded hypothesis, Smollett can dispense with the hypothesis of selfhood (supposing, which is unlikely, that he was even aware of it), and thereby gain freedom for play with incident and language. But Dickens, in massing his minor characters, is very much aware, even negatively obsessed, with the problem of self or identity. He is making a discovery of very large consequence: that most of the urban figures whom he renders as caricature or grotesque have no souls. In a valid artistic exaggeration, he "totalizes" their soullessness.

Some new and barely identifiable power in the world, destructive and crushing, has annulled whatever souls these figures might have had. For Dickens this comes as a great shock—walk through our cities today and it can still be a great shock. Dickens wheels in his Chadbands, Guppeys, and Smallweeds not just for entertainment, nor just to populate the "Dickens theater"—it is the soullessness of these figures that, through a demonic comedy, provides the ground for the entertainment. Dickens is also testing a hypothesis, in the one certain way a novelist can: through representation. Can he find in these creatures anything but soullessness? Occasionally, as with Snagsby in *Bleak House*, there is a shred of soul, but most of these minor characters turn out to be quite as he had feared, the waste of the city.

In the great novels of Dickens's last years, the minor characters may be slotted as mere accessories to the action, but they soon break out of these limits, so that in *Bleak House* and to a lesser extent in *Little Dorrit* and *Our Mutual Friend* they often become the center of interest while the ostensible heroes and heroines, too often paste figures, have to carry the plot.

Why should the minor characters come to seem so much more memorable than the major ones, indeed, come to be what the Dickens novel "is all about"? I offer a few speculations:

While formally enlisted in Dickens's elephantine plots, the minor characters are allowed repeatedly to step forward on their own, like performers in a skit, so that the plot can do little or no damage to their vitality.

The fine sentiments which the official Dickens feels obliged to drape about his major characters are largely abandoned when the authentic Dickens, fierce and corrosive, allows his minor characters freedom to exhibit or, as we now say, to do their own thing.

The minor characters are not burdened with an excess of civilized qualities; they act out of a direct and "primitive" (often really a socially decadent) energy, quite as if the "humor" were a basic truth about mankind.

With most of the minor characters there is no pretense of individuality; they can be uninhibited in their generic or even reductive traits, making of the type a monolithic, unshaded force. Indifference to subtlety brings enormous gains in graphic representativeness.

In their grouping and regroupings, their repeated appearances, the minor characters are truly of the city, inconceivable in any other setting, while a good number of Dickens's major characters seem to be transplanted to the city, alien there and unhappy. The minor characters are utterly at home.

In *Little Dorrit*, it is true, one major character, Arthur Clennam, is full-scale and persuasively subtle, but even there the gallery of the soulless, those on top who make things go and those on the bottom who do the going, occupies a large part of the book's foreground. Lacking a ready vocabulary with which to describe or place such figures, we call them grotesques. What Dickens is actually doing with these minor characters—more abundantly in *Bleak House*, with diminished fervor in *Our Mutual Friend*—is akin to what his literary cousin, Gogol, evoked with the phrase "dead souls." Evil is no surprise for Dickens; he has plenty of it in his early books. But by the late novels, evil has been somewhat subordinated as an active principle. Soullessness—that for Dickens is now more terrifying and familiar, the discovery of creatures formed in the image of man but operating as mere functions of the city.

This is a radically new vision of things. Notwithstanding some connections and similarities with Ben Jonson's "humors," it is also a radically new way of presenting characters, for Dickens sees them in their social specificity, as Jonson did not. Chadband and his monumental cant, the Smallweeds in their smoldering venality, the Barnacles in their sublime presumption—all are transfigured into varieties of comedy but embodying an increasingly acute sense of class and an utterly grim sense of the world. These are the antimen of greed, commerce, repression, the paltry carriers of the cash nexus. Entering the novel individually as minor characters, they mass together as a major presence.

BECOMING DOSTOEVSKY

To be true to one's self: this modern yearning takes the form of hoping, first of all, to discover what that self might be. Among writers it figures as a search for an authentic voice, which is to say, a public or literary voice, an outward simulation of self. But then, as the years pass, writers, fearing the humiliation that comes when fading of energy leads to self-imitation, want to break away from their true self. They want a second chance, another start. They want a new self won through transcending the old one. At the very moment of his death, Henry James, in his unfinished novel *The Ivory Tower*, was on the verge of creating a new Henry James, fiercely satirical in his view of society as he had seldom been before. Similar things could be said about Melville, George Eliot, Fitzgerald. But the most striking instance seems to me that of Dickens, who was only fifty-eight when he died, but who in his late great work—the four novels from *Bleak House* to *Our Mutual Friend*—was steadily becoming "another" writer.

In *Little Dorrit* there is a passage likely to excite the curiosity of any serious reader. It occurs in Book the First, Chapter 14. Little Dorrit, having been locked out of the Marshalsea Prison, walks with her weak-minded friend Maggy through the cold London night. They have no shelter. They meet an unnamed prostitute who at first takes Little Dorrit to be a child.

The supposed child kept her head drooped down, and kept her form close at Maggy's side.

"Poor thing!" said the woman. "Have you no feeling, that you keep her out in the cruel streets at such a time as this? Have you no eyes, that you don't see how delicate and slender she is? Have you no sense (you don't look as if you had much) that you don't take more pity on this cold and trembling little hand?"

She had stepped across to that side, and held the hand between her own two, chafing it. "Kiss a poor lost creature, dear," she said, bending her face, "and tell me where she's taking you."

Little Dorrit turned toward her.

"Why, my God!" she said, recoiling, "you're a woman!"

"Don't mind that!" said Little Dorrit, clasping one of her hands that had suddenly released hers. "I am not afraid of you."

"Then you had better be," she answered. "Have you no mother?"

"No."

"No father?"

"Yes, a very dear one."

"Go home to him, and be afraid of me. Let me go. Good night!"

    "I must thank you first; let me speak to you as if I really
were a child."

    "You can't do it," said the woman. "You are kind and
innocent; but you can't look at me out of a child's eyes. I never
should have touched you, but I thought that you were a child."

    And with a strange, wild cry, she went away.

    The prostitute assumes Little Dorrit is safe to approach
because she is a child, since a child will not rebuff her. Actually,
being quite indifferent to the world's judgments about "fallen
women," Little Dorrit would welcome her with kindness. But
the prostitute, even while recognizing that Little Dorrit is "kind
and innocent," cannot really credit her essential goodness, for
all experience dictates that such goodness in an adult is beyond
credence.

    Dickens offers no explanation of why he included this pas-
sage, nor does he bring back the prostitute on a later page, as
is his usual way with minor figures.

    Now there is a way of "absorbing" this passage into the
scheme of the novel, and that is to suggest that the prostitute's
response to Little Dorrit is an extreme refraction of the worldliness which, in this book as no doubt in the actual world,
denies the possibility of the kind of goodness represented by
Little Dorrit. This would seem to be a fairly plausible reading,
at least thematically, but it quite fails to account for what is
most striking about the passage—its intense, even overwrought
tone, the vibration of the prose. It is overwrought and pulsing
even for Dickens, with an excess of emotion beyond any cause
that we can plausibly locate in the story itself.

    Our natural desire to find a harmonious relation between

a local passage and the novel's dominant theme can easily lead us into the error—rather frequent in academic criticism—which takes it for granted that everything in a novel has a necessary function. If it's there, there must be a good reason for it, and the critic's job is to find the reason. The error consists in a failure to recognize the frequency with which, in extended works of fiction, there are and perhaps need to be loose ends, cues not taken up, false starts. No writer, not even the most self-conscious craftsman, is likely to keep every line under entire control.

Let me then propose a speculation. Dickens was the kind of novelist who kept looking past the work on which he was engaged, straining toward new insights and devices, retuning moral premises which, it might be, he had not yet fully developed in the book he was composing. None of his novels was quite like either its predecessors or successors: there is constant restlessness, movement forward and sometimes backward.

In the passage I have quoted, Dickens was anticipating that late in his career he might become Dostoevsky. There is a powerful urge, never completed, to enact a transition from the Dickens who was using his early comic grotesques in behalf of a stringent moral-social criticism to a dimly envisaged Dickens who would penetrate, as no English novelist had yet done, mixed psychological states, extreme versions of human personality and its disorders, and perhaps even negotiate the Dostoevskian vision of redemption through sin. The prostitute seems more like a character out of *Crime and Punishment* than out of any of Dickens's novels: there is really no urgent "need" for her in *Little Dorrit*, although the tone of the passage suggests that in ways we will never quite grasp Dickens felt a need to imagine her. And perhaps—I continue to speculate—if Dickens had gone ahead to "become" Dostoevsky, the figures of Little Dorrit and the prostitute, here briefly crossing, would have been conflated.

By the time Dickens came to write *Our Mutual Friend*, his last completed novel, he was struggling toward a view of the human psyche and, still more important, a prospect of salvation not realized in any of his earlier books, though anticipated in the chapter about Miss Wade in *Little Dorrit* and in the portrayal of Bradley Headstone in *Our Mutual Friend*. Done with a caustic innerness unique in Dickens's fiction, Bradley Headstone represents a fusion of class *ressentiment* and psychological malaise. Earnest, sweaty, rigid, Headstone suffers the exquisite pain of a plebeian risen, through costly exertions, to the status of respectability—he is a schoolmaster—but constantly aware of his clumsiness of person and speech. His dark-suited outer presence barely masks a seething mass of anger, frustration, self-hatred, and he knows that no exertions on his part will ever bring him the ease and polish of a gentleman. In this truly Dostoevskian portrait, Dickens projected both a sense of lingering plebeian rage and an equally powerful wish to subject his memories to punitive rebuke. The result is a great piece of work, even if ill-adjusted to other parts of *Our Mutual Friend*. We respond to such elements or strands in the late novels as to a musical composition which contains a phrase that will be fully developed only in a later work—which in the life of Dickens never materialized. So there is little point in asking what light the passage I have quoted from *Little Dorrit* sheds on the novel as a whole, for the passage really belongs, as it were, to another novel, one that might have brought Dickens to a triumph of self-transcendence but was, alas, never to be written.

That Dickens greatly influenced Dostoevsky is common knowledge (see Angus Wilson's "Dickens and Dostoevsky" in his book *Diversity and Depth in Fiction*). That Dickens knew only a story or two by Dostoevsky seems also well established—it is quite impossible that he could have been significantly influenced by Dostoevsky. What was at work were parallel developments and inclinations within two writers profoundly troubled by the life of nineteenth-century Europe and, more important still, profoundly moved by the possibilities evoked in the story of Christ. To become Dostoevsky could, I venture, have been Dickens's literary fate had he lived another seven or eight years. Or to phrase this notion more modestly, let us say that Dostoevsky is a name we give to the glimpsed desires of the late Dickens.

Farce and Fiction

MY DICTIONARY DEFINES farce as a work in which "broad improbabilities of plot and characterization are used for humorous effect." This definition, going back to Dryden, has a respectable lineage; but it won't do. The events of farce are quite as probable as those of tragedy. What is so improbable about slipping on a banana peel? Or a husband showing up when his wife is in bed with another man? Or a cream pie landing smack in your face? Or an old man revealing his impotence when he tries to make love with a lusty young woman? Such happenings seem as likely as the ordeals of Oedipus and Lear, perhaps more so.

Farce falls under the category that Wittgenstein describes as having "blurred edges," the kind about which he asks, "Isn't the indistinct often exactly what we need?" The "indistinct," in any case, is exactly what we are likely to get, so slippery is the idea of farce. But if we cannot satisfactorily define it, we can bound a few of its variants:

The Recalcitrance of Objects. At the simplest level, farce turns upon the ineptitude of people trying to cope with the perversity of objects. Doors won't open, screws won't turn, gears won't work. Sheer brute matter, as if gripped by malice, refuses to join in the satisfaction of desire. Farce of this kind is content with a small cast, often just one (Buster Keaton) or two (Laurel and Hardy).

In *The Navigator* Keaton fumbles ingeniously with kitchen utensils, his frustration so extreme it rises to farce. We feel delight, first because we share vicariously in Keaton's incapacity, but second because as spectators we can for a moment delude ourselves into establishing a certain distance from the fumbling. Chaplin develops two brilliant variations on this theme of recalcitrance. In *Modern Times* the automatic feeding-machine that is supposed to save labor-time refuses to behave, hurling soup in the worker's face; its intractability becomes a wild chaos that destroys the authoritarianism of the managers. In *Monsieur Verdoux* the intractable object takes the guise of a woman, Martha Raye, who simply cannot be murdered, no matter how ingenious Charlie's attempts. I cherish a fancy of old Tolstoy watching these films, impatient at first with their high jinks but then snorting gleefully at their confirmation of his belief that all attempts to rationalize life are irrational. Objects, processes, systems: everything beyond the fragile perimeter of self can reduce us to a farce of incompetence.

The Fall of Dignity. Farce often treats of blunt relations between people in which dignity is stripped away, status leveled, social standing wiped out. We laugh nervously, perhaps vindictively—farce does not make for charitable emotions. Mack Sennett, the silent film producer, once said—he is quoted in Albert Bermel's lively book *Farce*—that the task of farce is to act out "a fall of dignity." That's keen. Neoclassical farces about impotent old men trying to summon vigor, the bedroom farces of Feydeau reducing domesticity to deception—these form a mockery of postures, and what makes this mockery amusing is that it reduces us all to smallness. It is also what makes that mockery frightening.

Farce does not compromise; neither is it kind. It hits below the belt. It flattens out the refinements that sensitive people value. It is a sort of fart among the genres. It levels us all to an ultimate equality: man on his ass. There are few metaphysical consolations or ennobling ends in farce, certainly nothing like those we impute to comedy; there is only the putdown or the social demolition which reduces the world to a gleeful level (the Marx Brothers).

Nor does farce fool with transcendence. Its philosophy is a rude pragmatism, even if its ultimate negations assert a bitter truth—that sprawled out on the pavement or adorned with a pair of horns, we are all equally ridiculous—well, more or less. And farce does not provide an austere catharsis or good-spirited sociability. Even as it seems to undermine everything, finally it changes nothing. Egalitarian yes, progressive no.

Parallel Negations. Farce is to culture as anarchism is to politics: the enemy of existing norms. Fatty Arbuckle keeps falling into a barrel of water; Laurel and Hardy, cast as clumsy salesmen, destroy their customer's house. Anarchy is loose. Farce and anarchy disintegrate the claims of society, rendering pointless all pretenses to respect. In one of the Marx Brothers' films, a policeman gives Harpo a ticket, so Harpo writes out his own ticket for the policeman, whereupon the policeman tears up Harpo's ticket and, in a supreme gesture, Harpo tears up the policeman's ticket. With one rip, Harpo negates the state.

Since farce and anarchism are extreme positions, they must suffer the strains, perhaps also the ultimate incoherence, of extremism. It is easy enough to acquiesce in a moderate version of the anarchist critique—just about every sensible person does—but really to credit the idea of a society without the state and without law is very hard. So too with farce. Our acquiescence in its destructiveness is conditional, an *as if* indulgence, a moral holiday—but not completely; that would be too frightening. Farce and anarchism both take joy in negation, scoffing at the big questions, deriding common proprieties, thumbing their noses at rationales for power—and then they back off a little. Enticing us with their enchanting visions of total rejection—the miserable world in shambles—they smile innocently: that's not what we meant at all; everything will soon fall back into place. To wreck the world provisionally is easier than ploddingly to remake it.

We can take pleasure in the democracy of reduction that farce (or anarchism) induces, but not for long, since something within us, some need for balance and order, craves a passage across the shoals of negation.

Revolutionists are cool to farce.

Two incidents—they actually happened:

During a trip to Japan, my wife and I breakfasted in a hotel. My wife was eating some eggs and took a moment to smoke. An eager Japanese waiter grabbed her plate; indignant, my wife grabbed it on the other side; and for a moment the two of them pulled each side of the innocent plate—until the waiter yielded. This was pure farce, not very threatening, its struggle wildly disproportionate to its object. Buster Keaton could have performed it wordlessly, perhaps doing both parts.

The second incident is more complex. A friend who grew up in Warsaw between the wars led a protest of Jewish students against segregation in university lecture halls. As he was shouting slogans, the police started pulling at one arm and some fascists at the other. He was in danger of being torn apart until his brother, also demonstrating, cried out: "Let him go! He's a good guy! I know him!" Nonplussed, both the police and the fascists released my friend. The minute or so when, like the plate in Japan, he was being tugged in opposite directions was farcical, but not pure farce, since his brother's outcry introduced a touch of complicating social comedy, invoking, as it parodied, the values of his assailants.

Farce can be ominous. It brings pleasure through humiliation: knock him down, throw him into the water, hit him again. And then, a sort of magical cancellation: Fatty Arbuckle gets up, blinking with good humor—the world is restored.

In a brilliant essay called "Laughter," Henri Bergson fails to distinguish between comedy and farce, offering as an instance of comedy what I would call farce: a Punch-and-Judy show in which a policeman is felled with a single blow. "Up and down [he] flops and hops with the uniform rhythm . . . of a spring, whilst the spectators laugh louder and louder." But if the victim were a person, would they keep laughing?

Only, I think, up to a point—and half the art in farce is know-ing when to stop. In principle the Punch-and-Judy show allows for endless repetition, with the major risk being boredom; but if repeated with a human victim for more than a few times, the blows could come to seem too cruel, too real. A little cruelty is *all right*; Molière understood this. The aggression of farce, repeated too often, would take on lasting consequences and thereby cease to be farce. Mack Sennett grasped this keenly: "Something uncomfortable happening to the other fellow, but not *too* uncomfortable. Yes . . . Things must go wrong, but not too wrong. And to some fellow you feel reasonably sure can't be too much injured by it—just enough to make you laugh, and not enough to make you feel sad or cry" (cited in Bermel).

Is farce a branch of comedy? It is hard to decide. We say it is because we don't know what else to say, and that may be a good enough reason.

Still, if you accept Hegel's remark that what is "inseparable from the comic is an infinite geniality and confidence capable of rising superior to its own contradiction," then it seems du-bious to link farce with comedy. Much farce is by no means "genial." But we may partly reclaim farce for the comic mode since, just as comedy resolves depicted conflicts into harmo-nious "geniality," so farce will suddenly stop its chaos and settle into innocent calm.

But there are major differences. An unknown eighteenth-century author, quoted in Leo Hughes's *A Century of English Farce*, wrote: "Farce is more loose and disengaged [than com-edy], not cramp'd by Method or measure of time or other

Unity. . . ." Not only structure but tone is likely to be a point
of difference. Both farce and comedy can render streaks of
cruelty, but at least in writers like Shakespeare and Molière,
the intervals of farce are held in proper subordination by the
good humor of comedy.

Comedy speaks for civilization; farce bears an ill-
concealed, sometimes unconcealed animus against civilization.
Often against civility too. The difference is touched upon in
George Meredith's "Essay on Comedy": the heroines of comedy, those of Shakespeare, Molière, Congreve, Shaw, and
Wilde, "use their wits" yet are not "necessarily heartless from
being clear-sighted." Intelligent women bring critical point and
fine sensibility to comedy, while farce has little place for
them—indeed, little use for individual characterization at all.
When the pie swirls through the air, it hits a type-character.

Farce is mostly visual: there's slipping and falling, there's
hiding and tumbling and fleeing, there's the tug-of-war and the
chase. The farceur, writes nimble Hazlitt, "should have his
wits in his heels, and in his fingers' ends." Farce dotes on
situations and neglects stories; favors action but seldom plot.
Short-breathed, it strives for rapid effects, blunt, even gross,
and leaves little space for reflection. In farce, repetition takes
the place of development, or, rather, repetition *is* development.

Nor is there much spontaneity. Farce is studied performance, stylized, agile, dependent on style and timing, most at
home with nonrealistic modes, once in a while with a faint
allegorical undercurrent. The Kafka who laughed when reading
aloud his stories of fruitless quest might have regarded traditional farce as a partial source of his work.

I cannot imagine a writer like Hermann Broch or Robert Musil doing farce: they are too heavy, too cumbered with tradition and idea. Kafka could and did, seizing upon the unfathomable sequence of dream as the ground for actions in which farce melts into anxiety. The farce in *The Trial* and *The Castle* consists of repetitive encirclements, without visible end or seeming reason. Joseph K. calls his arrest "a farce"—and in Kafka it becomes all but impossible to distinguish between events resembling farce and relations evoking comedy, since both entangle the characters in a maze of unexplored selfhood, so that they come to their doom aware of its farcical shamefulness yet without much grasp of its significance. This might be called metaphysical farce, but then, all farce seems to have a metaphysical element, mute in Keaton and struggling to break out in Kafka.

A wretched little clerk named Lyamshin in Dostoevsky's *The Possessed*, playing the jester to an "enlightened" provincial circle, improvises a musical farce by interlacing the "Marseillaise" with "Mein Lieber Augustin," so that the "vulgar waltz" finally obliterates the French hymn, all emblematic of what Dostoevsky takes to be the farce of Russian enlightenment.

The modern master of farce is Samuel Beckett. The farce of *Waiting for Godot* has an obvious source in vaudeville horseplay: two bums clowning on stage. The farce of *Watt* is at first quite traditional, with the pliable Watt, on his way to a job as a servant, suffering a series of indignities close to those that might befall a Smollett picaro. He is kicked out of a train, knocked over by a porter, hit by a stone thrown by a nutty woman, and finally falls into a ditch. More difficult to specify,

there emerges a streak of farce in Beckett's very language, with
its plethora of thwarting commas and logical parodies. From
Watt:

> . . . we know that we are no longer the same, and not only
> know that we are no longer the same, but know in what we are
> no longer the same, you wiser but not sadder, and I sadder but
> not wiser, for wiser I could hardly become without grave per-
> sonal inconvenience, whereas sorrow is a thing you can keep
> adding to all your life long, is it not, like a stamp or egg col-
> lection, without feeling very much the worse for it, is it not.

I am not sure whether it stretches the idea of farce exces-
sively when we try to locate it in language; but if we can speak
of farce in language, then it is to be found in, of all writers,
Henry James. Striding along in his grave and stately prose,
James will suddenly drop headlong into a sentence or two of
farcical aggression. In *The Bostonians*, that frigid masterpiece,
he writes about a female character: "If she had been a boy she
would have borne some relation to a girl, whereas Dr. Prance
appeared to bear none whatever." The fleshly Mrs. Luna draws
on her gloves and the hero of the novel, Basil Ransom, "had
never seen any that were so long; they reminded him of stock-
ings, and he wondered how she managed without garters at
the elbows." James is especially inclined to farce when dealing
with journalists. George Flack, the odious reporter of *The
Reverberator*, "was not a specific person . . . [he] had the
quality of the sample or advertisement, the air of representing
a 'line of goods' for which there is a steady demand." In such

remarks James's wit is harsh and reductive: farce as a pratfall of language.

And farce in the novel? Only seldom can it be sustained over a full-length fiction. It cannot accommodate the complications a novel requires; it has to move along a short and straight line of incident. Perhaps, also, novelists feel there is something a bit disreputable about farce, a tacit violation of high standards, an affront to man and God. Often, about two-thirds of the way through novels that start happily with farce, writers will lapse into mere seriousness, as if to prove they too can be good citizens.

Farce serves most handily as subplot about plebeian buffoons (in theater, *A Midsummer Night's Dream*) or as relief to picaresque adventure (Smollett's *Roderick Random* and *Peregrine Pickle*) or occasionally as an interval within a serious comedy (the Molly Seagram churchyard scene in Fielding's *Tom Jones*). For Fielding the recurrent bits of farce serve to keep his inventions from becoming too fixed, bringing a welcome note of disorder.

One of the few more recent novels that keeps fast to the business of farce without declining into virtue is Kingsley Amis's *Lucky Jim* (1954). It does not flinch from the logic of Jim's philistinism, so that when he quits the academic world he so passionately detests, neither he nor Amis pretends to be asserting higher values. *Lucky Jim* is a fictional farce with the stamina to maintain its motive to the very end. Amis has the courage of farce, and that turns out to be quite a lot—indeed, rare.

History and the Novel: Variations on a Theme

DEFOE'S MOLL FLANDERS fears she will sink into London's depths; Balzac's Lucien races toward fame and fortune; Dostoevsky's Raskolnikov murders at least partly for money; Joyce's Bloom sells advertisements for a newspaper. Except for Moll, these fictional characters also cherish high motives and grand delusions, yet they are constrained by commonplace necessity. They must find a way to earn a living, they are pressed by circumstances quite as most of us are in reality. No such pressures, however, beset Aeneas, Tristan, or Faust—not even the most literal-minded reader can ever have worried about their finances.

In the novel there is no "once upon a time . . ." There is London in the 1840s, Moscow in the 1950s. The clock rules; place helps determine psychic formation; characters reach identity through social role. In the novel a complex of circumstances often emerges as a "slice" of time across the passage of history, since an illusion of historical stoppage is essential for that "thickness" of specification at which many novels aim: Chicago as it looked upon Sister Carrie's arrival, Paris seen through the eyes of Swann.

But the illusion of historical stoppage must also be linked to an illusion of historical flow. How this is done we hardly know, it is a secret of genius. A fictional "world," say, Faulkner's Yoknapatawpha County, is portrayed at more-or-less stationary points, yet the very act of so conceiving it also promotes the illusion of historical motion, somewhat the way a series of stills can result in a moving picture. Social circumstance melts into historical process.

Novelists write on the tacit premise of the self-sufficiency of history, the cosmic solitariness of mankind. Beneath heaven's "indifferent blue" we are now freed from the decrees of any external will, as the glow of faith is replaced by the hard light of causality.

It was deism that first taught us to accept the pain of historicity. By granting God powers of initiation and then putting Him to sleep forever, deism freed the mind from the puzzle of origins and cleared the way for historical consciousness. Without such a tacit premise, the novel could not have gotten very far, since it really has no room for a will superior to natural law. True, great novels have been written by devout Christians, but as writers they were something more or less than devout Christians.

In wrenching free from the dualisms of Christianity, modern novelists improvised historical dualisms of their own. Soon after the Enlightenment, the problem confronting the novelistic imagination was not only the gloom of being distanced from heaven; it was also the pain of estrangement from a society taken to be at least as indifferent to men and women as the cosmos was now recognized to be. In many nineteenth-century novels, society figures as more than the sum of its members; it takes on what we call "a life of its own," and that life is not our's. Society now hovers over mankind like a crushing weight, sometimes it seems with a willful malevolence. It is notable that conflicting visions of society bear a curious similarity to conflicting visions of God—and, for that matter, of God's disappearance. Remove the idea of a wrathful or loving God, and the distance from a neutral to a malevolent cosmos is not very great. Remove the idea of a naturally ordained social hierarchy, and the distance from a neutral to a malevolent social order is even smaller.

A parallel development can be noticed, I think, with regard to the idea of the self. As a historically liberating hypothesis advanced during the Enlightenment and the age of Romanticism, the self becomes a shadow of our public lives, created within the modern historical moment while often turning upon it as a critical adversary. The self comes to be treasured as a reserve of consciousness, a resource beyond the press of social forms. The child of history, it erects a defense against the assaults of history. The very assumption that we can locate a psychic presence that we call the self or that it is useful to suppose such a presence exists implies a separation of inner being from outer behavior—what might be called the dualism of the person.

With time, the notion of the self becomes frayed, breaking

into fragments of dissociation and estrangement. In Beckett's novels and plays it ends as a state of nullity, the self erased or reduced to mere waiting. Perhaps it is a simplification to see the history of the novel—or historical consciousness working through the novel—as a two-sided confrontation with demons of estrangement: those that bear down from without and those that surge up from within. With Kafka, this distinction collapses.

In other literary genres the pressures of history are registered obliquely—in much lyric poetry, where sensibility operates, so to say, in its own space. But in the novel the impress of history is often blunt. To achieve verisimilitude, something most novelists strive for instinctively, the novel requires historical specification: Melville knows nineteenth-century whaling as a trade, Dostoevsky experienced Russian squalor directly, Proust sets up as anthropologist of the French aristocracy, Nabokov became an aficionado of the American motel. None of these writers scorns information.

Henry James, not commonly regarded as a realist, writes in his preface to *Roderick Hudson* that by specifying its opening locale as Northampton, Massachusetts, that "perfectly humane community," he assumed an obligation to a degree of exactness. "To name a place, in fiction," wrote James, "is to pretend in some degree to represent it—and I speak here of course but of the use of existing names, *the only ones that carry weight*" (emphasis added). Why are those the only ones? Because they rouse a desire for specification—otherwise, why name them? To be sure, James adds a tricky proviso with his verb "to pretend": I think he means that in representing places (or persons) with "existing names," there can be some latitude, but within strict limits. Specifying Northampton, Massachusetts, James had to evoke an image of a small, "humane" New England town and nothing else.

Fictional images of historically situated places or persons are cast up and then cast away by the passage of history. Such images are far removed from those "eternal" motifs which some critics and many readers like to regard as the novel's true concern. The writer's power of imagination is exerted not in "transcending" but in realizing concretely, which also means transforming, the materials of history. We may be right finally to see the Paris of Balzac's *Lost Illusions* or the Dublin of Joyce's *Ulysses* as places of myth, but first they must register the authority of streets and quarters and they must do this with some precision. The approximate will not do. Balzac knew this in his bones, Nabokov would have railed against it—no matter, for Nabokov in his own way adhered to the principle of exactness quite as much as Balzac.

The historicity of the novel, writes Georg Lukács, is shown in its "derivation of the individuality of characters from the historical peculiarities of their age." Versions of morality, styles of sexual behavior, tokens of psychic anxiety—such elements of fictional characterization are shaped by the moment of composition as well as by the individual sensibility which conforms to or rebels against that moment. George Eliot's Dorothea strains toward a "heroic" surmounting of circumstance, but not only does circumstance limit her choice of vocation, but the very notion she holds of what a heroic aspiration should be is itself flattened out by the circumstances of her life. Turgenev's Bazarov may by now represent the generic figure of the thwarted rebel, but to gain this status he had first to be deployed as a narrow-minded positivist of a kind that flourished in mid-nineteenth-century Russia. Nor are they ready-made characters "placed" against a given or fixed historical background; they emerge out of the writer's historical awareness, out of a sense of a lived moment. The characters come from the writer-in-history.

But only out of historical awareness? Of course not. Individual natures, visions, idiosyncrasies all play a part; only as a convenience of discourse can we distinguish the historical from the individual. Still, the novel rests on the assumption that man is a consequence of himself, the outcome of a self-initiated activity over stretches of time. And woman too. The novel thereby refuses, or at least minimizes the claims of, a belief in unalterable human nature.

Ortega y Gassett, in a famous sentence, remarks that "man has no nature; what he has is . . . a history." This is a powerful overstatement, for even if man has only a history, there are constants and continuities within that history which might well come, in their accumulation, to be something like a fixed nature. In the absence of such constants and continuities we would be unable to make out fictional characters with any degree of intelligibility. So it might be better to say: "Man has no unchanging nature; what his nature does have is . . . a history." And in most or much fiction, such an assumption prevails.

Most novelists, I'm sure, never bothered their heads about this but felt their way empirically, sentence by sentence, character by character; but what about those who did hold to an idea of immutable human nature? We can only speculate. Insofar as novelists like Fielding held to a classical view of a fixed human nature, this had of course to make itself felt in their work, and many novels bear the imprint of world-views inherited from both classical Christianity and earlier literary genres—*Tom Jones*, for instance. Yet the fact that a novelist deliberately and frequently wrote out of a conscious belief in immutable human traits—especially useful, by the way, in comedy, where it allows a stable repertoire of habit—does not at all mean that his work is untouched by the signs of history. Again *Tom Jones*: Fielding's organizing conception of human nature may be suprahistorical but his treatment of Squire Western and Lady Bellaston reflects an acute historical consciousness. Fielding may see them as universal types, and so they are, but we also see them as peculiarly situated in a specific moment of English life. Even what a writer like Fielding takes to be immutable human traits may itself be marked by historical mutability.

One of the things we expect from novels—many of them—is that they answer the question put by Trollope's title *How We Live Now*. Daily existence with its scatter of contingencies and exhaustion of energies preoccupies not only the realists; it absorbs even novelists like Proust who reach toward philosophical scope or those like Lawrence who search for deeper grounds of existence. And also a writer like Beckett, whose bubbling nausea has a source in dailiness.

Still, we ought not to think of history as a tyrant imposing itself, as if from necessity, upon every novel within reach. As history seeps into the novel it becomes transformed into something else, what might be called history-in-the-novel. Nor does history make itself felt simply as a reproduction of the familiar world. For many acceptable novels a sort of moderate mimesis is sufficient, the kind about which we say, "Well, it gives a pretty faithful picture of life in Oklahoma during the Depression years." But as modern readers we have come to expect more. Accurate representation seems no longer enough, if only because journalism claims or pretends to offer as much. At least since the late nineteenth century we have imposed an enormous cultural burden upon the novel, coming to think of it as an agency of moral criticism and, still more remarkable, as a creator of values. *How We Live Now* becomes *How Should We Live?*, and then *Can We Live?*

During its two greatest periods, the mid-nineteenth and early twentieth centuries, the novel has maintained a deeply critical, even subversive relation to the social milieu in which it thrived. (Is literature "ungrateful"; does it bite the hand that feeds it? Perhaps so; but that hand needs an occasional sharp bite, and besides, it does many other things but feed.) What gets "swept" into the novel are not just depictions of how we live now; it also draws upon the line of critical thought, the fund of literary allusions, the play of street sentiment, and sometimes the ideology of revolt. Look, even, at the work of an unrebellious novelist like Thackeray and you will see that there is more in it than acquiescence to standard Victorian precepts; there is also a subterranean critical ferment, sometimes beyond the writer's intention. Once past the sorts of novels written for amusement or shock, a representation of life can rarely be separated from a criticism of values.

Is this true only for the modern epoch, so ruthless in its self-perceptions? I think not. Something about mimesis, the effort honestly to evoke a portion of shared experience, seems to mandate criticism. And probably there is no such thing as a mere record or "slice" of life, since all representations imply perspective and perspective entails criticism, though not necessarily of a kind to satisfy critics of a particular kind or moment.

An exaggeration: the novel has a history, the sonnet has a tradition. A more conservative genre than the novel and with its own stricter formal requirements, the sonnet has enjoyed a greater autonomy of development; it can turn its back on history, though there are sonnets by Milton and Wordsworth which do not do that at all. And of course novelists are, like poets, influenced by predecessors—a few decades ago it seemed as if every young novelist in the world was trying to imitate Ernest Hemingway. Still, because the matter of the novel is so "impure," so alloyed with topical reference, we think of its development as a history more or less parallel to the history of mankind, while, by comparison, the development of the sonnet can perhaps be seen as self-referential.

In the traditional epic, myth and legend replace history or, more accurately, become history. Yet after a time, history in the ordinary sense, that flow of event through time which we shape into patterns, renders the epic obsolete. Epics are not written in the age of the computer, and even those novels which, like *Moby Dick*, have borrowed thematically and structurally from the epic transform it in crucial respects. It is hard to imagine a time in which the epic would again flourish.

May the same obsolescence await the novel, a genre that

is not exactly thriving at the end of the twentieth century? I suspect not, since it is precisely the adaptability of the novel, its gift for quick changes in response to historical need, that should enable it to survive. Unlike the epic, it is not constrained by fixed expectations regarding action; unlike the sonnet, it is not constrained by formal requirements. Transience becomes the ground for endurance.

When you read a novel with a strong political-historical slant, you are faced with the delicate problem of balancing social rhetoric and imaginative representation. In certain novels by Dostoevsky, Stendhal, and Conrad, the two can hardly be separated, so that there follows among critics, as Joseph Frank remarks, "quarrels over the validity of the images of social life created by novelists." Works like *The Possessed, The Red and the Black, Nostromo* stir deep passions, and this makes a pure or disinterested literary judgment very hard.

In an essay about *The Possessed* (it appears in his book *Through the Russian Prism*), Joseph Frank draws upon an extensive knowledge of Russian culture to argue against critics like Philip Rahv and me, who greatly admire Dostoevsky's novel, recognize that it scores some hits against leftist dogmatism, and still believe that, on the whole, its attack upon Russian radicalism constitutes a historical distortion. Frank argues that Dostoevsky "does not transgress the bounds of verisimilitude" in *The Possessed*; it follows closely the career of the infamous Nechaev, the nineteenth-century Russian adventurer-revolutionary of iron will and terrorist deceit. Dostoevsky, continues Frank,

has invariably been charged with giving a misleading picture . . . of the Russian radical movement as a whole. Nechaev
was incontestably an isolated phenomenon among the radical
groups of the 1860s, and his systematic Machiavellianism was
alien to the other major organizations of the radical intelligent-
sia. . . . In point of fact . . . Dostoevsky never tries to give any
other impression.

One critic's "point of fact," however, may clash with another's "impression." I would argue that by populating his
radical group with scoundrels and buffoons, and by employing
a style of searing ridicule in his treatment of them (laced though
it is with a subterranean feeling of kinship), Dostoevsky *had*
to leave another "impression." He was after bigger game than
just the little Nechaev group; he was intent upon showing that
the murderous buffoonery, the "systematic Machiavellianism"
of Peter Verhovensky (the fictional double of Nechaev), is
inherent in or a logical extension of the more humane and
rational brands of radicalism. He wanted the part to be seen
as representing the whole.

If, as Frank writes, Dostoevsky acknowledged that the
circle around Peter Verhovensky was merely "an isolated phenomenon among the radical groups of the 1860s," and if indeed
this acknowledgment informed the plot of *The Possessed*, then
not only would his novel lose its claim to representativeness,
but it would shrink into a mere extended anecdote about a
strange fanatic. But *The Possessed* does advance, as any serious
novel must, a strong claim to some degree of representativeness,
what I would call a sort of "potential verisimilitude," one in

which the story is taken to form an anticipation of things to come.

So there is a disagreement here. To certain kinds of critics it would be profoundly uninteresting, since they do not regard verisimilitude as a significant factor in the criticism of fiction. But Frank and I do; we both respond to the heavy breath of history upon Dostoevsky's work; where we disagree is in estimating the specific relationship between historical event and Dostoevsky's rendering of it. For my present purposes, it hardly matters which, if either, of us is right, since what interests me here is in trying to locate a difficult critical problem.

Works of literature touching on the politics of a distant time we can read in a relaxed fashion—who feels strongly about, or quite remembers, Dante's politics? But novels that evoke our deepest biases, as *The Possessed* still can, make the act of reading into a moral risk, entailing what critics of a few decades ago used to call "the problem of belief." (For readers without beliefs there is of course no problem.) Readers with strong political opinions are likely to find that in responding to a novel like *The Possessed* it is all but impossible to separate ideological sentiments from literary judgments, for they read as whole persons, with a rush of feeling and idea that is stronger than any recognition of the book's local verisimilitude.

Let us suppose that Joseph Frank and I, sharing a high estimate of *The Possessed*, are not very far apart in our political views. How then are we to explain the differences between us? He believes that in demonstrating the faithfulness of the novel to the actual experience of Nechaev he has also demonstrated that "the usual accusations against [Dostoevsky regarding the historical implications of the novel] must be qualified," while I believe that together with brilliant insights Dostoevsky offered brilliant distortions. Probably my admiration will turn out to be more qualified or uneasy than Frank's.

Can we be certain, however, that these differences are due to political assumptions or literary valuations? Do we really know how to distinguish between them? The one thing that seems reasonably clear is that I respond more intensely to Dostoevsky's ideological intent than does Frank—but that of course does not mean that I respond more accurately.

At the end I am left with a severe problem, some would say confusion: How can you say that *The Possessed* is both a great work of literature and also a work that offers a distorted, even malicious treatment of its subject? How to answer this question I am not at all sure: perhaps by recognizing that the imperatives of literature and history can be at deep variance. In any case, I am entangled in this difficulty, and the tangle is exactly where I want to remain, since I believe it is faithful to the actual experience of reading such novels.

The impress of history is likely to seem especially powerful when we read novels in translation.

Andrei Bely's *Petersburg*, a classic of twentieth-century Russian literature, contains many of the devices favored in postmodernist fiction: the willful violation of transparency, the text's dependence upon allusions to and parodies of earlier work, the frequent resort to verbal play, the manipulation of jumbled time sequences, the refusal of conventional devices of suspense. *Petersburg*, however, appeared in 1916; Bely's amended edition, six years later.

History figures in this novel as a revision of accepted techniques, so that while reading it we think about the history of the novel, ranging back to Laurence Sterne and forward to Milan Kundera. It might not be too farfetched to read *Petersburg* as a novel "about" the history of the novel as a genre—if, that is, we knew Russian. Bely's play with language seldom survives translation. Largely deprived of what Bely's knowledgeable critics agree is the essence of the work, we find ourselves having to fall back upon the very historical references which both author and critics regard as secondary. Unavoidably, what remains in translation is mostly the historical frame.

But as it happens, 1905, the year in which the novel's action is set, was a fateful moment in Russian history, a rehearsal for the revolution to come, and Bely, for all his absorption with purely literary matters, knew this perfectly well. In reading the translation we therefore find ourselves shuttling back and forth in novelistic time—back to previous novels about revolutionary terrorists which anticipate Bely's story of a terrorist (Dostoevsky, Turgenev) and forward to postmodernist writers who may know nothing about Bely, yet, were they to read him, would find in him an ancestor. The novel we must read in translation is radically different from the original text, with the gap in language being filled, insofar as anything can do so, by an enlarged historical awareness.

"Ah," cries an impatient voice, "history, yes, but what about the eternal themes, those recurrent human experiences, those overarching myths which, as R. G. Collingwood once wrote, tell readers 'the secrets of their own hearts.' Themes like love and death, innocence and experience, goodness and evil, themes

linking Helen and Paris to Anna and Vronsky, perhaps to Lily
Bart and Selden? Are not these the abiding concerns of literature, reducing to a quite secondary level all reflected changes
of historical circumstance? Do we read Dreiser's *An American
Tragedy* for his knowledge of hotels or for his ability to enter
the sadly yearning heart of Clyde Griffith? And what about
the archetypal characters through whom the abiding myths are
dramatized, do they not survive—Oedipus and Quixote, Clarissa Harlowe and Tess—even into the age of the computer?"

Well, yes; but the point is that if you strip them to bareness,
the eternal themes come to seem commonplace. To affect us,
they must take on flesh that will decay, be located in houses
that will crumble. Eternity lodges in the temporal. Here is an
illuminating passage by William Troy about the scene in Zola's
Germinal where Etienne and Catherine are trapped in the mine:
"It brings us back to an atmosphere and a meaning at least as
old as the story of Orpheus and Eurydice. For what is the
mine itself but a reintegration of the Hades-Hell symbol? The
immediate and particular social situation is contained within
the larger pattern of a universal recrudescence. . . ."

I would prefer to say that the "larger pattern" can be fully
realized only through "the immediate and particular social situation," that is, that the "Hades-Hell symbol" reaches universality only through the graphic rendering of the mine. But
no matter; in either Troy's phrasing or mine, the centrality of
circumstance is clear.

Even powerful archetypes get worn down by the workings
of time. A few, like Oedipus, Hamlet, and Faust do seem to
survive a range of historical situations, in part because we assign
changing meanings to them. But Tristan—except perhaps in

Wagner's opera—does he exert the imaginative hold he once did? As for Richardson's Clarissa, that spotless exemplar of maidenhood, she has surely lost a good part of her authority. And even Oedipus had to be reinvented by Freud in order to maintain his status as archetype.

If we turn to a more modest variety, the sort for which we claim not universal scope but a large role in a particular culture, we find that these can fade quickly. Sinclair Lewis's Babbitt was elevated a few decades ago to a proper noun in the American language, so representative did he seem of petit-bourgeois philistinism. By now Lewis's novel is little read, Babbitt almost forgotten, the name familiar only to the elderly. Archetypes die too.

Simply because it is what it is, the novel can never quite free itself from the shaping pressures of history, but with some novels history is more than a mere felt presence; it is an all-but-completely dominant force.

Stendhal, a latecomer in the line of the French Revolution, writes out of an explicit recognition of historical disadvantage. The Revolution has been traduced; liberalism has suffered rout; for people like himself, those who admired Napoleon but refused his tyranny, there is nothing to do but wait. In *The Red and the Black* Julien Sorel strains against the confines of history, tries to escape through cunning and ruse, succumbs to values he had despised, and by way of concluding gesture, offers his head in payment. History comes here to form an accumulation of all the rubbish of a detested past. History batters the spirit, stamps out spontaneity.

Far more oblique, occasionally as farce tinged with a dry

sadness, is Stendhal's still greater novel *The Charterhouse of Parma*. Once its protagonist Fabrizio has left the battlefield of Waterloo and come to the mean little duchy of Parma, the story may seem to be at some distance from the gross historical pressures weighing upon Julien Sorel. In *The Charterhouse of Parma* the central trio—the worldly politician Mosca, the grand Duchess Sanseverina, the innocently guileful Fabrizio— must live by personal relations, because personal relations are all that history allows in the post-Napoleonic moment. Yet their sense of the skimpiness of a life focused entirely upon personal relations itself constitutes a mark left by history. They have known something better. Now they must submit to the authority of a comic-opera despot and a shriveled church. Resisting as best they can, they try to live out the Nietzschean prescription of "objection, evasion, joyous distrust and irony" but history is not to be cheated so easily.

In 1908 the young Trotsky confronts Leo Tolstoy with a mixture of admiration and disapproval: "To history [he] grants no recognition; and this provides the basis for all his thinking." A keen but not really accurate remark, for, as Isaiah Berlin shows in *The Hedgehog and the Fox*, it is not history as such to which Tolstoy "grants no recognition," it is, rather, to all intellectual formulations claiming to possess a key to history. Berlin speaks of "Tolstoy's violently unhistorical and indeed anti-historical rejection of all efforts to explain or justify human action or character in terms of social or individual growth, or 'roots' in the past; this side by side with an absorbed and life-long interest in history. . . ."

For Tolstoy, adds Berlin, "history does not reveal causes;

it presents only a blank succession of unexplained events." Tolstoy alternated between the hedgehog's search for a "single embracing vision" and the fox's "actual experience of actual men and women in their relation to one another and to an actual, three-dimensional, empirically experienced physical environment."

Yet there is no major novel of the last two centuries in which the experience of history—history as pressure, burden, encompassing atmosphere—is so strongly felt as in *War and Peace*: the very same history that Tolstoy believed to be devoid of rational structure or progressive development. History is *there* in all its abundance, felt in Kutuzov's fatalistic submission to the course of battle, in Pierre's epiphany upon being captured by the French, in Prince Andrei's discovery when wounded that "all is vanity, all is delusion except these infinite heavens," and even in Natasha's single-minded absorption in domesticity. If one can say with Tolstoy that history is the impenetrable sequence of human experience—that is, everything—and being impenetrable, it cannot order that experience—that is, nothing—then one can conclude that in *War and Peace* history is nonetheless everywhere visible as guide and dynamic in the conduct of his characters. The theorist of antihistory becomes the great portraitist of historical shaping. (He also involves himself in some amusing contradictions. Kutuzov is said to be superior to Napoleon because Kutuzov knows that the course of battle cannot be determined in advance—which is to say, that in denying historical determinism Kutuzov understands the history to which Tolstoy had denied rational order.)

The hedgehog searches and the fox portrays, but what the fox portrays is enabled, provided for by the hedgehog's search. It is Tolstoy's supreme achievement that, like Stendhal before him, each of his depictions of personal life bears the impress of historical consciousness, with the two inseparable.

In García Márquez's *One Hundred Years of Solitude* the elemental life cycles of a Central American country—the haughty decorums and sensualities by which people in the town of Macondo try to relieve the barrenness of their existence— become a power, a salvage which the sterile official history of the country, that sequence of revolutions and coups d'état, cannot quite destroy. García Márquez wishes to capture all that gradually slips out of memory and can perhaps be regained only through myth: he wishes to preserve the subhistorical "history" of his people as they try to preserve themselves in the midst of an endless civil war.

By itself the fabulous narrative of the rise and fall of the Buendía family in *One Hundred Years of Solitude* might come to seem a grandiose evasion, falsely upbeat, a sort of Central American operetta; but what gives this novel its quotient of ferocity is the repeated intrusion of the sterile official history, the often ridiculous politics and civil wars of the country so self-absorbed in its blood and waste as to point up the meaning of García Márquez's title. The sterile official history is juxtaposed to the fertile subhistorical myth, as a sort of comic transcendence. The matriarch who dominates a good part of the novel feels that "time was not passing . . . but that it was turning in a circle." The circle of generations and of solitude.

Bluntly entitled *History*, Elsa Morante's novel about the

poor quarters of Rome during the Second World War offers little historical interpretation. The book contains intermittent "broadcasts" of contemporary events, but they seem almost superfluous, for history now become dailiness needs no external signs. In the mind of the central figure, an insignificant schoolteacher who cares only for her bastard son and little dog, there revolve "the scenes of the human story (history) . . . which she perceived as the multiple coils of an interminable murder." In this fictional epitaph for the twentieth century, a time of "interminable murder," we have reached an end point for modern history, the point at which it dissolves into suffering.

I come to a disconcerting conclusion: History may be the rock on which the novel rests, but time crumbles that rock into grains of sand. The circumstances forming the matrix of fiction turn out to be, soon enough, inaccessible, distant, perhaps no longer arresting; come to seem alloyed by values we can no longer credit; or decline into mere reflexes of social bias.

Mansfield Park, the one Jane Austen novel her admirers find troubling, was the subject of an influential essay some years ago by Lionel Trilling in which he made out a case for this most conservative and least lively of Austen's works. Trilling confronted head-on a problem that disturbs modern readers: that when Sir Thomas Bertram, head of a solid family in the landed gentry, leaves for the West Indies, his children and their friends decide to amuse themselves by producing an amateur theatrical and that this project, which to us must seem the height of innocence, comes to be an occasion for moral uneasiness. The characters of firmer or traditional morality, Fanny Price and Edmund Bertram, express grave doubts about the propriety of dramatic impersonation, and Trilling persuasively explains why, in the circumstances, the amateur theatrical could be seen as morally dubious. Not many readers would today "agree" with Sir Thomas's portentous statement that "such a scheme" is marked by "impropriety," but at least we learn to give it enough conditional assent so that the business of the amateur theatrical does not interfere with our enjoyment of the novel.

But there is another historical fact that may cause greater uneasiness. Sir Thomas, though subject to moral criticism by Jane Austen because of his imperceptive rigidity, is still shown as a respected patriarch; his visit to the West Indies in behalf of his estate occurs at a time when slavery dominated those islands, which means that he must have been an owner of slaves. Now this occasioned neither criticism from Jane Austen nor comment from Lionel Trilling; but it is a serious ground for those discomforts which the passage of time, the flow of history, can cause in the reading of even great or near-great novels. One common defense of Jane Austen is that the workings of the West Indian estate is not central to the action of *Mansfield Park*; and then too we have to make discounts for an earlier time, as later times will for ours. In my years as a teacher I would say something of the sort to students, but now I wonder. Jane Austen could have sent Sir Thomas on plenty of other trips: the only requirement of the plot was to get him away from home. Yet, with the deliberateness that marks all her work, she clearly meant to write as she did: Sir Thomas goes to estates worked by slaves and is nevertheless seen as a morally upright if somewhat unimaginative figure. I find this much more troubling than the amateur theatricals, which I am content to accept as a convenience of plot. Am I wrong?

The kind of problems presented by *Mansfield Park* can be found in many novels of the past. What can we "do" about them? Seek to accommodate ourselves, or make allowances, or offer partially negative judgments. If we are very sophisticated, we tell ourselves that in reading a novel of the past—and not so distant past: say, Rousseau's *Julie* or Fielding's *Amelia*— we ought to have enough "historical imagination" to enter unfamiliar settings and recognize the integrity of other moralities. And we should also, of course, make it our business to learn about distant historical situations: say, those of Manzoni's *The Betrothed* or Cooper's Leatherstocking Tales. We should be able to understand, even if not share, the obsession with virginity that courses through Richardson's *Clarissa*—but see how I betray myself, since the very word "obsession" evinces a bias.

It is a splendid thing, this historical imagination, and everyone needs a supply of it, but the mere fact that we need to invoke it testifies to difficulties. We can no longer read some of these novels with a direct, spontaneous response; there must now be a complex act of "mediation" which entails all sorts of mental reserves. By contrast, nothing of the sort is required if we pick up Elsa Morante's *History*, at least nothing for any literate person over fifty. But for a twenty-year-old to whom the Second World War is almost as distant as the French and Indian War? And fifty years from now—introduction, footnotes, chronological table ("The Second World War, which forms the background to Elsa Morante's novel, broke out in 1939, when . . .").

History makes, history unmakes the novel. And this is true even for novels we love; it is profoundly disconcerting to see them slowly drained of their original power.

In the 1930s Hemingway's *The Sun Also Rises* was a work that many readers felt close to. We may have been irked by Hemingway's anti-intellectualism, or have scorned his macho posturing, and we certainly knew ourselves to be at a distance from his Parisian expatriates; yet we felt that through this story of lostness and its sad repressed language, Hemingway expressed a disenchantment we had inherited from the generation caught up in the First World War. Even if his notion of a "secret community" surviving historical disaster had a self-dramatizing aspect, it still related to our feelings of plight. There is more than one kind of "secret community."

In later years I still found *The Sun Also Rises* a deeply affecting novel, but by the late 1970s a dismaying change of response began to show itself among my students. They found the milieu of the novel merely exotic; its stylizations they saw as an affectation, and its tone—this was the worst of all—as self-pitying. A gap had opened between generations, so that the very novel which history had, so to say, pressed against our hearts had now fallen victim to history.

Still more so must this be true for the political novels of Malraux, Silone, Orwell, and Koestler. While not among the masters of modernism, these were writers to esteem, since novels like *Man's Fate, Bread and Wine, Darkness at Noon* were witnesses to a terrible moment in modern history.

Some decades have passed, these writers have died, and even those of us especially fond of, say, Ignazio Silone know that a work of such moral poise as *Bread and Wine* is not likely to stir younger readers as once it stirred readers of my generation. If a few young persons do open *Darkness at Noon*, a novel that roused violent argument when it first appeared, they may need explanatory notes about the Moscow Trials.

"Yes, dad, we know that for you and your pals the questions raised by Silone, Koestler, and Orwell were of great importance, and we can even guess why you got so excited by Koestler's one-sided depiction of Rubashov's confession— that's what you thought, wasn't it? But that was your story, and your story is an old story—all those memories of idealism and delusion. And besides, we have our own stories."

"When was it that you said the Moscow Trials took place? This fascism mentioned in Silone's *Fontamara*—what was that?" Should anyone remember? And isn't it wonderful that we have survived all these catastrophes? Yes, it's wonderful; but our hearts also sink before the ravages of time.

Kipling's Kim: *Ecstasies*

KIPLING APPROACHES THE India of the late nineteenth
century as a stepson, and scrutinizes it from the distance of a
stranger, though the kind of stranger who has yielded his heart
forever. India is for Kipling at once the cradle of remembered
happiness and, in some of his writings, the site of the Other,
unfathomable. Kipling loves the amiability of traditional Indian
life, its talkativeness, its casual gossip. He loves the sudden
shift from metaphysics to chatter. Life in India seems to run
more thickly than in the West. The traditional and the day-to-
day, the temple and the market; all entrance the young Kipling,
a stranger who has made himself at home.

Kipling is also a jingo and a bully, or at least a defender
of bullies. He is not the sort of writer we easily take to heart,
as one takes Thomas Hardy, or respects unreservedly, as one
respects Chekhov. There are really two Kiplings, the lyricist

of glowing memory and the thumper of fixed opinion. Both appear in *Kim* (1901), shrewdly set in contrast and interaction, though it is the voice of memory that finally controls the book. The result is a work of an exquisite radiance of spirit, breathing a love of the world such as few of his contemporaries, including writers we may regard as greater than Kipling, could match.

Kim starts with noises of sociality. A thirteen-year-old darling of the streets, a fast-talking urchin, white by birth and dark from the sun, Kim takes each day as a meeting with pleasure. Trading amiable epithets with the bazaar merchants, who call him "Little Friend of all the World," Kim is neither innocent nor naive. He has "known all evil since he could speak," but he does not let it overwhelm him; he absorbs and then puts aside that knowledge, as if breaking a skin, for there is always something to see and experience in the streets of Lahore, that "wonderful walled city." In these streets he is as shrewd as his distant cousin Huck Finn is along the shore; he has learned "to avoid missionaries and white men of serious aspect," and has also learned the fine art of doing "nothing with an immense success." Whenever he sidles up to a booth, the men of the city smile, knowing they will hear something clever and will enjoy his command of the Indian art of cursing. He is a young entrepreneur and apprentice con man, a quick-change artist who does not care for any fixed self because life offers so many selves to discover and try out. "Who is Kim?" he will keep asking himself, and the book will yield the happy answer that there are many answers. He loves "the game for its own sake"—the "game" standing here for both the British secret service, with which he will become enmeshed through his worldly self, and the entirety of the business of life. "The game" is not an adequate term, or concept; it reflects the all-too-familiar side of Kipling's sensibility that is adolescent and stunted.

When Kim meets the Tibetan lama, an ungainly rhapsodist who makes transcendence seem a familiar option, the two of them quickly find common ground. They share a meal, they bound their territory. To the boy, the old man represents a guru such as the mainland does not yield; for the old man, the boy is a guide through the bewilderments of India who will ripen into a *chela*, or disciple. Kim is possessed by the evidence of his senses, the lama with a vision beyond, and the book will make as its central matter an unfolding of the love between the two, that thrill of friendship which in nineteenth-century literature comes to replace the grace of God. A venture in fraternity, their friendship also forms a relation between master and disciple, with Kim repeatedly asserting that he is not a Sahib but one of "my people," that is, the people of India. In saying this he simplifies a complex and ambivalent condition, as he will come to see once he draws closer to both the lama and the British secret service. But finally, it is the discipleship to the lama that is the transforming matter of the book. And along the way, since Kim can never quite achieve the indifference to worldliness that the lama preaches, he does at least gain the niceties of what the lama calls "courtesy," a term implying a visible token of spirit in the relations among men.

At first Kim goes to beg food for the old man. "They ate together in great content"—so begin and end half the great stories of mankind. Awakened after a sleep brought on by the meal, the old man looks for the boy and is bewildered to find Kim in one of his transmutations, "a Hindu urchin in a dirty turban." We think to compare this moment with the trick Huck plays on Jim, but only to reject the comparison, since everything is far gentler in Kipling's India than in Twain's America, and Kim need not go through torments of conscience in order to declare himself "thy *chela*," certainly need not declare himself ready, like Huck, for perdition. Because he is utterly fortified in his sense of being at home in the world and feels some mild superiority to the unworldliness of the old man, Kim can also begin to see that the lama represents other possibilities for him: "I have never seen any one like to thee in all this my life. I go with thee. . . ." It is not yet a spiritual discipleship; it is simply a companionship of the road. Perhaps, Kim says, smiling, "they will make me a king" during the journey. To which the lama replies: "I will teach thee other and better desires upon the road."

The first five chapters of the book form a picaresque entry into "the great good-tempered world," first on the "te-rain" and then along the Great Trunk Road. It is an India refracted through adoring memory and, in its relation to the "real" India, complex beyond hope of disentangling. It is an India Kipling loves for its rough vivacity, its easy mixture of manners, its encompassing of gutter and cloud; and it is praised by him (as if to unsettle all those who declare settled views of his work) as the "only democratic land in the world"—by which he means, I gather, not the absence of rank or distinction but a readiness to live with and intermingle all ranks and distinctions. (At this point historical fact and imaginative vision may find themselves at odds: a problem by no means confined to Kipling.) In Kipling's India—Kim's playground—the boy is a trickster delighting in his tricks and expecting that his audiences will delight with him in seeing, and seeing through, them. A people raised with a sense of hazard appreciates the boy's virtuosity; shrewdly eyes his utterly this-worldly performance; yet also looks tolerantly and often worshipfully upon "holy men stammering gospels in strange tongues."

Kim and the lama now move through a world that is like a vast, disorderly bazaar. People are quick to embrace and to anger. They speak suddenly from the heart, as if any traveler may be a friend. They curse with the expertness of centuries ("Father of all the daughters of shame and husband of ten thousand virtueless ones, thy mother was devoted to a devil, being led thereto by her mother . . ."). Running errands for Mahbub Ali, the freethinking Afghan horse trader who initiates him into the British secret service, Kim charms a fierce-tongued old Indian lady (straight in the line of Chaucer, one pilgrimage to another) into helping him and the lama. He trades stories with retired soldiers, jests with travelers, even pokes a little tender fun at his lama—for this is Kim's world, a stage for his multiple roles as urchin, beggar, raconteur, flirt, apprentice spy, and apprentice *chela*. Picked up by some British soldiers who propose to educate him ("sivilize," says Huck), Kim tells the lama, "Remember, I can change swiftly." It is the motto of every boy trying to evade the clamp of civilization.

And the world's evil? The poverty, injustice, caste rigidities which must have been so grinding in the India of a century ago?

Kipling's book releases a distinct, which is necessarily to say, a limited vision. It seeks to give life a desirable look; it brushes past social misery as more recent novels brush past personal happiness; it neglects the shadows as others neglect the lights; it sees the world as fresh, alluring, and young—young, in India! But *Kim* is not an idyll, not a retreat from the world; it is a celebration of the world.

The book has no assured answers to the questions of Indian poverty, injustice, and caste rigidity, partly because it does not choose to give them priority, though we know that it is not an evasive or willfully "positive" book. All the wrongs and evils of India are there, steeped in the life of the people, yet these do not keep them from grasping the sensations of their moment, or from experiencing the appetites and ceremonies they rightly take to be their due. What so wonderfully distinguishes Kipling's characters is their capacity for shifting from treble to bass, from pure spirit to gross earth, from "the Search" to "the Game." It is as if their culture actually enables them to hold two ideas in their heads at once. The India of Kipling is a place in which people live by customs and caprice, fixed in ways given them yet ready to move past those ways when they feel a need to.

One great flaw in the reforming passion is that in its eagerness to remedy social wrongs it tends to neglect, certainly to undervalue, the experience of those whose lives it wishes to improve. It does not honor fully enough the life-hungers, the life-capacities of the oppressed. Now Kipling, it is true, did not see India as particularly oppressed, and I am as ready as the next liberal or radical to deplore this failure; but he did see the people of India as vigorous, full of humor and energy, deeply worthy. How are we to explain that in the pages of this apologist for imperialism, the masses of India seem more alive and autonomous than in the pages of writers claiming political correctness?

Regarding Kipling's apparent indifference to the social evils of India there remains another and more radical "answer." Though in much of his work he shows a quite sufficient awareness of evil, even at some points an obsessive concern, he really wants to persuade us that in the freshness of a boy's discoveries and the penetration of an old man's vision, evil can become ultimately insignificant, almost as nothing before the unsubdued elation of existence, almost as nothing before the idea of moral beauty. Others, long before Kipling, have said as much, though few have embodied it with the plastic vividness that Kipling has. I will confess here to not entirely grasping the import of this vision of ultimate goodness or harmony; I find it a kind of moral slope, at once very slippery and very attractive. Yet in reading *Kim* we may yield to this vision, just as we might for a moment come to accept beatitude upon actually meeting a saint. Nor should one try to get round the problem by remarking that *Kim* is a children's book. For it seems intolerable that the best things in life should be supposed available only to children. Older bones have their rights too.

Kim is unsubdued by the malignity at the heart of things. Whatever evil it does encompass tends to be passed off onto bumbling Russian spies who muddle along on the northern borders of India, about as alarming as Laurel and Hardy. *Kim* is at ease with the world, that unregenerate place which is the only one most of us know, and because at ease, it can allow itself to slide toward another possible world. All this may constitute a literary scandal, especially if one goes so far as to make a claim for the seriousness and greatness of the book.

There is greater scandal. *Kim* evokes and keeps returning to sensations of pleasure, a pleasure regarded as easy, natural, and merited. Kipling's book accepts the world's body, undeterred by odors, bulges, wrinkles, scars. *Kim* takes delight in each step of its journey, delight in our clamor, our foolishness, our vanity, our senses, and—through the lumbering radiance of the lama who comes from and goes back to the hills of Tibet—delight in an ultimate joy of being which beckons from the other side of sensuous pleasure but which, implies Kipling, those of us not lamas would be advised to seek through pleasure.

Part of the pleasure that *Kim* engages is that of accepting, even venerating, sainthood, without at all proposing to surrender the world, or even worldliness, to saints. *Kim* embraces both worlds, that of the boy and of the lama, the senses and beyond, recognizing that anyone who would keep a foot, or even a finger, in both of these worlds must have some discipline in adjustment and poise—otherwise, what need would there be for the lama's or any other serious education? But never for a moment does the book propose to smudge the difference between the senses and beyond, or, worse still, to contrive some facile synthesis. The "Wheel of Things," to which we are all bound in this world, and the "Search," by which we may penetrate another, have each their claim and dignity. The two speed along in parallel, but what they signify cannot readily be merged.

Naturalism and Taste

LITERARY REVOLUTIONS BEGIN as an assault upon standards of taste. Apostles of the new sense that literary doctrines can be overthrown easily enough, but that taste as the distillation of a culture's sentiments and norms, taste as the esthetic sign of its world-view—there's the enemy. No mere stubbornness spurs people to cling to their taste: they recognize, with or without words, that it serves as a token of identity. Taste speaks through a turn of phrase, a curl of the lip, a shrug of the shoulder: it makes an atmosphere. So when a literary revolution denounces the dominant taste as a reflex of social bias or as hostile to all that is fresh and spontaneous, that signifies the start of a fierce conflict. For a time, the new enjoys most of the tactical advantages—who wants to be labeled an enemy of the fresh and spontaneous? Think of the way "Victorian," at best a neutral historical category, was twisted into a term of abuse during the first few decades of this century.

The debut of a new taste—or style—carries with it a thick charge of emotion. Writing about the rise of modernism, Meyer Schapiro notes that

> the avowals of artists . . . show that the step to abstraction was accompanied by great tension and emotional excitement. The painters justify themselves by ethical and metaphysical stand-points, or in defense of their art attack the preceding style as the counterpart of a detested social or moral position. . . . The philosophy of art was a philosophy of life.

That is also true for the defenders of tradition. They declare themselves the party of true belief, sound morals, and, most urgent of all, Good Taste. They feel no great need to specify what Good Taste might be, since they regard it as a heritage of breeding—you either have it or you don't. The bohemian riffraff, the plebeian louts clearly don't. For the traditionalists, taste is an immutable capacity for discernment and perception, often made clear through rapid intuitions. Good Taste is not argued; it is expressed. Defending themselves against the new, the traditionalists attack its advocates as fostering a taste that panders to momentary fashions. But there is a problem here: How can that one word "taste" contain two such contradictory meanings—immutable discernments and momentary fashions? The answer is: It does. It does so in the brilliantly perverse way language has of exhibiting ambiguities of thought.

Here, as an instance, is Henry James struggling over a period of more than two decades with the novels of Emile Zola, a writer with whom he was not finally in sympathy but whose talent he could not ignore. In 1880 James writes about *Nana*:

> Decency and indecency, morality and immorality, beauty and ugliness, are conceptions with which "naturalism" has nothing to do. . . . The only business of naturalism is to be—natural, and, therefore, instead of saying of *Nana* that it contains a great deal of filth, we should simply say of it that it contains a great deal of nature.

The pretense here is description, the intent hostile. For Zola is by no means the cold-blooded "scientist" of nature, the dispassionate recorder of an incorrigible reality, that in his critical writings he claims to be. In his novels he reveals a strong, sometimes rather oppressive, concern with decency, morality, and all the attendant virtues. It is true that he violates the kind of taste which held nineteenth-century English fiction in a grip of prudery, but he does so out of a persuasion that this is a way of breaking into truth. In his opening engagement with Zola, James is venting the displeasure of those who felt that the literary depiction of a character like Nana necessarily abuses Good Taste. There are things a gentleman does not write about.

More than twenty years later, now a master novelist who has soaked up a good amount of European culture, James turns again to Zola. Works like *Germinal* and *L'Assommoir*, he writes in 1903, create "a world with which taste has nothing to do." As a first step toward description, this is not bad. James then hastens to add that the absence of taste, "this precious elixir," he calls it, "was positively to operate" in Zola's novels "as one of his greatest felicities." Now, it is not easy to know exactly what James meant here, but I venture a gloss (or a guess): The absence of those received norms of taste which Zola had chosen to violate enabled him to confront long-suppressed aspects of human experience, to reveal long-ignored segments of society, that had previously been missing from European fiction. But in the course of making this sensible observation, James may also be caught up in a contradiction such as besets almost everyone who ventures to say anything about taste: He starts by noting the absence of this "precious elixir," which in his view has constituted a legacy of civilization, yet acknowledges that this very absence, which might be supposed a major lack, has somehow become a "felicity." I suspect that this is really a backhanded way of saying that in Zola's work there operates *another*, that is, a new standard of taste—so that the Good Taste that is never defined by James, because he supposes his readers will know exactly what he means, must now give way to a relativism of taste largely determined by historical pressures. If I am right, then the case has largely been ceded to Zola.

Yet not entirely—for Good Taste might be defended as the accumulated residue of many previously transient tastes, the "immutable" as itself a product of historical change. Even readers sympathetic to Zola can acknowledge that in his revolutionary innovations of subject matter he sometimes revels in excess, taking an all-but-sadistic pleasure in rubbing our noses in the dirt he has every right to depict. Occasionally then, and in a quite limited sense, Zola may be said to display "bad taste."

But let us return to James: In the same 1903 essay, only a few pages later, James falls back from his keen perception of what Zola is up to and writes that his late novels show that

"there is simply no limit . . . to the misfortune of being tasteless.
. . . It eats back into the very heart and enfeebles the sources
of life." James is quite correct about Zola's late writings, which
are at once grandiose and hollow; but if this is what James
means by "tastelessness," then the rubbery term is being used
in still another sense, as a synonym for the lack of compositional rigor and not with respect to the display of unsavory
aspects of human behavior.

There really is no possibility of abandoning the word
"taste" in literary discussion: better one ambiguous term than
several slippery surrogates. James's struggle with the term and
its interweaving significations reflects genuine critical difficulties by no means confined to him. For all his fine capacities as
a critic, James could not bridge the gap between Zola and
himself—but then, why should he have? For what separated
them was nothing less than a revolution in taste. Naturalism
as a literary school would soon disintegrate, but during its brief
moment of strength it succeeded in changing forever the thematic boundaries of the novel.

The usual academic discussions of literary naturalism stress its
relation to, or dependence upon, philosophical-scientific theories of the late nineteenth century: determinism, skepticism,
Darwinism, and so on. The less cautious among such com-
mentators turn to Zola's misguided essay "The Experimental
Novel," in which he permits himself such crudities as "The
same determinism should regulate paving-stones and human
brains"; the more cautious find a linkage of atmosphere and
tone between the naturalist writers and the work of scientists
like Darwin and Huxley. That Zola was badly confused, suc-

cumbing to a kind of vulgar reductionism in his critical pieces, hardly needs demonstration. He clung to a mechanical scientism with the credulousness of a peasant; he kept insisting what his novels, especially if taken one by one, do not really show: that heredity determines the life of his characters; and he mimicked uncritically the physiological theories of Dr. Claude Bernard as if these had forever settled the quandaries of life.

Still, it should be stressed that when novelists like Zola and Dreiser were drawn to the scientific writings of their time, they were really looking for cues with which to understand the experience of human beings. They hoped, naively, that the lens of the most "advanced" theories would yield a sharper picture (quite as some writers in the years after the Second World War succumbed uncritically to existentialism). The clumsy philosophizing of the naturalists, their stumbling efforts at conceptual synthesis, their belief that they had found or were soon to find fundamental "laws" of human behavior—all were, finally, maneuvers in their struggle to establish fictional "worlds" that would capture the sufferings of their historical moment. They hoped that the "advanced" philosophical theories would help explain or justify why their own sense of life had darkened so visibly since the Victorians. They were looking for intellectual props in behalf of perceptions and moods already deeply implanted in their consciousness.

It seems to me a critical error to suppose that we can understand literary naturalism by studying or "applying" the theoretical statements accompanying it. When Stephen Crane remarked that "environment is a tremendous thing and often shapes life regardlessly," he was expressing a strong personal impression based on his experiences and observations (*Maggie* did not emerge from a textbook). But this is still a remark, an insight, a yield of eye and ear, something very far from Zola's dubious notion that "the day will come when the laws of thought and the passions will be formulated" or the still more dubious quotation from Taine which he used as an epigraph for one of his novels, "Vice and virtue are products like sugar and vitriol."

But when Zola pulled away a little from both publicity and polemic, he could be a good deal more modest and tentative, as in a talk he gave in 1893:

> In our generation, even among those least conscious of it, the long effects of positive philosophy and analytic and experimental science came to fruition. Our fealty was to Science, which surrounded us on all sides; in her we lived, breathing the air of the epoch. I am free to confess that, personally, I was even a sectarian, who lived to transport the rigid methods of Science into the domain of Literature. But where can the man be found who, in the stress of strife, does not exceed what is necessary?

All that matters about the naturalists by now is their passionate engagement with the life of their moment, what they actually saw day by day, the foulness, degradation, and hopelessness of the cities of Europe and America which Huysmans in his naturalist phase called "the sores of society." So it was in the realm of taste, ultimately signifying the realm of morals, that the naturalists did their work. They advanced and helped create a *low taste*—low in the sense that they forced readers to look down to the social bottom (the kind of subworld, say, that in our own time Hubert Selby would depict with absolute integrity in *Last Exit to Brooklyn*) and low in the sense of evoking the foul and the filthy, all that formed the silt of society. The first sense of low concerns social class; the second, morals and manners; and of course the two were closely linked. They were linked in Zola's novels, in Gissing's stories about workers and prostitutes, in George Moore's account of a servant girl, in Hardy's description of agricultural labor, in Alfred Döblin's portrait of the Berlin underworld, in Richard Wright's account of black pathology.

Nor was this low taste something perverse or frivolous. "On what authority," Henry James had grandly asked in his review of *Nana*, "does M. Zola represent nature to us as a combination of the cesspool and the house of prostitution?" And James answered his question: "On the authority of his predilections alone." No, not at all! Had Zola chosen to reply he might have said: "I speak with the authority of what I see each day in Paris and you, were you to look about you, would see each day in London. I speak with the authority of experience."

The whole matter—this conflict of taste and value—is summed up in a fascinating conversation between Maxim Gorky and Tolstoy recorded in Gorky's memoirs:

> "You've seen many drunken women [asked Tolstoy]? Many—my God! You must not write about that, you mustn't."
> "*Why?*"
>
> He looked straight into my eyes and, smiling, repeated: "Why?" Then thoughtfully and slowly he said: "I don't know. It just slipped out. . . . It's a shame to write about filth. But yet why not write about it? Yes, it's necessary to write about everything, everything."

The revolution in taste enacted by the naturalists was not of course an isolated event. There was, first of all, the far greater revolution of Romanticism, starting with Wordsworth's call for a poetry of common life. There was Flaubert's relentlessness in capturing the drabness of daily life, not too many steps away from naturalism. And there was also the steady development of French art since the 1830s, as it moved from neoclassical and historical painting to a growing concern with ordinary places and ordinary people. To enjoy Courbet in 1850, writes Meyer Schapiro, "one had to accept works with banal subjects, painted without an evident rhetoric of classical or romantic beauty, and revealing a personality whose response to nature and social life . . . seemed uncultured and even boorish beside the aristocratic inventiveness of Ingres and Delacroix."

This enlargement of social themes and sympathies cut across the various tendencies and schools of nineteenth-century French art. Attacks upon Manet, astonishing for their violence, bear a resemblance to attacks upon Zola: "Why," asks a contemporary critic of Manet, "do the Realists choose unclean women as their models and . . . reproduce even the filth that clings to their contours?" (cited in T. J. Clark, *The Painting of Modern Life*). To us today the tonal distance between Impressionist art and naturalist fiction may seem very considerable, but in the struggle to establish themselves through revolutions of taste the two groups were seen by Zola and his friends as natural allies.

After a time brutal moralistic attacks upon naturalism give way to a more subtle and sometimes justified criticism. Naturalism, because of its philosophical dogmatism, is said to shortchange human nature; it fails to take into account the variety and resilience of our experiences, it fails to recognize our occasional moments of transcendence, it fails sufficiently to honor the human desire for freedom. Jean-Paul Sartre has summed up these charges in his remark that "the determinism of the naturalistic novel crushes life and substitutes for human action the uniform responses of automata."

Here, it seems to me, we encounter Sartre the ideologue of existentialism, not Sartre the attentive reader. He is right in a small way—right with regard to the declared doctrines of some naturalists, right about some of the merely documentary portions of naturalist fiction (quite as any criticism of a literary school may be right when it seizes upon its weakest instances). But Sartre is wrong about the major works of the naturalists, who portray not the "uniform responses of automata" but the often-defeated struggles of human beings against overwhelming odds or the efforts of such people to achieve, in their very lack of articulation, some capacities of speech. Anyone who has read the concluding pages of *Germinal* in which Etienne stumbles into the world, beaten but with some glimmers of understanding; anyone who has read the seriocomic chapter of *L'Assommoir* describing the marriage of Gervaise and Copeau, with its all-too-human pomps; anyone who has read the portions of Dreiser's *An American Tragedy* in which Clyde and Roberta grope toward an experience of affection, almost wordless yet with depth of feeling, must realize how ill-conceived, indeed, ill-tempered is Sartre's dismissal. That the characters of naturalist fiction often sink into defeat is of course true—

there would seem to be some warrant for this in actuality, would there not? But they struggle with their destiny, as if even they merit a touch of freedom.

To write as an exponent of a new or "low" taste means to indulge in a certain roughness, even coarseness of expression, an often deliberate rejection of what had been taken to be "good style." It is an interesting question: Was this really necessary for the creation of a new kind of literature or was it due to the pressures of more or less accidental circumstances? I see no need for certainty. If there is no reason to suppose that poverty or social degradation can be adequately portrayed only through a style of crudeness, still, we would hardly expect the styles of, say, *The Ambassadors* or *The Good Soldier* to be appropriate for the kinds of material employed by the naturalists. (But even this cautious generalization may be questioned, for there is the example of *Ulysses*, a novel absorbing some of the devices of naturalism, which deals with poverty in a highly elaborate prose style. All efforts to link theme and style in the novel are necessarily problematic.)

Writers like Zola and Dreiser, Gorky and Döblin were driven by a need to overwhelm both subject matter and readers, to pile up unassailable evidence, to exhaust their subjects (and sometimes themselves), as if thereby to persuade that they were portraying not exceptional horrors but common realities. The naturalists may have begun with a wish to shock, but, as it turned out, their strongest impulse was to stun—to stun the reader into unwelcome recognitions. Subtle epiphanies, symbolic flashes, maneuvers of implication, all the devices made famous by James and Turgenev, Conrad and Ford seemed unsuitable, even irrelevant to the naturalists. They wished to pummel the public into acceptance, and to pummel meant to accumulate: relentless, wearisome step by step. "We novelists," wrote Zola, "are the examining magistrates of men and their passions," and good magistrates act only upon evidence beyond a doubt. We must suffer along with the creatures that suffer in the novels, and we are to take a kind of pleasure in the ordeal of exposure. From an entertainment, the novel would become a trial.

Naturalism had to be short-lived. Its power to arouse indignation gave way to a dulled acquiescence, a wearing-down of response. In reading, for instance, James T. Farrell's *Studs Lonigan*, famous only yesterday, we respect the seriousness of the writer, but his soggy repetitiveness leaves us with a feeling of helplessness. The main literary problem of the naturalist novel is, I think, that of pacing (a matter about which literary criticism has had little to say). The naturalist novel moves along as a steady march, from one demonstration to another, usually on a downward path. It is hard to imagine a short naturalistic novel—heaviness seems part of its very being. After a time, an experienced reader learns to anticipate the inexorable slippage of the characters, and may grow impatient with the writer's insistence that it is all a matter of necessity. The form tends to tire itself out.

If pushed to an extreme, naturalism has a way of turning into something other than itself, often into a kind of gross expressionist nightmare or an autonomous grotesquerie—this happens now and again in Zola and Döblin. The mania for documentation, because it saps the writer's imagination and perhaps even his will, has a tendency to become melodramatic, something the early American naturalist Frank Norris shrewdly noticed: "Terrible things must happen to the characters of the naturalistic tale. They must be twisted from the ordinary, wrenched from the quiet, uneventful round of everyday life and flung into the throes of a vast and terrible drama that works itself out in unleashed passions, in blood and sudden death. . . ."

Still, for all its brief span, naturalism left a permanent mark upon the modern novel. It declared all of experience to be the writer's province; it refused to accept barriers of taste that would ban the ugly and painful; it struggled for a more generous perception of truthfulness. Its conquests endure, only its program has died.

Novels of Academic Life

THEY AGE BADLY. In the 1950s, when I first read Mary McCarthy's *The Groves of Academe*, Randall Jarrell's *Pictures From an Institution*, and Kingley Amis's *Lucky Jim*, they seemed wildly funny. Reread a few decades later, they evoke little more than a grin of recognition.

The novel of academic life usually runs a narrow gamut, from farce to burlesque. It assaults pomposity, it discards shame, it packs in jokes and gibes, some accessible only to the professors who are both its victims and its audience. Evidently, something about academic life is utterly, hopelessly ridiculous, or at least so its participants often feel.

But what is so ridiculous? And why is it more ridiculous than, say the goings-on at a Washington bureau or a multi-national corporation? One plausible answer is that struggles within government and big business entail large stakes of power and money, while most academic disputes are over petty control and prestige. There's a certain smallness to the academic milieu which even its least sensitive members cannot help acknowledging. Disputes within the academy can seem especially ridiculous because they are often conducted through an exalted rhetoric, no less than "the cultural heritage of the West" or "the rights of the oppressed." Nor is the main problem with academic life one of outright fakery, though some of that is present too. What makes academics embarrassed or nervous is a suspicion of hypocrisy within the ranks, a discomfort at the thought that they do not live up to their proclaimed standards. Some sleep, more fret away their lives.

The novels of McCarthy, Jarrell, and Amis start in a spirit of malicious fun, on a note of pure farce, and for about a hundred pages continue in that way: McCarthy dismembering the fatuous president of a progressive college, Jarrell picturing an acidic lay novelist (not unlike McCarthy) who studies the natives at the same sort of institution, and Amis sighting a weekend party at an English redbrick university where a poor sod of a medievalist must pretend an interest in "culture" while lusting for beer and a girl.

Indifferent to the limits of verisimilitude, farce drives everything to excess. It is programmatically unreasonable, twisting plot and characters into a steady breakage of rules. The difficulty is how to sustain this for two hundred fifty pages. Somewhere around the middle, there occurs in these novels a lamentable sag into amiability, as if the writer were suddenly overcome by an attack of conscience. A fatal blunder!

How can we explain this drop into a middling outlook and

a middling prose? Perhaps by noting that most academic novels are written by intellectuals uneasy about their connection with the academy: they would like to see themselves as "free." So they write their novels with a punitive intent. Especially among the American writers—this may constitute a flaw in national character—there erupts a streak of fairness, a recognition that some of the issues discussed at faculty meetings may, despite the stuffy rhetoric, have a genuine importance. While this may speak well for their characters, it wreaks havoc on their art, since farce by its very nature must be blind to fairness.

Even that eminently unfair writer Kingsley Amis succumbs a little to the lures of fairness, though he does fight hard against them. (He is, after all, an Englishman brought up to resist notions of equity.) Amis makes his Lucky Jim into an un-abashed philistine railing against "the academic racket" and spewing contempt for "filthy Mozart." Yet, now and again, Amis feels obliged to suggest that he doesn't really share Lucky Jim's low views, even as for long stretches he clearly revels in them. And his novel profits from the reveling. For Lucky Jim, a university man by mere mischance, is a determined lowbrow who remembers in time the plebeian axiom that hands which feed are meant to be bitten.

So deeply ingrained is the style of farce in fictions about academic life that it seems all but impossible for a more "bal-anced" outlook to prevail. C. P. Snow's efforts to make drama out of middlebrow academic humdrum largely fail because he is himself largely middlebrow humdrum. For a serious fictional rendering of the academy to succeed, it has to run toward an extremism of tone and outlook quite as radical as that of farce.

I know of but one novel in which this feat is managed, and that is John Williams's *Stoner*, a neglected book with a very modest following.

In depicting a professor of pedestrian integrity, *Stoner* is as uncompromisingly grave as the novels of McCarthy, Jarrell, and Amis are farcical. Seemingly aware that he must position himself through a polar distance from farce, Williams takes academic life with an absolute, indeed a grim, seriousness. His protagonist—the name tells all—is a not-very-distinguished professor of English literature whose career is marked by fierce honesty and modest talent. Uncelebrated among his colleagues and unknown to any larger public, Stoner nevertheless forms part of the fabric of a living culture, as it weaves ungloriously through the generations. For years he struggles against a colleague, flashier than he but badly flawed as scholar and teacher. A climax occurs when the two battle during an examination for a graduate student, with Stoner ruthlessly, yet in complete and necessary justice, exposing the flimsiness of the colleague's protégé, a "brilliant" student. That so routine (and often dreary) an academic occasion could be used effectively to dramatize the tensions of moral life seems almost beyond credence. Perhaps the lesson is that the occasions for drama, if not to be found everywhere in ordinary life, are still more frequent than many novelists suppose.

By the end of the novel Stoner has done little in his profession: a single book, unread and by no means a neglected masterpiece. Still, what makes Stoner so impressive a figure—impressive in his very failure—is the intensity of his devotion to the idea of honest scholarly work.

What relation can there be between a Stoner and a Lucky

Jim? Suppose they met: what would happen? Probably a flat uncomprehending silence on both sides, or possibly an exchange of insults. But perhaps there is a slender link between the animating values out of which Williams and Amis have written their two radically different versions of academic life. Only the most oppressive seriousness can find a bond with lawless farce.

Obscurity in the Novel

WHAT DO WE mean when we say that a novel is obscure? We do not, or should not, mean that it is difficult—that is something else again, though difficulty often gets entangled with obscurity. Read for the first time, *Ulysses* is a difficult novel, packed with references and allusions that can be readily grasped only by a reader who knows the topography of Dublin and commands the scope of English literature. But with time and help, such difficulties can be eased, and we may then decide that *Ulysses*, or most of it, is not obscure. For all its complexities of structure and language, it presents a fairly clear and forthright story, and we may suppose ourselves able to form a reasonably secure sense of its meanings.

Nor is obscurity quite the same as opacity, that which cannot be penetrated. When we say that a work of literature is obscure, we usually have in mind a darkness of implication, a radical uncertainty regarding matter and meaning, but also that some gleams of light may break through this darkness. If we persevere or are blessed with quick intuitions, we may be able to reach a firm understanding. It is not just that the work in question can sustain a multiplicity of readings—that seems true for any serious piece of imaginative writing. It is that there is no entirely persuasive, let alone strong, case to be made for any reading. Obscurity teases us, lures us into speculations we cannot fully support, elicits lively if also dubious critical judgments. Confronted with an obscure work, the honest critic has no choice but to admit the tentativeness or incompleteness of his reading.

A further distinction I would suggest is that between obscurity as an internal condition and obscurity as an intended theme or subject. In the former sense, there is usually the implication of at least a partial failure: something has been blurred or left out or something has gone askew, so that we miss those signals of suggestion through which a writer would have us "take" his fiction. The reader has worked as hard as may reasonably be expected (not many of us can devote to a single work the lifetime that Joyce requested), but a margin of darkness remains which, it seems, cannot be removed. Even the resourceful William Empson cannot help.

Now, the obscurity I shall be attributing to Defoe's *Moll Flanders* is different in kind from that which pervades Mallarmé's poetry, since the latter entails a far richer consciousness and greater executive control than we can attribute to the former. Reading Mallarmé, we might be dissatisfied with a chosen method, but with Defoe we cannot be certain that there is one, or if there is, what it might be.

So obscurity as an internal condition needs to be distinguished, at least in preliminary analysis, from obscurity as intended theme or subject. In Henry James's great novel *The Awkward Age*, through a deliberate withholding of knowledge in behalf of focused perception, there is obscurity as a chosen theme or subject. Neither virtue nor failing in itself, such obscurity signifies insofar as it embodies or enhances the controlling vision of the work. In *The Awkward Age* the troubled isolation of consciousness within a sophisticated social group forms an essential theme, and the uncertainties about the outcome of the story contribute to the working-out of this theme. Or so, at least, I shall argue. And finally, there will be a few words about Ford Madox Ford's *The Good Soldier*, a novel much praised in recent decades but one in which I find obscurity in both of the senses I have mentioned.

To read *Moll Flanders* is like wandering through a vast city where all seems familiar at first: there are street signs—we can make out what they say—nevertheless we grow uneasy, we lack a sense of orientation and may even come to feel lost. Looking for some guidance from a controlling intelligence, we can never be sure whether such guidance is there or we have really "gotten" it.

At first this response seems strange, since, at least among ordinary readers, *Moll Flanders* is taken to be an "easy" book—and, after all, such readers feel, what's the point of looking for needless troubles? The happenings in the novel are clear, the writing is blunt, and there are few, if any, perplexing allusions. In terms of commonplace realism, the book seems transparent, meriting all the praise it has won as a pioneering fiction. Moll is a recognizable sort of woman, tough-minded but generous, unscrupulous but not mean. Thrown upon her own resources in a hostile city, she acts in behalf of survival and then, if any options remain, in behalf of pleasure—which means an array of men, mostly husbands, who can provide for her but toward only a few of whom she has strong feelings. She will, if necessary, steal and cheat: a woman has to live. Here is our Moll in one of her candid moments: "The Case was alter'd with me, I had Money in my Pocket, and had nothing to say to [men]; I had been trick'd once by *that Cheat call'd* LOVE, but the Game was over; I was resolv'd now to be Married or Nothing, and to be well Married or not at all."

The rambling voice and episodic structure elicit responses that range from intense interest to mild lassitude, but what seems most likely to hold attention is the fable as a whole, charting Moll's ingenuity in struggling for a place in the world, above all, her anxiety lest she fall through the bottom. When Virginia Woolf praised Moll as a generous rogue who in her own way anticipated somewhat the values of feminism, she may have been guilty of a romantic exaggeration, but she was closer to the spirit of the book than are those critics who put down Moll as a mere reflex of the commercial ethos. *Moll Flanders* the novel and Moll the character induce admiration for sheer energy; they relax, though they do not remove, our inclination to moral judgment.

The story is told in the first person singular, with very few passages in which Defoe as author can establish a critical distance from the narrator—something always difficult in novels with a first-person narrator. Every narrative method can be employed in behalf of or can succumb to obscurity, though this is probably least likely in novels written from the omniscient point of view. (God knows.) The particular weakness of first-person narrative is often a confinement of vision that results, so to say, in the world collapsing into the narrator's voice. Some writers employing the first-person singular manage to avoid this, as, for example, does Robert Penn Warren in *All the King's Men*, where the narrator's limitations of mind are set in ironic contrast to what the text as a whole induces us to believe. But in *Moll Flanders* the external world is granted little autonomous space, being largely subordinated to Moll's solitary sense of things.

Defoe the master of notation and Mallarmé the symbolist poet may occupy opposite poles of the literary spectrum, yet they share a desire to undo the strategies of traditional literature, Mallarmé by precise intention and Defoe by shrewd intuition. Neither accepts the premise of Aristotelian "imitation," that the literary work, while of course distinct from, also draws upon the external world. Mallarmé wishes to purge his poems of contingency, while Defoe virtually collapses his fiction into the world, so that the reader can readily feel that Moll's story *is* reality, unmediated by a clear authorial presence. Moll crowds out or usurps that presence, so that her story comes to seem more a record of event than a worked-up narrative.

What is missing is an inflected narrative voice or even a shadowy authorial presence which, at need, can move closer to or farther away from Moll. The dominant tone is a worldliness at once shrewd and naive, which makes for a strange blending yet is by no means unfamiliar; it is a tone that Defoe seems to have shared, perhaps because he wrote out of a secular consciousness still tied to the vestigial religious emotions he occasionally got around to remembering. All of which makes unlikely that there will be (what modern readers would regard as) an appropriate distancing of perspective in Defoe's relation to Moll. There are, it is true, local ironies, often entertaining in their own right, which Defoe grants Moll and which indicate that this writer knew a lot about the ways of the world; but these are incidental touches that, in my judgment, do not settle into a larger pattern. What happens in *Moll Flanders* we always know; what to make of the happenings we are never quite sure. Hence, the endless critical debate as to whether Defoe shares Moll's rather crude morality or provides an implicit criticism of it. Both sides in this debate offer valid citations; neither can quite clinch its argument. There just isn't enough evidence.

We might, to be sure, fall back upon a postmodernist "open" approach, which would see both, indeed, any number of readings as acceptable in a playful spirit; but this would merely be a way of acknowledging the substance, while denying the cogency, of the debate. For in any acceptable reading of *Moll Flanders* a radical indeterminacy of meaning remains, a margin of obscurity.

If *Moll Flanders* survives as a prime example of artless creation, Henry James's *The Awkward Age* is surely one of the most artful of fictions. Yet, oddly, the two novels seem, at first glance, to share certain technical characteristics: both lack a guiding omniscience or a clearly placed inner focus of consciousness, both leave us decidedly, even nervously, unsure of the writer's intentions, and both are thereby open, if in sharply different ways, to the charge of obscurity.

The Awkward Age is written almost entirely in dialogue, as if it were a play; we grope toward an understanding of the relationships among the characters but without the help that in the staging of a play can be provided by the actors. Elusive, sometimes maddening, this difficult novel has at least as strong a claim for realizing the perplexities of human relationships as does the traditional well-plotted novel in which everything is neatly arranged and the ambiguities we take for granted in daily life tend to be flattened out. To be sure, it seems unlikely that even among the English upper classes there could have been a social group quite as dazzlingly articulate as the one at the center of *The Awkward Age*—*that* we have to accept as a literary convention, quite as we accept Hamlet's eloquence. It should be added, however, that the difficulty of James's novel stems not just from the characters' readiness of speech but from their habit of cutting one another off midway, as if quick understanding rendered speech superfluous.

When we read this novel, we are likely to experience something like that nervous groping for hints and clues that we engage in upon entering an unfamiliar social milieu. Even among sophisticated readers there is likely to ensue an epistemological insecurity so extreme that they may beat a hasty retreat from James's novel. Yet that nervousness is testimony not only to James's technical skill (which sometimes does become a cause for distraction) but also to his accuracy in evoking the feelings that accompany any effort to make out, to "see," a cluster of human beings. Artifice in this novel becomes a clue, perhaps an equivalent to the way (some) things are, since life too, if less artfully than Henry James, does employ a range of artifice. And the artifice also mirrors the atmosphere of decadence, something shady, even mildly sinister, which hovers over the action of the novel, with a number of the secondary characters contributing especially to that atmosphere.

The *donnée* of *The Awkward Age* is fairly trivial: how to arrange the "coming-out" of an English girl in a late-nineteenth-century house where the talk is free and sometimes fast. It is hard to suppose that this could be sufficient matter for more than a short comic novel, and in *The Awkward Age* it turns out to be little more than the precipitating incident. We then come upon the intimate circle of the roguish and witty Mrs. Brookenham's house, where her daughter, Nanda, wise but bleak, must soon be invited to mix with the adult visitors. Gradually we become entangled with the complex, almost indecipherable relationships among the central trio: Mrs. Brook and her two close friends: Van, elegant, clever, and poor, and Mitchy, ugly, benevolent, and rich. There follows a series of conversations increasingly tense, evoking what F. W. Dupee called "the simple wear and tear of existence," or what might also be called the price exacted upon nerves and flesh by a highly stylized mode of civilization as it is slipping into a mild decadence.

The story itself moves along traditional lines, somewhat as in a Jane Austen novel: a stable community is unsettled by the intrusion of an alien figure, with the role of Mr. Darcy being shared by young Nanda and old Mr. Longdon, a family friend who speaks for a fading traditionalism. I will not here entangle myself with the mechanism of plot: suffice it to say that the central trio is encircled by a second group, some of them vulgar and corrupt, which in turn calls into question the self-admiration of Mrs. Brook's "temple of analysis" by suggesting that in or near this "temple" there are less exalted appearances of financial greed and sexual jealousy. The whole structure of the central group is then shattered by Mrs. Brook in a marvelous comic scene which achieves the result, probably by her intention, of persuading Mr. Longdon to take Nanda off to the country in an alliance possibly ambiguous. Thereby one of the traditional motifs of nineteenth-century fiction is put to Jamesian use: the retreat from urban corruption to the supposed health of the countryside.

Although Mrs. Brook's circle seems "exposed" at the novel's end, it would be a misreading to see in this nothing but exposure. For the inner group that has been coming together in Mrs. Brook's drawing room *is* a carrier of civilization, if not of high culture; it does adhere to values of friendship and personal cultivation. What one feels strongly after reading *The Awkward Age* is the extent to which suffering can be a cost of consciousness, indeed of civilization itself. The plot makes demands on our credence, the speech of the central characters can seem implausible, but the characters themselves are utterly persuasive in their need and pain.

About the happenings in this precious little circle James invites us to speculate, very much as we do in the encounters of our daily life. He provides no more knowledge than we customarily enjoy or, for the purposes of this novel, need. All the perplexities of motive and conduct we struggle with and either resolve in part or learn to live with—why Mitchy will marry a little trollop or Van backs away from Nanda's love or Mrs. Brook overturns the structure of her group. This mixture of concealment and revelation justifies James's famous remark "Really, universally, relations end nowhere, and the exquisite problem of the artist is eternally but to draw, by a geometry of his own, the circle within which they shall happily *appear* to do so."

As novelist, James is here in almost complete control, reaching a tragicomic mixture of brilliance and sadness, the sleek surface of civilized relations and the chaos seething beneath it. All this is put at the service of the novel's ultimate epistemology, which is to say, its constant posing of the problem of knowledge: what do we know of one another? how can we know one another? Together with the characters, we struggle to make things out, piece by piece, insight by insight, blindness by blindness. So the obscurity in this novel forms the very matter of perception, becoming thereby a lucid theme, lighting up the obscurity that inheres in the life of men and women.

Ford Madox Ford's *The Good Soldier* has been praised by a generation of New Critics who saw in its technical resourcefulness a model of what a highly wrought fiction can be. For a long time I shared this estimate, but a later look—ah, the risks of disenchantment!—has persuaded me that, despite some remarkable segments, the novel suffers from a darkness of implication or what I have here been calling obscurity as an internal condition. It was of course Ford's wish, as it was Henry James's wish, to make out of the obscurities of life a compelling novelistic subject. *The Good Soldier* is arranged as a sequence of gropings, false leads, blind alleys, reconsiderations, and skeptical conclusions that conclude with very little. Abstractly put, the difficulty of secure knowledge about others and ourselves forms a dominant theme of this novel; where the disagreements of valuation converge is with regard to the uses of Ford's technical ingenuities.

In the opening paragraph we hear the dispirited, droning voice of Dowell, the narrator, or, as he calls himself, the storyteller, who keeps striking a single key: the hopelessness of supposing that even after many years of friendship we can know much about the most important aspects of our friends' lives. What he is now going to tell us is "the saddest story I have ever heard," a remark that keeps recurring like a leitmotif—though to at least some skeptical readers it suggests that poor Dowell cannot have heard many sad stories. Unless, the thought occurs, Ford is slyly mocking Dowell through Dowell's lugubrious voice.

The plot, taken in isolation, is lurid. Dowell is married to a false and hysterical woman, Florence, who fakes a heart condition in order to keep him in a state of submission and meanwhile to carry on an affair with their close friend, the English Captain Ashburnham, handsome, profligate, and sentimental, a lecher who somehow is to represent the traditional virtues of the generous if also obtuse Torydom toward which Ford displays kindly feelings. The Captain's wife, Leonora, is a strict Catholic who puts up with her husband's wasteful philandering, even sometimes lending a hand in his efforts. Toward the end of the story there also appears a ward of the Ashburnhams, the lovely young woman Nancy, with whom the Captain falls utterly in love but out of a desperate sense of noblesse oblige refrains from seducing. The down-at-the-dumps Dowell also loves Nancy, but to no avail. In a climax that might faze a Jacobean dramatist, Nancy goes mad, Florence and the Captain take their lives, Leonora contracts a routine second marriage, and poor Dowell, now finally aware that he had been duped for years but still abrim with admiration for "the good soldier," remains alone and miserable.

My summary, I admit, is unsympathetic and fails to do justice to the novel, though it seems to me fair enough about the plot. For this story is a melodramatic shocker, and even the novel's ardent admirers recognize that their claims for it must rest elsewhere: on, say, admiration for its technical virtuosity (which no one disputes) and also on the sense of the wordless suffering which even these wretched figures can feel.

If, however, the story itself is shrouded in the skepticisms of multiple points of view that admit of only the most ambiguous moral conclusions, and if, no matter how we take it, the story itself does not possess much interest, what then remains? "What remains," writes Denis Donoghue in an interesting defense, "now that nearly all the ostensible significance of the facts [in this novel] has been drained from them by Dowell's skepticism? And the answer is: Dowell himself." This is a shrewd critical maneuver, since it diverts us from what Dowell is "ostensibly" remembering and focuses instead upon the activity of his mind and memory; but finally, I think, it constitutes a virtual abandonment of any great claims for the book, since Dowell's mind is feeble, his recollections are dispirited, and when there are some striking passages of reflection we are tempted immediately to suppose that this cannot be Dowell speaking, it must be Ford himself breaking past or through Dowell. The vibrations of response that such interventions by Ford solicit turn out to be greatly in excess of the matter that is supposed to have evoked them.

As the novel proceeds, the distance between Ford and

Dowell—particularly between Ford and Dowell's extravagant admiration for Captain Ashburnham—keeps shrinking. Does Ford himself want us to suppose that this is "the saddest story"? Or is he soliciting a measure of irony in letting Dowell say such things? If the former, then Ford is making claims for his action which cannot be justified; if the latter (which at least in the second half of the book seems unlikely), what is left but the pathos of a wretched group of self-deluded figures?

It may be said by way of reply: But is this not true for much modern fiction? For, say, *Madame Bovary*? Yes; but it should be remembered that when Flaubert said, "*Emma Bovary, c'est moi,*" he was saying that no one, and least of all he, had a right to feel morally superior to the Emma Bovarys of this world; he was not casting any sort of romantic glow about her, as Ford does, ambiguously, it's true, about the Captain. Flaubert's clear-minded valuation of Emma, like James's of the characters in *The Awkward Age*, is beyond question, while Ford's relation to his two male characters, and especially to the judgment that one has of the other, is uncertain and flecked with sentimentalism. For all its brilliant surface, this novel has a soft center.

In *The Awkward Age* there are outcomes of the story that we find hard to fathom: this is a sign of the obscurity of human existence. But in *The Good Soldier* there is an obscurity regarding Ford's relation to his material and the reasons for the strong responses he wishes to—and often does—get from us. *Moll Flanders* may be artless and *The Good Soldier* astonishingly artful, but after reading both we are left with the question: What are we to make of it all?

Punitive Novels

IN THE LATE 1950s an Englishman resorting to the pseudonym E. A. Ellis published a novel called *The Rack*. Like most novels, this one came and went, and I am probably one of the few people who remember it. Awkwardly written but emotionally intense, *The Rack* is set in a tuberculosis sanitarium and portrays the agonies of a young man, apparently the author himself, who spends two years there as a patient and then hears himself sentenced to the likelihood that he will have to remain there for the rest of his life.

Not many of the usual rewards of fiction can be had from a book like *The Rack*: not many in the way of plot, style, and characterization. What evidently mattered most to this writer was piling up, with a grim insistence, the evidence of pain. Nor does the depicted suffering carry any clear moral significance: the central character is a nice-enough fellow, but not at all remarkable in his responses, and, indeed, the whole point of *The Rack* seems to be that physical pain has no meaning; it is something that just happens, like rain or thunder. And of course there is a certain truth to this: pain does not illuminate. What I remember most vividly from this novel is its exact clinical descriptions: sternal punctures, mysterious fluctuations of fever, secretions of fluid from the pleura, endless jabbing needles. Quite free of spiritual chatter about "transcendence," the book forces us to stare at the terribleness to which the body is subject—and to do so without relief of any kind.

If there is a conclusion to be drawn, it is simply an acknowledgment of how arbitrary our existence can be, how pointless are all our diseases and afflictions. When I first read *The Rack* I was a young man and was somehow able to put up with the relentless pain it both portrayed and caused; now, decades later, I doubt that I could bear to read this book, honest and estimable as it is. My feeling is that I have since learned enough about pain. And even when I first read *The Rack* I felt that I was being punished, not for any wrongdoing of which I was aware, but simply because I was the kind of person who reads books. I have since come to wonder. Is this a punishment I am morally obliged to endure, even welcome, perhaps out of a sense of human solidarity? Or is there something gratuitous, even excessive about such writing?

I found myself thinking about a greater novel, Thomas Mann's *The Magic Mountain*, but quickly abandoned the comparison. The sanitarium in which Mann set his novel is used for dramatic concentration and intellectual tournament, with the aim of advancing the writer's vision of life in the twentieth century. With the cruelty that comes readily to spectators, we soon "rise above" the sufferings of Mann's characters. Someone like Ellis or his protagonist might say that Mann makes it all too easy for his readers by providing a contrived resolution (not, of course, a happy ending). But Ellis's novel is severely representational, without any claim to symbolic resonance; it does not "use" a sanitarium, it depicts what happens in a sanitarium. And it ends with the protagonist staring bitterly at the walls of his sickroom, trying to accept the blow of treatment without end. He recalls Shakespeare's lines:

> . . . he hates him
> That would upon the rack of this tough world
> Stretch him out longer.

What, I want now to ask, is the value of such writing? Where, among the many branches of literature, are we to place it? Surely *The Rack* is a serious work, but just as surely it does not yield the pleasures that esthetic theories say a work of literature should yield. Ever since the rise of realistic fiction in the last two centuries there has been a number of such novels—what I am inclined to call punitive novels, which make pain an all-consuming theme and its endurance a sign of virtue, with the apparent end of forcing readers to share in the suffering. And why should we not?—since we suspect that to shirk this burden may be a cause for shame.

Punitive novels do not settle attention on an imagined autonomy of character; they do not stir us to moral indignation or social rebelliousness; they provide little catharsis. What they do is to solicit pain and hoard guilt. The pain and guilt have to do with conditions beyond remedy, and the intent of the authors of punitive novels is often to affirm a somewhat narrow sense of realism, that is, to display circumstances of existence that have been previously ignored or blinked in literature.

It is notable that we tacitly bring to bear different norms of judgment when reading memoirs or history. I have read a good many Holocaust memoirs which accumulate horrors upon horrors, and although some of these books can be charged with a measure of sensationalism in exploiting their subject, I have found myself accepting or at least enduring most of them. For most of them tell the truth as best they can; their main purpose is to leave a record of what happened. But with imaginative writing things are different; our acceptance is not so readily extended, for we expect something "more," something beyond mere factual accuracy. We look for some portion, however modest, of what Proust in *The Past Recaptured* called "the essence of things," at least an insight into whatever lies beneath the surface of our world.

I am aware of how risky it is to compare novels with other kinds of writing, and I invoke the Greek drama for a strictly limited comparison. It is true, of course, that a staged play entails a strong visual aspect that is bound to seem more immediate than words put down on paper; yet I think that the sense of moral decorum which led the Greek playwrights to refrain from showing certain events on stage may also be invoked with regard to the novel. Such restraints, or, as many would now say, such inhibitions, have increasingly been discarded in the modern era, and by now the program of realism makes us receptive to fictions of total exposure. Nothing need be shielded, nothing confined to offstage. In a modern version, we might see the blood dripping from the eyes of Oedipus.

But let us return to the novel. Some of George Gissing's

—*Born to Exile*, for example—approach the condition of the punitive novel. There is a short novel by the gifted Austrian writer Thomas Bernhard, *Wittgenstein's Nephew*, set, like *The Rack*, in a sanitarium but somewhat richer in emotional texture, since together with overwhelming pain, Bernhard's book has some renderings of friendship. And there is a novel, *Tender Mercies*, by a fine American writer, Rosellen Brown, which records the sufferings of a young couple after the wife has been badly injured in an accident and the husband must tend her. About such books I find myself wondering: What end can the narrative accumulation of pain serve? Which literary or moral end is served by such punitive exercises? Or does even asking such questions betray a loss of nerve, the faltering of age before harsh realities?

Some decades ago, when naturalistic fiction thrived, similar questions used to be put by "humanist" critics hostile to the writings of Zola and Dreiser. But these questions, often prompted by an ethic of narrow propriety, were misdirected, since in the novels of Zola and Dreiser we hear strong voices of compassion and understanding. After reading, say, *Germinal* or *An American Tragedy* or Dos Passos' *USA*, we experience feelings that go beyond the mere registration of pain. If, however, we were to go back to the film version of *Sister Carrie*, in which Laurence Olivier played Hurstwood, Dreiser's main character, the "humanist" complaint might have some point, because the film lacks the aura of compassion that we find in Dreiser's narratives and what remains on the screen is a bare, blind portrayal of a descent into wretchedness.

Now the problem I am raising is hardly a new one, though my phrase "punitive novel" may be. It could be said that *King*

Lear also imposes a large quantity, perhaps even an excess, of anguish. Indeed, Dr. Johnson wrote that he could not "apologize" for "the extrusion of Gloucester's eyes, which seems an act too horrid to be endured in dramatick exhibition, and such as must always compel the mind to relieve its distress by incredulity." He had not been able, wrote Dr. Johnson, to reread the last act of *King Lear*, so painful had been his earlier reading. Notice that Dr. Johnson does not say that he finds "the extrusion of Gloucester's eyes" incredible—he is not concerned here with a test of realism. He speaks instead about the self-protective behavior of "the mind" in trying to ward off an unbearable dose of pain.

There is, to be sure, a sense of purgation, even a kind of solemn elation, at the end of *King Lear*, so that we can feel—perhaps too easily—that more than "incredulity" emerges from this "too horrid . . . dramatick exhibition." Still, it would be no disrespect to Shakespeare if we were to mutter that in the concluding segment of the play there is a little too much howling.

I am familiar with the standard critical view of the problem I have raised. It will probably remain the standard view: Great works show the many-sidedness of human experience and thereby surmount the suffering they must exhibit and evoke. But the novels you call punitive—so goes the dominant opinion—simply transmit pain unable to go beyond itself and must therefore be judged as failed works of literature.

I do not find this standard view satisfactory: it dissolves, rather than copes with, a difficult problem. While none of the punitive novels I have cited can be called great works of literature, they are all honest, competent, and, in some instances, even distinguished. What needs to be confronted is not the standard claim that the novels I call punitive fail to render the fullness of human experience—of course; nor do they attempt to. Their authors focus, perhaps obsessively, on one aspect of experience: the rule of pain.

It is also true that there are works of literature that elicit pain yet do not seem punitive. Reading Chekhov's *Ward No. 6*, also set in a hospital and suffused with suffering, we do not feel ourselves being punished, for we recognize in the ordeals of Chekhov's characters a pathos of wasted life. Reading *Summer 1919*, the concluding volume of Roger Martin du Gard's *roman fleuve, The Thibaults*, in which the doctor, Antoine Thibault, scrupulously records his physical disintegration after being gassed in the First World War, we again do not feel we are being punished, since through this doctor's notations we can share to the end the reflections of a lucid mind. Reading J. M. Coetzee's novel *Waiting for the Barbarians*, we can suppose that its depicted brutalities are due to oppressive societies and therefore remediable by an uprising of the victims. With all such novels we may conclude that, at least in part, they are at the service of an ultimately redemptive value.

The trouble with the punitive novel, I would suggest, derives from an esthetic misconception: the notion that there is no subject or situation exempt from novelistic treatment. For there are truths, grim and blunt, which can make no claim to being "redemptive"; and these are of a kind most writers pass by because they threaten to undermine both the reconciliations of comedy and the recognitions of tragedy. It may also be that our inherited notions about the catharsis available from tragedy constitute something of a delusion, providing us with consolations that mask the unbearableness of what literature hesitates to approach.

Walter Scott:
Falling Out of the Canon

IN 1825 WILLIAM Hazlitt observed that "Sir Walter Scott is undoubtedly the most popular writer of the age"—to which he shrewdly added, he "is 'lord of the ascendent' for the time being." That "for the time being" would stretch out for perhaps a century, during which Scott not only remained the great favorite of the reading public but also exerted a major influence on writers in Europe and America. But then—it's hard to give an exact date—something remarkable happened. Scott lost his grip on the imagination of the public and, except in high schools where *Ivanhoe* was still wearily assigned, he came to be treated as a worthy historical relic. The writer whom the brilliant Hazlitt had admired and whom, more than a century later, the Marxist critic Georg Lukács would treat with notable respect, dropped out of the canon. Dropped out so quickly that we must ask: What can have happened to account for such a drastic change in literary taste?

This change can hardly have been a consequence of sharp revisions in critical judgment, since many of the faults that now seem glaring in Scott's fiction were already being noticed by his contemporaries. That his prose is stuffed with elegant filler; that his plots have a way of dwindling into shapeless anecdote; that his "high" characters speak in exalted fustian rather than any language known to man or woman; that he is better at sketching the postures of bodies than at penetrating souls (even with regard to the much-praised Jeanie Deans, the plucky maiden of *The Heart of Midlothian*); that his minor characters often do not know, as minor characters should, when to make their exit—such criticisms are quite as old as the admiration that generations of hearty Englishmen have given him.

To go back to his contemporaries is to experience bewilderment. Goethe thought his "scenes and situations . . . the summit of art." Heine found his "partiality for the past . . . wholesome for literature." But Stendhal saw in Scott only "historical merit," the kind "which will grow old the soonest" and declared his "mannered approximations" to be "distasteful." Rounding the French dismissal, Balzac has a character in *Lost Illusions* say "there is no passion in Walter Scott; either he himself is without it, or it is forbidden by the hypocritical laws of his country." Yet neither praise nor attack made much difference to Scott's nineteenth-century reputation: he seemed invulnerable.

Scott wrote neither a pure nor a pungent English. He nattered on insufferably. His mind was decently pedestrian, without much moral energy. ("The spiritual sleep of that man,"

said George Eliot, "was awful.") But Scott did have one considerable advantage as a writer: he was in possession of, or
possessed by, an urgent subject, one that spurred him to nostalgia and contradiction in large and numerous fictions.

Hazlitt called Scott "a *prophesier* of things past," and by
this striking phrase I take him to mean, among other things,
that Scott was so deeply immersed in his native culture through
stories, legends, ballads, and memories that one could readily
imagine him living, say, in 1745 and accurately forecasting
Scotland's future. Scott had a real claim to a historical imagination, a sense of how history carves out its paths regardless
of individual desire. He was a witness to the slow death of the
hopes for an independent Scottish nationality, and this forms
a major theme in his novels. He conveyed, in the words of
David Daiches, "a tragic sense of the inevitability of a drab
but necessary progress, a sense of the impotence of the traditional kind of heroism, a passionately regretful awareness of
the fact that the Good Old Cause was lost forever and the glory
of Scotland must give way to her interest."

Except for Daiches's opening phrase, "a tragic sense," this
is keen. I would say that in his writings Scott rarely achieves
the severity of perception, the single-minded concentration on
a line of fatality, that we call tragic. The Scott character who
approaches genuine pathos is Rob Roy in the novel of that
name, a stubborn semioutlaw living by the collapsed tradition
of his clan in opposition to English rule; but even this, while
perhaps grand, is not tragic. For if Scott is an old Tory at heart,
his mind settles quite comfortably into new Whig. He is
shrewdly aware that the power of the state in London is a
reality it would be foolish to deny, and often this results in a

recognition that the old Scots order of heroic deeds and sublime vistas is done for.

It may be objected that my view of Scott's theme is too distant for a full imaginative engagement, but I would reply that this is precisely the trouble with Scott himself: he often does not fully engage with his theme. For all the flashy battles and verbal bravado of his costume dramas, Scott is extremely cautious in dealing with Scottish nationalism as it proceeds through several historical variants. His nostalgia can seem a literary convenience, handy for pageant-romances and adding "color" to his brushings in the Flemish mode. But finally he is too much the canny rationalist and too relaxed in mind— Walter Bagehot said he had "the enjoying temper"—to yield himself with tragic force to a fading past. For that, you have to be blessedly crazy, just a little, like William Faulkner. Scott was sane.

What I am saying may hold a little more for a later novel like *Redgauntlet* (1824) than for Scott's earlier novels in the Waverley series. *Redgauntlet* evokes the Scottish cause in its phase of decline, a recall of sentimentality. In an imaginary episode departing from Scott's usual rough adherence to historical actuality, there is a brief appearance by the Pretender, now middle-aged and stiff in the joints, and a strong appearance by the Jacobite fanatic Redgauntlet, for whom a defiance of history has become his life's credo. But about two-thirds of the way (the point at which a number of Scott's novels collapse), the Jacobite plot suffers a rapid disintegration, almost falling into farce. Scott has known all along that the Stuart cause is hopeless, so that little of *Redgauntlet*, though one of his better novels, can really be called "tragic." The narrative dissipation is finally a reflection of the writer's discomfort with his theme.

By now, also, the historical circumstances on which Scott's novels depend have slipped out of common knowledge: what might have seemed alive in the nineteenth century hardly seems so today. Who is likely to be clear in mind about the Covenanters and the Cameronians, the Erastians and other sects? A reprint of *Rob Roy* (1817) or *Old Mortality* (1816) would now require copious annotation, about both the religious tendencies and political groupings of Scotland in the seventeenth and eighteenth centuries and the sequences of uprisings that Scott depicts. Perhaps that is the fate of all historical fiction. A few years from now *Darkness at Noon*, which evoked furious debate on its appearance in 1940, may need descriptive footnotes.

There have been several efforts to revive Scott's reputation. One of these follows the lead of Georg Lukács, who, in *The Historical Novel*, praised Scott as a "great writer," not because he seemed especially delighted with any of his novels but because he found in Scott a schema of historical transformation from the "feudal" clans of traditional Scottish society to the commercial order dominant in Sir Walter's day. Lukács's historical schema was ready-made, and he fit it to the novel with a few tokens of gratification. For readers not well acquainted with Scott's works, Lukács's laying out of their progression can have a certain persuasiveness, but when he writes that Scott's "greatness lies in his capacity to give living human embodiment to historical-social types," we hasten to dissent. Scott's characters and scenes are mostly of the picturesque variety; long before Hollywood, Scott was using Technicolor. Not only is he a careless writer in English (his Scots dialogue is often sharply piquant), but his large-scale confrontations and dramas are often slipshod, the "mannered approximations" Stendhal spoke of.

A more sophisticated defense of Scott comes from critics who say that his books should not be judged by the standards of the novel, for they are really romances. Insofar as the term "romance" sanctions departures from verisimilitude, it may indeed be applied to Scott's fictions; but call them what you wish, the lassitude of language and tedium of depiction remain.

A still more modest defense is that there are "good things" in Scott. Of course there are. He can do a florid, stagey set piece. He has a few figures, like Rob Roy, memorable in their decline. He puts together strong mob scenes. He can elicit a throb from Jeanie Deans's long tramp to London in *The Heart of Midlothian*. And in *Old Mortality* he contributes a very funny chapter depicting a clutter of demented fanatics exhorting a rebel gathering of Scottish Presbyterians in an exercise of "participatory democracy" unnervingly similar to some I witnessed in the 1960s.

Yet these defenses of Scott evade the critical question: What do you make of the novels (or the romances, if you prefer) in their own right? My own reading suggests that it is *Old Mortality* which holds up best, perhaps because it is the one novel in which his distaste for fanaticism, of both the Royalist and Covenanting varieties, is allowed full imaginative play.

Why then was Scott so beloved, not only among the mass of readers but also by some of the eminent literary people of the

nineteenth century? I must confess to not having a fully satisfactory answer: there is a critical gulf here that seems im-
passable. What is clear, however, is that nineteenth-century
readers could yield themselves more readily than we do to the
rouge of spectacle. There was still much wonderment about
exotic places, sustaining a taste for the picturesque. And evidently readers a century ago were more tolerant of Scott's
garrulousness than we are likely to be. They did not feel our
need for novels to *move*.

The whole idea of what a novel should be was changing
radically even in the years of Scott's early popularity. A generous man, he praised Jane Austen's art without apparently
realizing that it had dealt a severe blow to the kind of fiction
he had been writing. At first, the culture of Romanticism wel-
comed his gift for the picturesque, which necessarily entailed
a rough typicality in the sketching of character; but then that
culture came to favor a complex psychology of character that
was quite beyond Scott's reach. Dickens and George Eliot
borrowed here and there from Scott, but they also left him far
behind.

Still, if sensitive and intelligent nineteenth-century readers
did not mind Scott's long-windedness, could follow his tangled
plots, and took pleasure in his comic interludes, why should
we now find Scott so tiresome? (I assume most of us do, though
a few hardy souls will be outraged by my every word.) Perhaps
because Scotland has dropped out of historical consciousness.
Perhaps because the idea of nationalism no longer evokes the
innocently heroic sentiments that it did in the time of Garibaldi.
Perhaps because we have come to regard the novel less as an
entertainment and more as a vehicle for the testing of values.

Not many of Scott's contemporaries would have grasped what D. H. Lawrence meant when he called the novel "the bright book of life."

There is still another, and I think fundamental, reason for Scott's decline in literary standing. It may at first seem a narrowly literary reason, but it is actually rooted in the depths of history. Scott wrote as if not only he but all his readers enjoyed world enough and time. That narratives might be foreshortened, conversations clipped, and tempos hastened seems never to have occurred to him—except in the last fifty or so pages of his books where he seems eager simply to get it all done with. The clock does not check his imagination. Must every scene be painted to the last tint? Every byplay of minor figures rendered to the last turn of dialect? Every hero orate in swollen prose? I fancy the thought of Scott edited by Beckett.

I exaggerate, but only a little. There are variations of tempo in Scott, and he can work up a climax of suspense (though it seems always to droop into detumescence). But given the sense of time he inherited from his culture he had little need to clip, skip, focus. Pageants are not to be rushed.

Nor is this a matter of length. The feeling that his novels drag has more to do with pacing than length. Some of Dickens's novels are longer than those of Scott, but there is a nervous tension in Dickens that signals a kinship with our age. Scott did not know the tempo of the city.

Pacing is a crucial element in the novel, often a tacit reflection of a writer's world-view. Between readers who a century ago adored Scott and those brought up on Borges and Beckett there are differences of assumption so profound as to resist definition, differences that reveal themselves in the varying speeds with which the eye follows a line of type and the mind takes in its matter.

The Self in Literature

NO ONE HAS ever seen the self. It has no visible shape, nor does it occupy measurable space. It is an abstraction, like other abstractions equally elusive: the individual, the mind, the society. Yet it has a history of its own which informs and draws upon the larger history of our last two centuries, a time in which the idea of the self became a great energizing force in politics and culture.

Let us say that the self is a construct of mind, a hypothesis of being, socially formed even as it can be quickly turned against the very social formations that have brought it into birth. The locus of self often appears as "inner," experienced as a presence savingly apart from both social milieu and quotidian existence. At its root lies a tacit polemic, in opposition to the ages. In extreme circumstances it may be felt as "hidden."

There is probably some continuity between the idea of

the soul and that of the self. Both propound a center of perci-
pience lodged within yet not quite of the body. Soul speaks
of a person's relation to divinity, a participation in heavenly
spark, while self speaks of a person's relation to both others
and oneself—though soul may in part serve this function
too. In these ideas of soul and self there is a dualism of self-
consciousness that forms, I believe, a historical advance. And
there is a similar link between the idea of the self and modern
notions of alienation, since both imply a yearning for—with
knowledge of a usual separation from—a "full" or a "fulfilled"
humanity, unfractured by contingent needs.

Once perceived or imagined, the self implied doubleness,
multiplicity. For what knows the awareness of self if not the
self?—division as premise and price of consciousness. I may
be fixed in social rank, but that does not exhaust, and may not
even quite define, who I am or what I "mean." By asserting
the presence of the self, I counterpose to all imposed definitions
of place and function a persuasion that I harbor *something else*,
utterly mine—a persuasion that I possess a center of individual
consciousness that is active and, to some extent, coherent. In
my more careless moments, I may even suppose this center to
be inviolable, though anyone who has paid attention to modern
history knows this is not so. To say that the world cannot
invade the precincts of the self is to indulge in bravado, and
yet, even while sadly recognizing this, I still see the self as my
last bulwark against oppression and falsity. Were this bulwark
to be breached, I would indeed be broken.

In the long past of modernity, there have been numerous
prefigurings of selfhood. Hamlet spars with his sense of self,
both cradling and assaulting it. Saint Augustine's *Confessions*

have been called a "manifesto of the inner world," though I doubt that he postulated a self in the modern sense of the term. Jacob Burckhardt writes that by the end of the thirteenth century Italy was beginning to "swarm with individuality: the ban upon personality was dissolved." But the ban upon that personality assuming historical initiative was not dissolved.

In the latter part of the eighteenth century, through the Enlightenment and Romanticism, a deep change begins in mankind's sense of its situation. In the Enlightenment educated Europeans experience "an expansive sense of power over nature and themselves" (Peter Gay). The self attains the dignity of a noun, as if to register an enhancement of authority. Earlier intimations of selfhood give way to the *idea*, or at least sentiment, of the self, slippery as that proves to be and susceptible to criticism as it will become. The idea of the self becomes a force within public life, almost taking on institutional shape and certainly entering the arena of historical contention. For what occurs is not just a new perception of our internal space, but its emergence as a major social factor. Once, as in Hegel's phrase, we celebrate our "existence *on its own account*" (emphasis added), that is, being for being's sake, we have stepped into a new era.

All this does not occur in a realm of pure spirit; it is entangled with worldly affairs, social changes, and class conflicts. I accept as reasonable a remark by Lucien Goldmann that "the most important consequence of the development of a market economy is that the individual . . . now becomes, both in his own consciousness and that of his fellow men, an independent element . . . *a point of departure*" (emphasis added), though I also think it no catastrophe to suggest that the sequence of causality might be reversed. What must, however, be strongly objected to is the vulgarized sociology of knowledge that judges value by imputed origin, tending to depreciate the individual as a "point of departure" because this idea may be a consequence of the growth of a market economy.

So far as I can tell, the prominence of the self in the writings of that brilliant intuitive psychologist Denis Diderot, notably in *Rameau's Nephew* and *Jacques the Fatalist*, does not lead to any expectation or even desire for a fusion of self and role. The split between the two is accepted as a given. There can be no return to any "state of nature," whether taken to be historical fact or tacit allegory. We may at first suppose that the *Moi* of *Rameau's Nephew*, that "honest soul" marked by a "wholeness of self," constitutes an image of ordinary, solid mankind, while the *Lui*, or the "disintegrated consciousness" about whom Diderot keenly remarks that "he has no greater opposite than himself," is a literary construct anticipating modes of character still to come. But the reality is quite the opposite. The very fact that Diderot's books were composed at the historical moment they were suggests that it is "the whole man" who is the imagined creature, a figment of desire, while the nephew, reveling in chaos, approaches a condition of actuality.

Once the notion of the self becomes entrenched in Western culture, there follows an acceptance of multiplicity within being. There may also follow a sort of pride in what each of us regards as unique stampings of personality. The Enlightenment, writes Kant, signifies "man's emergence from his self-imposed minority": which is to say, signifies the possibility of autonomy and the probability of division. The release of his-

torical energy through the Enlightenment means that the self
will now come forth in confident aloneness, declaring its goal
to be both a reformation of and an optimal distance from society. This also means that our frequently deplored alienation
can be seen as a human conquest, the sign that we have broken
out of traditional bonds. Psychologically: because the pain of
estrangement can be seen as a necessary cost of the boon of
selfhood—if we bemoan "deformed" selves, we may be supposed to have a glimmer of the "true" selves. And morally:
because it is all but impossible to postulate a self without some
intertwined belief in the good and the desirable. For the self
is not just an intuited supposition of a state of being; it is also
a historically situated norm.

The self turns out to consist of many selves, as Walt Whitman happily noted: partial and fragmented, released through
the liberty of experiment and introspection. It is also an interpretation of new modes of sensibility, and of interpretations,
as we have often been informed, there need be no end. So I
hasten to note just a few of these conflicting selves—songs,
chants, and whispers.

• The self may evoke an original state of nature, not yet stained
  by history, as if all were still at rest in the garden. "I dared
  to strip man's nature naked," said Rousseau, and, naked, there
  emerged the features of goodness.
• The self does service as a heuristic category enabling criticism
  of modes of existence taken to be morally crippling.
• The self can be envisaged graphically, with "higher" and
  "lower" segments, or perhaps as fluctuating up and down

between them, so that the two—some hold out for three—come to be seen as both intertwined and separable.

• The self becomes a lens of scrutiny with which to investigate psychological states, and is especially helpful for the study of anxiety, a condition that grows in acuteness as awareness of self increases.

• The self can become an agent of aggrandizement, an imperial expansion into a totality encompassing or obliterating the phenomenal world.

• Like all powerful ideas, the self can falsify itself through parody, becoming a masquerade of faked inspirations, hasty signals of untested intuitions. Jacques Riviere writes keenly about this:

> There is nothing more deceitful than what is spontaneous, nothing more foreign to myself. It is never with myself that I begin; the feelings I adopt naturally are not mine; I do not experience them, I fall into them right off as into a rut . . . everybody has already travelled along them. . . .

> My second thoughts are the true ones, those that await me in those depths down to which I do not go. Not the first thoughts alone are thinking in me; in the very depths of myself there is a low, continual meditation about which I know nothing and about which I shall know nothing unless I make an effort: this is my soul.

• The self is an ideal possibility, sole resident of utopia—a notion enabling humanity to extend its moral capacities. Schiller writes: "Every individual human being . . . carries within him, potentially and prescriptively, an ideal man, the archetype of a human being. . . ."

- The self implies an acceptance of the sufficiency of the human condition, so that divinities, myths, and miracles slip into obsolescence. Deism frees the mind from the puzzle of origins—God is granted primal power and then gently put to sleep—thereby clearing a path for human autonomy.

- As against atomistic theories positing a space "outside" society, the self may be seen as a social formation, a corollary of advanced civilization. A character in Henry James's *Portrait of a Lady* remarks: "There is no such thing as an isolated man or woman. . . . What do you call one's self? Where does it begin? Where does it end? It overflows into everything that belongs to us—and then it flows back again."

- The self entails a provisional unity of being, yet this occurs, if it does at all, during transformation and dissolution. For the self, as a felt presence, is inescapably dynamic, at once coming into and slipping out of being.

- The self [see Proust] creates a created self, manifested in works of art as a kind of double, different from, yet linked to, the putative empirical self.

- And in our own time, the self becomes a redoubt, the last defense against intolerable circumstances, precious even when lost. In Pasternak's novel, Dr. Zhivago writes in one of his poems:

> For life, too, is only an instant,
> Only the dissolving of ourselves
> In the selves of all others
> As if bestowing a gift—

Given this multiplicity of possible selves, is there any value in continuing to speak of "the self"? The question is of a kind that occurs in many contexts, as in the famous discussion of whether Romanticism "exists" in view of the numerous definitions proposed for it. The answer is provided by our experience: despite our awareness of how slippery a term "Romanticism" is we cannot avoid using it. Without such slippery terms, we cannot think.

The versions of self I have mentioned might be called interpretations in static cross-section. What gave them, historically, a tremendous charge of meaning and energy is that the idea of the self came to form a social and a moral claim. A strong claim for space, voice, identity. A claim that man is not the property of kings, lords, or states. A claim for the privilege of opinion, the freedom to refuse definitions imposed from without. A claim advanced by all who had been herded into orders and guilds. A claim against the snobbisms of status. In sum, the claim advanced by a newly confident historical subject. And a claim upon whom? Upon anyone and no one, launched into the very air—though at a given moment perhaps chiefly against despised governments. The revolution in moral consciousness, with its steadily magnified complex of claims, is by no means completed; it never will be; it is the one truly permanent revolution.

Let me offer three instances, from very different writers, with one speaking about time, the second about nature, and the third about society, yet all linked by common perceptions that bind men within a historical moment.

Rousseau writes about Jean-Jacques that he

loves activity, but detests constraint. Work is no strain on him
provided he can do it at his own rather than at another's time.
. . . It was one of the happiest moments of his life when . . .
he got rid of his watch. "Thank heaven" he exclaimed in a
transport of joy, "I shall no longer need to know what time it
is!"

As it happens, the world Rousseau helped usher in is one
where everybody needs to know what time it is, yet the rebellion of self that his refusal of clock time announces, is still
a recurrent cry of the heart: man against his rules.

Wordsworth in the Prospectus for his long unfinished
poem *The Recluse* declares that he, the poet, commands a subject even greater than that of Jehovah, so mighty is the idea of
man:

> Not Chaos, not
> The darkest pits of lowest Erebus,
> Nor aught of blinder vacancy, scooped out
> By help of dreams—can breed such fear and awe
> As falls upon us often when we look
> Into our Minds, into the Mind of Man. . . .

Here transcendence becomes an aspect of subjectivity, or
in the words of Wallace Stevens, writing in a Wordsworthian
mode, men shall "chant" in self-celebration, "Not as a god,
but as god might be."

Stendhal, exalting the freedom of the person against all
structured hypocrisies, has Julien Sorel make a speech to the
jury at the end of *The Red and the Black*. Accused of a personal

crime, Julien speaks as if he were a political prisoner: "Gentle-men, I have not the honor to belong to your class. . . ." In this astonishing remark, self emerges as historical definition.

That the idea of the self should be mobilized as a mandate for action is part of the development of the liberalism—both political and metaphysical—that comes to the fore in the late eighteenth century—liberalism not just as social program or political movement, but as a new historical temper.

Liberalism in its heroic phase constitutes one of the great revolutionary events of our history. The richness of modern culture would have been impossible without the animating lib-eral idea. The self as a central convention of modern literature depends upon the presence of liberalism. The dynamic of plot in the novel, based as it is on new assumptions about human mobility, would be quite inconceivable without the shaping premises of liberalism.

All of these terms—self, liberalism, Romanticism—have a way of melding into one great enterprise of renewal. "The deepest driving force of the liberal idea of the Enlightenment," writes Karl Mannheim, "lay in the fact that it appealed to the free will and kept alive the feeling of being indeterminate and unconditioned. . . ." This new moral and imaginative power promises a dismissal of intolerable constraints, speaks for pre-viously unimagined rights, declares standards of candor and sincerity. For the whole of modern culture, liberalism releases energies of assertion, often as energies of opposition. Without some such cluster of values and perceptions, how could the nineteenth-century novelist so much as have conceived a *Bild-ungsroman* in which the self attains itself through a progress within and against society, or struggles to escape the locked frames of social role?

Let me now glance at a few central texts, starting with Rousseau's *Confessions*.

Not the whole of Rousseau, not the Rousseau whom Ernst Cassirer presents as the author of a coherent political philosophy, not the Rousseau of that problematic notion "the general will"; but the Rousseau who said about himself that he was more changeable than "a Proteus, a chameleon. . . ." If we choose to see Rousseau as moving from speculative thought to personal apologia, we can focus upon his as an exemplary and undisciplined—exemplary, in part, because undisciplined— personality, one of those whose tumult and self-penetrating chaos ushers in the modern age. William Hazlitt, a critic born sixty-five years after Rousseau but of a romantic generation which could still read him as its contemporary, observed: "The only quality which [Rousseau] possessed in an eminent degree . . . was extreme sensibility . . . an acute and even morbid feeling of that which related to his own impressions. . . . He had the most intense consciousness of his own existence. . . ." This "intense consciousness" was both a sign of a moral revolution being enacted in his time and what Jean Starobinski calls "a manifesto from the third estate, an affirmation that the events of his inner life . . . have an absolute importance. . . ."

Saint Augustine confessed to God; Rousseau to a packed house, sometimes filled with enemies, sometimes with merely his own shifting selves. Saint Augustine hoped to make confession into a discipline; for it would be an affirmation, at once humbling and flaunting. Saint Augustine sought to bend himself to Christ, Rousseau to justify the contortions of self to anyone who might listen. Saint Augustine sought truth, Rousseau sincerity. Seeking truth, Augustine found, at the least, sincerity; seeking sincerity, Rousseau unleashed a memorable persona with a lively touch of scandal. For Augustine, anything like the self would be a barrier to relation with God; for Rousseau, the self is the public creation of a private face, sometimes a scolding judge before whom he pleads guilty with every expectation of going free.

Rousseau's *Confessions* opens with the declaration that he has resolved on "an enterprise which has no precedent." He will offer "a portrait in every way true to nature, and the man I shall portray will be myself." A few sentences later occurs the crucial word "sincerity," that mode of feeling through which he, Jean-Jacques, at once "vile" and "noble," will bare his soul to the "Eternal Being"! A not inconsiderable project, and as I read this slippery character, he is quite aware of how improbable his "enterprise" is. Which only prods him, with a sort of malicious sincerity, to further displays of self, a subject of which he never tires.

Yes, he will be sincere, he will reveal the truth about his inner being, he will strip everything away to reach an essential self that the world has only glimpsed. It is unique, this self, he declares with a pride that to a Christian must seem appalling (as it did to Kierkegaard, who in his *Journal* remarks that Rousseau "lacks . . . the ideal, the Christian ideal, to humble him . . . and to sustain his efforts by preventing him from falling into the reverie and sloth of the poet. Here is an example

that shows how hard it is for a man to die to the world"—
something that a writer with one thing more to write will rarely
do).

But the fact is that the more Rousseau reveals his turmoil,
his inner conflicts, his misdeeds through the flaring chaos of
his self, the more persuaded we are likely to be that, yes, he
is unique; and, still more odd, the more we are persuaded that
never before was there anyone quite like this Jean-Jacques, the
more we feel that this touching monster shares many traits with
us; and, oddest of all, the knowledge that there are contradictions here does not trouble us; we may even feel that this tangle
of response approaches a sentiment (if not a statement) of truth.

Everything that can be said about the versions of the self
in literature composed during the age of Proust, Kafka, and
Beckett—"I wanted," says Hermann Hesse's Demian, "only
to try to live in obedience to the promptings which came from
my true self. Why was that so very difficult?"—has already
been said by Rousseau. So it is not quite true, as historians of
consciousness sometimes claim—I will be making the same
mistake in a few moments—that the self in literary representations has "disintegrated" over time. The self in Rousseau
begins as a state of disintegration, a state it abides with ease,
sometimes with a tear of shame or a smirk of remorse.

The writer who declares he will be utterly sincere, indeed,
the first truly sincere voice in the history of mankind, ends
as a virtuoso of performance. As Starobinski remarks, "The
discovery of the self coincides with the discovery of the
imagination: the two discoveries are in fact the same." Pro-
gramatically to make a claim for sincerity may already entail
an element of bad faith, may itself contain an alloy of insincerity

(the reasons for this having been grasped by Rousseau himself in his attack on the theater). Sincerity is not likely to make its appearance as an announcement. If it can be had at all, it must (Whitman again) sidle in as a portion of speech; always more halting and less articulate, surely less well-rounded, than Rousseau's wonderful prose. But why should his effort to reach an unprecedented sincerity have resulted in a performance in which "natural man" turns out to be a shifty historical actor? Because his enterprise yields the hubris of supposing that a human being, even one so keen as Rousseau, is capable of sufficient self-knowledge. Because it means replacing the fragments of candor with the fullness of program—and a program, be it "noble" or "base," signifies a performance undertaken to some outer measure.

Still, may not the partly sincere or even insincere performance of sincerity—this contrived public self—be in some way authentic? May this not actually be Rousseau's "true self," that is, the only self available to him, as against the much-invoked "inner self" we have all been taught to look for? May not, still further, the "true self" consist in the performance which is perhaps all we have in life?

Rousseau was quite sincere in his yearning for sincerity, but everything about him, especially the public being he had so artfully constructed, militated against that. As he shrewdly noticed, his downfall began the moment he published his first *Discourse*, since from then on, alas, it was all uphill, toward the construction of the most dazzling if frequently repulsive persona of the modern era. His vision of natural man was only a phantasm of civilized man, a compensation for having no escape from civilization and its not-unglorious discontents.

By now, Rousseau has found his place in literature. His thought seems hopelessly entangled by time and commentaries, but his figure looms brilliantly, our ancestor in division, who made his self into a myth of literary consciousness, quite as Byron would, and after him, Lermontov. There is no "real" Rousseau to be ferreted out in research; the Rousseau of the writings is the salvage of time. If I may parody Wallace Stevens: The self is momentary in the mind, but in performance it is immortal.

Brushing aside their enormous differences in style and temper, Hazlitt linked Rousseau and Wordsworth. He saw that the linkage was historical: whatever binds radically different personalities within a defining epoch, perhaps an overflow of consciousness variously mirrored. The self, for both Rousseau and Wordsworth, figures as creed, goal, burden, necessity, sometimes as token of revolution. Wordsworth, wrote Hazlitt, "may be said to create his own materials; his thoughts are his real subjects." Even when placed against great historical events or a natural setting glowing with sublimity, his thoughts center upon the molding of self, that growth which enables him to claim identity ("Possessions have I that are solely mine, / Something within which yet is shared by none").

In his autobiographical poem *The Prelude* Wordsworth cultivates a historically novel sense of the self as emergent, internally riven, and therefore constantly open to misstep, yet finally providing a provisional security of being out of which he the poet, here representative of humanity, can look back upon his earlier years, measuring his personal history against the history of his time. If Rousseau's self is a virtuoso, Wordsworth's is a sober narrative. The self we discover in *The Prelude* seems more hooded and less volatile than that of Rousseau, but what the two writers share is a persuasion that this self, be it psychic actuality or mere shadow of desire, is not fixed unalterably in either nature or historical circumstance. It is created, nurtured, the mark of our freedom. The self is its own child.

Still, what can it mean, in the Wordsworthian climate, to say that man is his own creation? Partly this is a testimony to the powers of imagination, not always distinguishable from the powers of will. The entirety of Wordsworth's thought can be read as a meditation upon the interrelation, sometimes the bewildering mutual disguising, of imagination and will. To imagine a self beyond immediate reach, *to be able* to imagine such a self, is to prod the will to action; it is to awake from the metaphysical slumbers of the past; it is to assert a new history. Tacitly, then, *The Prelude* seems to signify a rejection of all those who dismiss the idea of the self as a mere fiction of unity. Wordsworth locates any possible unity of the self as an arena of conflict, buffeted by historical flux. It is this which prompts one to think of *The Prelude* as an epic of selfhood in which "the transitory Being," as Wordsworth refers to the contemplative "I," replaces the hero of traditional mythic quests.

Is there, however, in Wordsworth's view of things an "original self," an integral prehistorical being endowed by nature? We must beware of reducing a poem to a proposition; what Wordsworth cares about is the experience more than the idea of the self. Still, he does write as if the infant, not yet

soiled by consciousness, awaits that fortunate fall which signals
the growth of the self. Because not yet homeless, the infant is
not yet burdened with self-awareness:

> No outcast he, bewildered and depressed:
> Along his infant veins are interfused
> The gravitation and the filial bond
> Of nature that connect him with the world.

The self carries the brand of alienation, the consciousness
of consciousness, that which we have left after expulsion from
the garden or after being torn from the mother's breast. There
are intimations in *The Prelude* of the therapeutic notion that,
as an endowment of nature, we may recover gifts of childhood
in a journey through a series of false and inadequate selves—
rather like the trail of a romance hero confronting a sequence
of ordeals—and that this will culminate as a healing of self and
a unity of peace. But this journey is perilous, and it is to the
perils that *The Prelude* introduces us. The poem can be seen
as a chronicle of false starts and bewitched wanderings; from
the "unnatural self / The heavy weight of many a weary
day / Not mine, and such as were not made for me," which
is one consequence of the city's false sociality, to those treach-
eries the self can so cunningly generate ("Humility and modest
awe, themselves / Betray me, serving often for a cloak / To a
more subtle selfishness . . ."). Nor is there any reason to
suppose that in this *Bildungsroman* Wordsworth indulges a
notion of a fixed, unitary self, ready like a premade box for
instant use; he speaks, rather, of seeing himself at times as
"Two consciousnesses, conscious of myself / And of some
other Being. . . ."

Nor does the precious if fragile unity of being celebrated at the close of *The Prelude* constitute an end, for there is no end, only quest. This implies a quasi-religious if hardly Christian vision, finding its strongest imprint in "spots of time," set pieces focusing upon lighted moments of memory. These "spots of time" evoke an achieved (not a given) capacity for the peace that might yet surpass understanding, through a loving submission to nature—yet (a Wordsworthian paradox) also through the activity of the imagination. In J. V. Cunningham's words, this entails "the problem [of] the relationship of a man and his environment, and the reconciliation of these two in poetry and thus in life."

The journey at rest but not concluded, there may follow what Geoffrey Hartman calls "the special consciousness that can bring a man home to himself"—a home not soon found, not without confusions and misdirections, even to the journey's end.

There is a lovely passage in *The Prelude* about "the Boy," apprentice in selfhood, who stands by "the glimmering lake" and blows "mimic hootings to the silent owls / That they might answer him. . . ." "A lengthened pause / Of silence . . ." follows, and the boy would yield himself to the environment, so that "the visible scene would enter unawares into his mind / With all its solemn imagery, its rocks, / Its woods, and that uncertain heaven. . . ." Like many other nineteenth-century writers, Wordsworth enacts a spiritualization of nature—and also an accommodation of nature to human ends—as the basis for healing, which is also a questioning, of the self. And, note well, heaven remains "uncertain."

The interaction of nature and mind postulated by Wordsworth remains a difficulty, perhaps a mystery, for us and for him. It represents a desire, a yearning, in which it may be, as Geoffrey Hartman says, "nature [does] the best it can to act as Heaven's substitute." Nevertheless, through this uncertain struggle, with the imagination as prompter, the self is formed.

I have read *The Prelude* largely in terms of Wordsworth's own perception of the formation of his self, but there is of course another reading, one that sees his strong valuation of selfhood as a consequence or sign of a displacement of political aspiration, a turning inward after the disappointment of political hopes—which makes the poem an anticipation of post-totalitarian literature in our own century, also charting journeys from public to inner life. At various points Wordsworth himself seems to endorse this reading, as a subtheme to his main one. These two ways of approaching Wordsworth's journey of selfhood can, with a bit of jostling, be reconciled, but what matters, in any case, is that the realization of self be seen as a consequence of costly journeys, whether toward revolutionary Paris or the poet's idyllic birthplace. The Wordsworthian theme, however placed, is that our inner existence can become a mode of heroism too, even if without sword and shield, and that it is we who can make it such.

In no other writer does the idea of the self—the self as host and shaper of consciousness—attain such centrality as in George Eliot; and in no other writer does the self become the object of such severe moral scrutiny. The novels of the later George Eliot treat consciousness—for her, the very stuff of selfhood—as a gift; but then, in accord with her "religion of humanity," that grey solace for the fading of the gods, consciousness becomes a *project* for mankind. It is only conscious-ness that keeps us from slipping into the abyss of egotism and its nihilist reduction; yet, as if to recall that at heaven's gate there is a byway to hell, consciousness also comes to be its own intimate betrayer, breeding Wordsworth's "more subtle selfishness. . . ."

Egoism engulfs the self. The freedom that is the reward of consciousness swells into despotic possessiveness. If conscious-ness is indeed to serve as a solacing companion, it must now turn upon itself, ruthless in judgment. The "abstract individ-ual" of the eighteenth century gives way in George Eliot's novels to a social individual who exists only by virtue of the presence of others. To this acceptance of solidarity, the only alternative, as George Eliot graphically demonstrates, is the kind of moral monster—also a self, indeed, preeminently a self, as fearful parody—who dominates her last novel, *Daniel Deronda*.

But is there not something terrifying in George Eliot's invocation of consciousness? Is that all? Nothing else beyond or within? Yes, that is all we have, replies the sibyl with her steely warmth, and precisely because she knows how weak a bulwark the self can be, she makes her fictions into muted calls for sympathy, hoping, as she puts it, to "mitigate the harshness of all fatalities."

Those characters in *Middlemarch*—Dorothea, Lydgate, Casaubon—who serve as centers of consciousness also become, in consequence, its victims. Almost all of them yield to the low clamor of self which, by a turn of mischief, can also mask itself as a favorite of consciousness. Still, her characters wrest a few moments of insight, if only in grasping how sadly limited these can be. Her major characters think and, thinking, suffer.

The stress upon consciousness in her earlier novels had implied, I suppose, at least a partial attribution of positive moral value. How could she not have slipped into the assumption, so tempting to the secular mind, that a history of consciousness must display signs of progress? But in *Daniel Deronda* she faces up to the chasm between consciousness and value, self and ethic. Through the character of Grandcourt, that supercilious aristocrat who embodies a *system* of dehumanized relations and who, as she remarks in passing, is ruthless enough to "govern a difficult colony," she invokes the barbarism that shadows civilization as a double of the cultivated self. Grandcourt cannot be said to lack consciousness—he has it in abundance—yet he takes a peculiar pleasure in employing it for a "principled" brutality. The structured self here becomes a pleased witness of the very things George Eliot had supposed it would enable us to resist. In creating Grandcourt, this monster in and of civilization, George Eliot the novelist achieved a triumph, but at the expense of George Eliot the moralist, who must now acknowledge that before the spectacle of a Grandcourt consciousness—hers, ours—may be helpless.

Trapped in dilemmas to which her truth-seeking imagination has driven her, George Eliot turns in her novels to that sustained flow of commentary, at once impassioned and ironic, severe but not systematic, which forms the moral spine of her work. So commanding is the Eliot voice that we can readily suppose that the rendered consciousness of her characters is a tributary of the consciousness of their creator. The voice of George Eliot as narrator envelops her characters in an arc of judgment and compassion. It is a voice that comes, so to say, to serve as the source of the characters' existence, the self that is the mother of all these imagined selves.

It is in Whitman's poetry, and especially "Song of Myself," that the idea of self takes on its most benign expressions and copious modes, a sort of luxurious, relaxed experimentalism accommodating both the private and the transcendent. Democratic man is transfigured into a democratic hero: "plumb in the uprights, well entretied, braced in the beams / Stout as a horse, affectionate, haughty, electrical." Whitman's images are plebeian, those, you might say, of an ecstatic carpenter. At once individual and "en masse," Whitman's democratic hero, cast in American easiness, sees no problem in adopting numerous tasks, venturing a wide variety of roles, and then skidding back to the solitary self.

"Song of Myself" carves out a transit between self and all that is nonself, between the Walt hugging secrets to his bosom, a furtive, somewhat deracinated bohemian, and the assured self that enters into, merges with, and shares an easy moment with all other selves. But Whitman's notion of the self is sharply different from that of Rousseau, in that he has little taste for revelation or display, and different also from that of Wordsworth, in that he cares more for simultaneous enactments, shifty changes of role, than for a coherent, formative history. In Whitman the self serves as a normative supposition projecting the democratic hero who is of and with "the roughs and beards and space and ruggedness and nonchalance. . . ." Prototype of a "new order"—we have still to see it—in which "every man shall be his own priest" and carry himself "with the air . . . of [a person] who never knew how it felt to stand

in the presence of superiors," this envisaged self yokes Prot-
estant individuality with New World friendliness and is treated
by Whitman with humor, even mockery—as if to acknowledge
the impudence of native visions!

The self of the poem is fluid, defined by unwillingness to
rest in definition, committed, with both an ingenuous faith and
comic skepticism, to the belief in *possibility* which so delights
and bedevils Americans. At times the self of the poem comes
to resemble a protean demigod absorbing all creatures who yet
avoids grandiosity by the grace, rather infrequent among demi-
gods, of having a sense of humor. After one of his rhapsodic
catalogues, Whitman writes: "And these one and all tend inward toward me, and I tend outward to them, / And such as
it is to be of these more or less I am." That *more or less* is
priceless as an intimation of Whitman's distancing fraternity.

At times the self of the poems sinks to an almost mineral
tranquillity, a quasi-mystical dissolution of consciousness. The
famous "oceanic" impulse that disturbs some readers because
it seems to blur distinctions in quality of being, is here acceptable because we see that the self of the poem also acts out
of a deep anxiety and loneliness. Reduce the cosmic straining
of "Song of Myself" from philosophical grandiosity to a common human tremor, and Whitman's possession of all possible
selves, like his corresponding withdrawal from them, becomes
familiar.

"I have no mockings or arguments, I witness and wait."
"Agonies are one of my changes of garments." Such lines are
spoken by a stranger in the midst, planted in the very milieu
from which he moves apart. In a splendid phrase Whitman
speaks of the "knit of identity," that is, the self composed of

a multitude of experiences, feelings, and intuitions, all braided into a loose unity. The self becomes an agent of potentiality, and Whitman, most amiable of pragmatists, tries on a range of new ones, yet keeps returning to his own center: "I have pried through the strata and analyzed to a hair / And counselled with doctors and calculated close and found no sweeter fat than sticks to my own bones."

The rejection of the self as mere mental consciousness finds its keenest novelistic voice in D. H. Lawrence.* He invites us to respond to his characters as Ursula, in *The Rainbow*, responds to the life about her: "She could not understand, but she seemed to feel far-off things." These "far-off things" are not only of immensities and absolutes, the "infinite world, eternal, unchanging"; they are also close within, deep down, untapped. Lawrence said he wanted to drop "the old stable ego," or what we call the coherent self, and move toward "a stratum [of being] deeper than I think anyone has ever gone in the novel."

In *The Rainbow* he strives to represent states of being which his characters feel to be overpowering yet find hard to describe. "There is another seat of consciousness than the brain and nervous system," wrote Lawrence in a letter to Bertrand Russell, "there is the blood-consciousness, with the sexual connection holding the same relation as the eye, in seeing, to the mental consciousness. . . . This is one half of life, belonging to the darkness."

Through metaphor and analogy, since he cannot find a

---

* Much of the material in the following paragraphs on D. H. Lawrence appears also in "Lawrence: Another Language Almost."

denotative vocabulary for this "deeper stratum," Lawrence explores "the other seat of consciousness." Might this "other seat" be what we usually call the unconscious? Admittedly, the distinction between "blood-consciousness" and "the unconscious" is vague; if we could speak with clarity about such matters, there would be no need to speak at all. But I venture that there is a distinction of sorts between the two: because Lawrence spoke of a variant of consciousness, and because this "deeper stratum," unlike the unconscious, can now and again be reached by his characters on their own.

Through long, loping alternations of submission to and resistance against this "state of being," some of the Brangwens (the family in *The Rainbow*) know this "state" or at least can feel themselves in its grip. Acutely or drowsily, they sense that in some nether layer of consciousness there swirls a supply of energy, and that this energy is not to be controlled entirely by will or intelligence—on the contrary, these characters feel that fulfillment can come only through yielding to these deep-seated rhythms, rhythms in which they move toward union with another person and then withdraw into the solitariness. Lawrence's characters live out the thrust and pull of the forces churning within themselves; sometimes throw up sterile barriers of resistance; but except for Ursula, who represents the third and youngest generation of Brangwens, they do not propose or think it possible to name these forces.

Naming things, identifying the deeper surges of instinctual life, becomes a possibility only for Ursula's generation, though by the previous or second generation, that of Will Brangwen, there is a groping after meanings that elude words. This wish to describe the inner actions of psychic life coincides with and may even be a consequence of a yearning to move "upward" spiritually, a yearning that can be felt even when Lawrence's characters are still in the drowse of sensual experience.

Naming things is something about which Lawrence feels sharp inner conflict. He sees the urge to name things as a striving after "higher" values, but also as a sign of the sickness afflicting an overrationalized consciousness. He admires those who live in "another seat of consciousness than the brain and the nervous system," he even makes them into exemplars of his fiction; yet he is himself, like those characters, such as Ursula, who are closest to him, a creature of "the brain and nervous system." The writer who would abandon or at least minimize that "system" cannot help resorting to it. Lawrence writes most familiarly about characters who have entered what he calls "the finer, more vivid circle of life," the circle of mental consciousness. For only the latter are capable of so much as imagining "another seat of consciousness"—those already lodged there do not know or need to know it.

The "deeper" stratum Lawrence seeks to evoke consists of intervals in long swings of psychic-emotional energy, into "the darkness" and then back to the outer air. There are mergings with others, sometimes ecstatic, as if to break into the marrow of being, and sometimes sullen, as if in fear of losing identity; and then comes a bruised solitary apartness, the stuff out of which a self is formed.

Yet a reading of *The Rainbow* leaves one with a question. We can readily say that the solitariness of Lawrence's characters, their periods of withdrawal, are the stuff out of which a self is formed: that, after all, is a familiar notion to readers of the nineteenth-century novel. But may not the phase of merging into "the darkness," also be—not a blotting-out of self—but another way of renewing the self? May not Lawrence's enterprise be one of prompting a series of tentative, connected selves, available upon need and retracted when not? And may these not be present within a deeper stratum, call it "blood-consciousness" or the unconscious? The Lawrence who would probe beneath mental consciousness is also the Lawrence who aspires to its "higher" levels. So the self is not obliterated. It may for a time be "lost," it may be transformed or immersed within some collective flow; but it returns, a witness to its subterranean adventures.

I would have liked to look at the vicissitudes to which the idea of the self has been subjected in twentieth-century literature, through both monstrous expansion and radical shrinkage of characters, as well as through the manifestations—imperial, disintegrative, muffled—of the authorial presence. An extreme instance would be that of Samuel Beckett, in whose work occurs a dispossession or emptying-out of characters as selves, so that in a play like *Endgame* a world of feeling remembered and mourned for comes into juxtaposition with an emptied present, the "zero-level" condition in which Beckett's characters suffer. But in Beckett's work the self also emerges as an overpowering presence: his own voice, with its lucid speech and biting wit: "You must go on, I can't go on, I'll go on."

I approach the end, without having finished or, perhaps, being able to finish. In recent literary and, to some extent, political theory, the self has suffered demotion, even dispossession. I have tried to get a handle on this school of thought, but with shaky results. There is the problem of verbal opacity, which I find a formidable barrier. So I can only venture a few possible reasons for the demotion of the idea of the self.

- It is said that the idea of the self is phallocentric, a sign of traditional male domination. This claim is partly true, but since it is made through or as a historical approach, it is not in principle so different from the one I have been using here: namely, to see the self as a concept with its own history forming a narrative within history at large. If there is value to such an approach, then there is no reason why the idea of the self need be or remain phallocentric, no reason why it cannot be extended to serve as a basis for rectifying inequities of gender.

- The idea of the self, providing lonely moderns with "metaphysical consolation," is a notion, we are told, that a postsymbolic view of language—language self-subsistent, perhaps autonomous—can now dispense with. There is a philosophical tradition, reaching back to parts of Nietzsche, which rejects the idea of the self. But the evidence compiled by Professor Stanley Corngold in his learned study of German literature seems decisively to show that in some version the idea of the self has been central to the work of many major literary figures these past two centuries, and, more problematically, that even Nietzsche, while at some points disdaining the idea of the self, inclines at other points to recoup a version of it. The self, it would appear, can be banished only by a banishing self. At least for purposes of literary discourse—I cannot enter the philosophical discussion—this historical evidence takes on significant weight.

- A fairly innocent reason for demoting the idea of the self is provided by Richard Poirier. Writing in a quasi-Emersonian vein, he argues that the very idea of the self, fixed because defined, blocks further vistas of possibility, closing off a "circle" in that endless sequence of "circles" which forms the schema of Emersonianism. One such possibility—but now Poirier seems to write in a Foucaultian vein—is "the abolition of the human," and the question whether this "is a good or bad idea," he adds, "is not to be decided by a show of hands." Indeed not! Exactly what "the abolition of the human" might mean Poirier does not make crystal clear, nor do I suppose he can, although the nonchalance with which he puts forward the notion strikes me as breathtaking. But is it really true that to hold to an idea of the self is to foreclose on the endlessness of the Emersonian "circles"? Cannot our idea of the self expand with the expansion of those "circles" of possibility, perhaps now and then to reach an "oceanic sense" of a transindividual or collective self, and may it not also contract with the contraction of the "circles" into a grim acknowledgment of nothingness?

• Perhaps the most powerful assault on the idea of the self is one that identifies it, tacitly or explicitly, with the historical disabilities of humanist liberalism. I cite two telling passages from Michel Foucault:

> By humanism I mean the totality of discourse through which Western man is told: "Even though you don't exercise power, you can still be a ruler. Better yet, the more you deny yourself the exercise of power, the more you submit to those in power, then the more this increases your sovereignty." . . . In short,

humanism is everything in Western civilization that *restricts the desire for power* . . . (emphasis in original).

And

It is a source of profound relief to think that man is only a recent invention, a figure not yet two centuries old, a new fold in our knowledge, and that he will disappear again as soon as that knowledge has discovered a new form.

Foucault's first passage bears a distressing resemblance to the notion that "bourgeois democracy" is a mere façade for class domination. As for the second . . . well, we can only wait and see what the "new form" replacing man will be like. So far, most candidates have not been very attractive. But what interests me most is not so much the question why is this being said as the question why have these statements somehow become apparently plausible at this historical moment.

Have we reached a breaking point? Is it possible to argue the question of the self, especially with its more intransigent opponents? Do we not have here two sharply contrasting narratives of modern experience which can only be placed side by side in the hope of a later enlightenment?

So let me declare my bias. The idea of the self has been a liberating and revolutionary step, perhaps the most liberating and revolutionary, toward the goal of a communal self-humanization. I will cite, for support or comfort, two utterly different writers: Karl Marx: "The critique of religion ends with the doctrine that *man* is the highest being for man, hence with the categorical imperative to overthrow all conditions in which man is a degraded, enslaved, neglected, contemptible being." And in two lines of verse, Hölderlin:

> *Der Mensch will sich selber fühlen . . .*
> *Sich aber nicht zu fühlen, ist der Tod.*

> Man wants to have a sense of self . . .
> Not to have a sense of self is death.

Style and the Novel: Some Preliminary Paragraphs

[*Note: When he died, Irving Howe was at work on several entries about style and fiction for* A Critic's Notebook. *None was completed but each had several paragraphs that seemed worth including in this book. They follow here as a series of ideas rather than as a developed argument.*]

I HAVE NO grand or overarching theory of style in the novel, only some empirical observations concerning what one can and cannot say about style in the novel. I have invoked the help of several novelists and critics, for this is a subject about which one needs all the help one can get.

The very nature of the language employed imposes upon writers distinct patterns, qualities, and limitations, perhaps more than they recognize. The English language leaves its stamp upon the work of all prose writers who employ it, and so too do the Russian and Hebrew languages on the writers who employ them. Even so basic a matter as the presence or absence of articles is not left to individual decision.

Novelists employing a "common style," which may be no more than the favored style of their moment, are harder to identify, at least through their stylistic devices, than those who "deviate" into idiosyncratic styles. Laurence Sterne is easier to identify stylistically than Henry Fielding.

If, as Robert Frost once said, poetry is what gets lost in translations of poetry, style is what gets lost in translations of prose fiction. I cite an instance from personal knowledge. Several decades ago the novels of a popular Yiddish writer named Sholem Asch were put into English by a gifted literary man, Maurice Samuel. Not known for reticence, Samuel once told me that in rendering Asch's fiction into English he had frequently to "lower the temperature." In the Yiddish world Asch was famous for a "tempestuous" style, brimming with pathos and high rhetoric. It was a style that stirred many Yiddish readers, though not all Yiddish writers. What Samuel offered the readers of Asch's novels was translation—it might, in Robert Lowell's phrase, have been called "imitation"—in which the rhetoric was eased, the pathos dried, the style chastened. In a sense Samuel was rendering Asch a service, since a literal rendering would have seemed overheated in English.

Prose style is lost as poetry is lost, yet we need translations. It is style that can provide a measure of what translators can and cannot do, style that forces upon them improvisations of difference.

Many of the seeming choices of language, which are seen as the signals of style regarding epistemology, are actually given by the language itself.

In George Meredith's novels there's just too much mannerism of language, too much dandyish display—the sort of bad prose that is sometimes praised as prose poetry. Actually, Meredith's best novel is his great sequence of short poems, *Modern Love*, in which he writes with a gravity and restraint one wishes for in his novels. The man was infatuated with language, mad for metaphors, wanton in exuberance. He loved his style, loved it too much, and his style turned out to be his downfall, not because it is complicated (so is Proust's, so is Conrad's) but because it is an exercise in vanity: lyrical apostrophes, sonorous approximations set up for display.

There was a time, some decades ago, when novelists were frequently praised as stylists. The lines of division seemed clear. Flaubert and Henry James, Elizabeth Bowen and Virginia Woolf: such writers were stylists. By contrast Trollope wrote with a pedestrian drabness, Dreiser wrote like a lumbering oaf, and Frank Norris (joked John Berryman) had the style of a shaggy wet dog. Behind the praise for the fictional stylists there was an assumption that what matters in a novel is language as an autonomous and crucial element—diction of a disciplined elegance or an epigrammatic pointedness. If such novelists were not quite poets, they were near-poets.

In discussing style in prose fiction there is a problem not often remarked upon: large parts of most novels consist of dialogue. Now, in some novels, like those of the late Henry James and a few of Joseph Conrad's, the characters speak in a highly stylized language, not at all naturalistic—a language that uncannily, sometimes uncomfortably resembles that of the author. What the writer seeks in such novels is not the rendering of common speech such as we may suppose people in actual life might employ. The characters in *An Awkward Age* speak Jamesian English, quite as if it were their birthright—as in a sense it is—and it hardly matters whether, by the largest stretch of charity, we can imagine any group of actual English men and women speaking in this highly "artificial" but also strikingly brilliant way. What matters is that their stylized speech contributes efficiently to the total effect of what James wishes to achieve. So, to a notable extent, there is a stylistic continuity between James and his characters: they exist in a special world we might call Jamesland.

What does this style suggest? First, ambiguity, the difficulty of assured perception, the likelihood of error, and the probability that different observers will see different things. The style also suggests a certain amount of hedging: the action of a mind moving through different observations and tones, from high gravity to low farce, yet hesitant before the awesomeness of understanding and the responsibilities of naming. And then, the style points to a certain musing: the mulling over of a mature intelligence, extremely worldly yet disenchanted with worldliness, holding these two attitudes in balance, looking upon human affairs from a notable distance, as if preparing for an exit from all the troubles these entail.

A style may become habitual, even obsessive, reflecting a writer's deepest, often unconscious, habits. The style of the late Henry James is not just "appropriate" to the themes of his last several novels; it is by now his "natural" (that is, highly stylized) mode of expression, an emanation, as it were, of his ways of thinking and feeling, and it is used in radically different situations as the very medium through which his imagined actions must flow and imagined characters must be regarded. The elaborate syntax, the qualifying phrases, the sudden shifts from abstraction to colloquialism, all reflect the processes of Henry James's mind.

Most novelists do not have one consistent style; they shift from one linguistic plane to another, like composers who change key. The greater the desire for fictional verisimilitude, the more likely will the novelist brush aside refinements of style. Not always; what I have just said does not hold for Proust or Nabokov. But then, I was only making a rough generalization.

Some devices that may help create a style: heavy dependence on abstraction, frequent use of present tense, habitual evocation of similarities through parallel structure, a tendency to place feelings in syntactical positions of agency, a trick of underplaying causal words, hackneyed hyperbole for comic effect, heavy use of professional idiom (Smollett, Dickens). When we see a verbal effect (Faulkner's long sentences, or Shabtai's), we tend *post hoc* to find a rationale for it. Sometimes rightly, sometimes not.

Any language persuades its speakers to see the universe in certain ways, to the exclusion of other ways. It thereby limits the possibilities of choice for any writer.

There are clearly subjects that cannot be accommodated by certain styles. To cite a somewhat comic instance: Can anyone imagine the material of Norman Mailer's story "The Time of Her Time" in the language of the late Henry James? Or can one imagine the material of Smollett in the language of Virginia Woolf? Well, just barely—perhaps by a great master like Joyce, who could do almost anything.

Tolstoy: Five Comments

Did Anna Have to Die?

In his book *Personal Impressions* Isaiah Berlin prints an account
of a lengthy conversation he had in 1945 with Anna Akhmatova, the great Russian poet. Why, Akhmatova asks him,

> Why did Anna Karenina have to be killed? . . . As soon as she
> leaves Karenin, everything changes; she suddenly becomes a
> fallen woman in Tolstoy's eyes. . . . Of course there are pages
> of genius, but the basic morality is disgusting. Who punishes
> Anna? God? No, society; that same society the hypocrisy of
> which Tolstoy is never tired of denouncing. In the end he tells
> us that she repels even Vronsky. Tolstoy is lying: he knew better
> than that. The morality of *Anna Karenina* is the morality of
> Tolstoy's wife, of his Moscow aunts; he knew the truth, yet he
> forced himself, shamefully, to conform to philistine convention.
> Tolstoy's morality is a direct expression of his own private life,

his personal vicissitudes. When he was happily married he wrote *War and Peace*, which celebrates family life. After he started hating Sofia Andreevna, but was not prepared to divorce her because divorce is condemned by society, and perhaps by the peasants too, he wrote *Anna Karenina* and punished her for leaving Karenin. When he was old and no longer lusted so violently for peasant girls, he wrote *The Kreutzer Sonata*, and forbade sex altogether.

To this vivid account Berlin adds the remark, "Perhaps this summing up was not meant too seriously: but Akhmatova's dislike of Tolstoy's sermons was genuine. She regarded him as an egocentric of immense vanity, and an enemy of love and freedom." Just how seriously Akhmatova meant her attack on Tolstoy we will never know, but it is interesting that D. H. Lawrence, a writer utterly different from her, had a similar view of Tolstoy's novel, though in somewhat cruder form. Lawrence wrote:

> Why, when you look at it, all the tragedy comes from Vronsky's and Anna's fear of society. . . . They couldn't live in the pride of their sincere passion, and spit in Mother Grundy's eye. And that, that cowardice, was the real "sin." The novel makes it obvious, and knocks old Leo's teeth out.

Well, old Leo's teeth are not so easily knocked out. Provocative as the remarks of Akhmatova and Lawrence may be, they suffer from a common fault: they fail to consider Anna Karenina as a character in a novel, as she actually appears in Tolstoy's pages.

Anna is so sexually vibrant, so striking in her beauty and

charm, that one can easily forget how limited are her social views and circumstances. The wife of a high czarist official, Anna is a woman completely part of the Russian upper classes. At no point does she express any explicit criticism of the values that inform her society and her class, let alone any rebellious sentiments. She is not a George Sand or a Frieda Lawrence, not even a George Eliot. Tolstoy is quite clear about this in a passage that comes shortly after Anna has told Karenin about her affair with Vronsky:

> She felt that the position she enjoyed in society, which had seemed of so little consequence that morning, was precious to her after all, and that she would not have the strength to exchange it for the shameful one of a woman who has deserted her husband and child to join her lover; that, however she might struggle, she could not be stronger than herself. She would never know freedom in love. . . .

Especially telling are the words, "she could not be stronger than herself"—something that a self-declared rebel might be supposed to be. Until this point Tolstoy has shrewdly, with what might be called his sexual cunning, persuaded us of Anna's attractiveness. He relies very little on direct statement, knowing that it is seldom effective in this respect, but instead registers the impressions Anna makes on other characters, most strikingly in the incident toward the end of the novel where the upright Levin, meeting her, with his disposition toward righteousness, succumbs to her completely. Anna's power of attraction clearly rests on a strong, increasingly asserted sexuality, especially of course for Vronsky; when he first pursues her, she experiences "a feeling of joyful pride," the pride of a beautiful woman. Her sexuality is not aggressive, except a little toward the end, when unhappiness prods her to an exercise of her powers; but in the main, it is a sexuality that is simply part of her splendid being. Yet even though she is able to rise above, or, if you prefer, sink below, the norms and customs of her social milieu, she makes no effort to deny or reject these. Her passion is neither sustained nor spoiled by an idea.

And that is precisely what makes Anna so interesting. An intellectual rebel against the norms of nineteenth-century Russian society might well engage our sympathies, but in a way less dramatic, less internalized than by the situation Tolstoy creates. Anna Karenina is not struggling for a new mode or path in life, either for herself or for her sex; she cares only about being with the man she loves, quite apart from any larger social or moral issues. Yet this soon becomes the root of her dilemma. The love between Anna and Vronsky, based as it is on a fine mixture of sexual attraction and personal sympathies, brings her into a deadly clash with society, a clash she never desires nor quite understands. Indeed, I would say that the power of the novel depends on the fact that Anna remains a conventional woman—intelligent, sensitive, even bold—but still a conventional woman driven by the strength of her feelings into an unconventional role she cannot in principle defend. She feels her love to be good, she believes her behavior is bad.

If my account, so far, has any merit, then the question to be asked is not Why must Anna be killed? A real-life Anna would probably not kill herself, but would drag out her years unhappily, with or without Vronsky. For certain kinds of readers, her death is to be seen as a mere novelistic convention, a device for rounding out the plot. But I think the real question, drawing upon the entirety of the action provided by Tolstoy, is not the death of Anna; it is the impossibility of the life she has chosen with Vronsky—an impossibility that finds its final realization in her suicide. In saying this, I should add that, as drawn by Tolstoy, Vronsky is a decent and honorable man who loves Anna and suffers because of her suffering. The two are trapped simply because it is impossible for people like them—which is to say, almost everyone—to live "outside" society. Portrayed as it is with a protective tenderness, the love of Anna and Vronsky seems deeply affecting: Tolstoy offers no judgment, either for himself or on behalf of his aunts; but this love remains unsupported by any principle (or delusion) strong enough to enable them to resist the judgments of the society in which they must continue to live.

There is a revealing incident when Anna and Vronsky go off to live comfortably in Venice. Cut off from his usual pursuits, Vronsky decides to take up painting, perhaps with some hope for self-fulfillment, perhaps simply to pass the time. ("Soon he felt a desire spring up in his heart for desires.") Anna and Vronsky meet a Russian painter named Mikhailov, an irritable fellow but a serious artist, and through his unspoken but harsh judgment of Vronsky's painting we recognize a dismissal of artistic dilettantism. Vronsky himself, acknowledging as much, abandons his painting and returns with Anna to Russia. He is a nobleman, an officer and sportsman, unable to live for long apart from his "natural" milieu. Meanwhile Mikhailov's view of Vronsky's painting has a certain impact on Anna's passing notion that she will write children's books. Art and literature cannot provide a sanctuary; step by step Tolstoy tightens the noose of their isolation.

Unlike Vronsky, Anna can for a time live by love alone ("To have him entirely to herself was a continual joy"). Now I suppose this might be taken as evidence of Tolstoy's sexual bias—the belief that while personal relations suffice for women, men need a larger arena of public life. But it is also possible —I think, plausible—to conclude that Tolstoy is showing that, for all their individuality, Anna and Vronsky cannot wrench themselves away from the mores of their historical moment. Even Anna comes to feel that a life devoted entirely to love can be stifling and that, like everyone else, she needs the comforts of sociability, so that when her sister-in-law Dolly comes to visit the house she shares with Vronsky, Anna is delighted.

Just how does society press down on the two lovers? Not through a lack of money. Not through social cuts, though they suffer a few. It is the verdict of society that deprives Anna of her son, Seryozha, and Vronsky, with the best will in the world, cannot quite grasp, let alone share, the pain this brings her. The most severe pressures, however, are internal, within Anna and Vronsky themselves. They introject society's judgments, they feel uneasy in the presence of others, they make others feel uneasy in their presence. The very atmosphere of their life forms a kind of social pressure. Without normal social relations, Anna and Vronsky, even while deeply in love, begin to get on each other's nerves, become suspicious and hurt, start protecting themselves from the wounds each feels the other is inflicting even while aware that neither intends to. It is all insidious, terrible, part of the destructiveness so often interwoven with a great love. Society manifests itself in the most painful way: through their self-consciousness. All this Tolstoy understood with an intuitive exactness, and nothing he ever wrote matches in honesty his portrait of the disintegration of their love.

No, Anna does not have to be killed. She had only to be defeated in the central adventure of her life; after that, the killing hardly matters.

THE RUSSIAN FLY

"He wouldn't hurt a fly," we say about someone of gentle disposition, implying perhaps that such gentleness is ill-suited for the ordinary course of life, since most men would indeed hurt flies. It is normal to destroy them and no moral blame is attached to doing so. The fly serves no visible purpose; it merely gets on our nerves. Yet this wretched little creature, without utility or charm, seems entrenched in the very nature of things. We cannot really imagine a world without flies.

The fly also occupies an ambiguous place in literature, buzzing its way through some of the great Russian novels. One might even speak of a distinctly Russian fly hovering over the heads of Russian heroes and heroines. What the novelists make of the fly they do not say; they do not need to, since the fly lends itself readily to symbolic representation. Some decades ago, in an essay called "The Hovering Fly," Allen Tate remarked upon the passage in the concluding chapter of Dostoevsky's *The Idiot* in which Prince Myshkin, the holy fool, and Rogozhin, the debased sensualist, stand together over the body of the murdered Nastasya Filoppovna. Here, in David Magarshack's translation, is the passage:

> But his eyes had already got used to the dark, and he could make out the whole bed; someone lay asleep on it in an absolutely motionless sleep; not the faintest movement could be heard, not the faintest breath. The sleeper was covered, from head to foot, with a white sheet, but the limbs were, somehow, only faintly visible; only from the raised outlines was it possible to make out that a human being was lying there stretched out full length. All around, in disorder, on the bed, at the foot of the bed, on the arm-chair beside the bed, even on the floor, clothes were scattered—a rich white silk dress, flowers, ribbons. On the little table at the head of the bed diamonds, which had been taken off and thrown down, lay glittering. At the foot of the bed some sort of lace lay in a crumpled heap, and on the white lace, protruding from under the sheet, the tip of a bare foot could be made out; it seemed as though it were carved out of marble, and it was dreadfully still. The prince [Myshkin] looked, and he felt that the longer he looked the more still and death-like the room became. Suddenly a fly, awakened from its sleep, started buzzing, and after flying over the bed, settled at the head of it. The prince gave a start.

If mortality is figured in that "tip of a bare foot" which looks like marble and is dreadfully still, then, adds Allen Tate, the fly "comes to stand in its sinister and abundant life for the privation of life, the body of the young woman on the bed. Here we have one of those conversions of image of which only a great literary talent is capable: life stands for death, but it is a wholly different order of life, and one that impinges upon the human order only in its capacity of scavenger. . . ."

I see what Allen Tate is driving at: a reading against which the buzzing fly will not protest. But neither will it protest against another reading. I would say that the fly "stands for" the sheer indifference of everything not human to everything human. The fly evokes the indifference, perhaps the heartlessness of nature. Generations of men and women come and go, but the Russian fly will remain, nuisance that it is, to reduce our life to a still-smaller speck. It serves here as one of those "natural" symbols creating an all-but-unbounded range of associations.

The Russian fly has also found its way into the work of Tolstoy, at a critical point in *War and Peace*, where Prince Andrei, wounded in the Napoleonic war, lies in a semidelirious state experiencing intimations of death and glimpses of some transcendent force greater even than death, "a happiness beyond the reach of material forces . . . a happiness of the soul alone, the happiness of living!" (Rosemary Edmond's translation).

Prince Andrei hears "a rhythmic murmur of music" and feels "as though a strange, ethereal edifice of delicate needles or splinters was rising over his face, from the very center of it, to the sound of this whispered music." What this music and those needles signify it is hard to say precisely, and perhaps we do not need to; my own sense of it, advanced without certainty, is that they may be sensory signals regarding a possible vision or power that can bring the soul to accept and even triumph over death. (A bit later, knowing that he is "going to die," Prince Andrei feels "remote from everything earthly" and "is conscious of a strange and joyous lightness in his being.")

But Tolstoy, harsh realist that he is, does not stop there. He knows, or at least the rationalist within him knows, that death is not to be conquered. Even when Prince Andrei is experiencing his ecstatic delirium, he also hears "the rustle of cockroaches and the buzzing of a fly that flopped across his pillow and his face." And "each time the fly brushed his cheek it burnt him like a hot iron. . . ."

Again the Russian fly, doing its job, coming to remind Prince Andrei of the transience of flesh and the sovereignty of matter. In this contest between cockroaches and flies against music and needles, Tolstoy embodies his own unbearable struggles of desire, fright, and recognition. We commonly say that the angel of death brushes the cheek of its victim—might not this angel come in the guise of a Russian fly?

Dostoevsky's *The Idiot* and Tolstoy's *War and Peace* are virtually contemporaneous, the former having been published in 1868 and the latter in 1863–69. It is possible that one of these titans borrowed from the other—no one has a monopoly on flies. But it does not really matter, since the perception of the fly is ingrained in common human experience, always the firmest basis for a literary symbol. Tolstoy seems to have resisted more strongly than Dostoevsky the finality of death, but both knew that they, and we, would turn to dust, while the fly—that generic Russian fly—would remain.

The Unheroic Hero of War and Peace

Almost everything about Pierre Bezukhov seems slightly ridiculous. He is painfully clumsy, his body oversized and his movements awkward (in the Rostov drawing room he keeps "blocking the way for everyone"). At his first appearance, he stumbles into a stupid prank, drunkenly tying a policeman to the back of a bear. Called to his father's deathbed, he looks helplessly to a female relative for a cue as to appropriate behavior. In a circle of Russian noblemen, he shouts his enthusiasm for Napoleon. At the climactic moment of his courtship of the poisonous Hélène—an episode that is pure farce—she has to instruct him, "Oh, take off those . . . those . . ." while she points to his spectacles. Remembering, finally, what one is supposed to say on such ecstatic occasions, he mutters, *"Je vous aime!"* Pages later, disillusioned with the French, he harbors a fantasy that he will arrange the assassination of Napoleon.

Such incidents place Pierre Bezukhov in a comic light, even as a bit of a *shlemiehl*, a bumbling baby-giant devoid of style or glamour, and with little social tact. Tolerated at first because of his goodness of heart, and later because of his large inheritance, he is hardly the sort of young man a Russian matron would want for a son-in-law. He cannot charm society, nor win glory in battle, nor become a leader of his country. His life consists of a mixture of thought and embarrassment.

In all this, I would guess, there is a touch of Rousseau, the writer whom Tolstoy, with much admiration, turned to for some of his central ideas. The Rousseau of the *Confessions* is also a clumsy bumbler, poor in speech, prey to fits of embarrassment, helpless before women, yet, like Pierre, keen enough to make himself into a subject for self-mockery. The comparison should be taken lightly, since the overbearing egoism of Rousseau is not really present, or, perhaps more accurately, is gradually disciplined and contained in Pierre. What Tolstoy has done here is to create a comic character bearing some of Rousseau's external traits, but also with a kindly "Russian" mildness that hardly seems to fit Rousseau.

Striding, more often stumbling, across the vast panorama of Tolstoy's epic, Pierre is deliberately molded as a figure rejecting the melancholy posturings of early-nineteenth-century Romanticism, indeed, as a foil and contrast to the Byronic hero, in Russia most notably the hero of Lermontov. Pierre carries nothing of the high mysterious aura that surrounds Prince Andrei, his opposite in the scheme of *War and Peace*, but neither does he suffer from the nihilism which saps Andrei's moral life. This contrast is deliberate, part of the Tolstoyan strategy of undermining the very ethos of national glory which a good part of the book exalts. Throughout his work Tolstoy dramatizes an inner struggle of completely opposed values— in this instance, between the pacific ways of Pierre and the self-sacrificing heroics of Prince Andrei. Another way of putting this might be: between the modest claims of personal life and the larger scheme of national struggle.

Pierre is one of literature's antiheroes, bringing together strands of filiation with both Don Quixote and Sancho Panza, though finally more with the latter. Even in his moments of sublimity—and there are some toward the end of the novel, especially during his captivity by the French—there is a touch of the ridiculous. He accepts this doubleness of his character with a tonic self-derision that keeps him from being contaminated by the caste pride that afflicts so many figures in *War and Peace*. (Pierre is a count, but we do not think of him as an aristocrat.) By contrast, Platon Karatayev, who speaks for the Tolstoyan world-view, is too good or too bland to be true: he is a figment of ideological will. But Pierre, embodying the waywardness of life, rising a little from the slightly ridiculous to the mildly dignified, becomes the central man of the Tolstoyan world.

Now and then Pierre engages in philosophical reflections ("What is wrong? What is right? What should one love and what hate? What is life for and what am I?" etc.), but he does this without a visible yielding to religious faith. And instinctively he knows when to stop, for these are questions he can no more answer than we can. The important thing is to keep asking them. He is, I might add, the least Dostoevskian of Tolstoy's heroes. None is very Dostoevskian, but characters like Prince Andrei and Levin do strive for a spiritual rebirth, if not through a Dostoevskian religious affirmation then at least through a this-worldly moral cleansing. Still, there is a shared desire for spiritual rebirth. Pierre, however, while occasionally tempted by the idea of such a rebirth, finally settles for something more modest: a good life within the world as it exists. Through Pierre, if I may twist a sentence of Kafka's, Tolstoy "takes the side of the world," which means, not least of all, to appreciate the charm and vivacity of Natasha. Of all Tolstoy's major characters, Pierre is the farthest from Dostoevskian aspirations.

True, Pierre is a "seeker," but not of mystical states or sublime moments. He feels that this life is the only one we have or can know, so we might say that he is a restless antihero, a comic seeker battling the limits of flesh and time. It is not as if Tolstoy is always satisfied with this aspect of Pierre, since Tolstoy wants more (he always wants more), but the artist within him, loving what exists, stands firm in behalf of Pierre, so that he becomes the most securely realized character in the book. His interlude with the Masons—though the passage of time may have dulled its significance—is presented as a solemn absurdity but also as an honest quest; gradually Pierre comes to see that, while possessing the appearance of spirituality, they lack the spirit itself. Still, he does not whip himself with remorse; he has the dignity of a man who knows it is his lot to make mistakes.

At the end a family man, moderate in manner and expectations, free of those ascetic creeds that lead men to dismiss small pleasures, tolerant of others and therefore of himself, Pierre seems to live by the code of Shakespeare's "quiet days, fair issue and long life." This is not the stuff from which romantic heroes, or revolutionary ones either, are made. So it comes as a bit of a surprise, but a pleasant one, that in the final chapter of *War and Peace* Pierre seems to be ready to join with the oncoming Decembrists of 1825 in their struggle against absolute monarchy. Perhaps, then, not such "quiet days" after all. But think of how Natasha, who opens his letters day by day, will torment him if he threatens the security of their family life. *War and Peace* ends before the clash between husband and wife can materialize, and Pierre, a man of good will, is spared the test of his convictions. Comedy is protective.

THE OLD MAGICIAN

The old magician stands before me, alien to all, a solitary traveler
through all the deserts of thought in search of an all-embracing truth
which he has not found—I look at him and, although I feel sorry for
the loss, I feel pride at having seen the man. . . .

—MAXIM GORKY,
Reminiscences

Reading the aged Tolstoy stirs the heart. He will not yield to
time, sloth, or nature. He clings to the waist of the lifeforce.
Deep into old age, he battles with the world, more often with
himself, returning in his diaries, fictions, and tracts to the un-
answerable questions that torment him. Blessed old magician,
he is free of literary posture and the sins of eloquence.

"And what truth can there be," he demands of Chekhov,
"if there is death?" Death will not pass him by, and its certainty
dissolves all claims to meaning. (Levin in *Anna Karenina*:
"Here am I working, wanting to accomplish something, and
completely forgetting it must all end—that there is such a thing
as death.") Yet a need for meaning allows him no rest, and
finally it overcomes, provisionally, the absurdity in which he
thinks all must end. The state is evil, a "conspiracy" for "de-
moralizing" and "exploiting" the people, but the artist, as companion to reality, must acknowledge the power and thereby
perhaps the charms of the state. In all but his late writings, the
state takes on a human aspect, by no means the mere enemy
that his "Christian anarchism" would make it out to be. Sexuality comes to seem deeply suspect, a blossom of evil, but

the old man, still in the grip of male vanity, teases Chekhov: "I was an indefatigable fornicator" in my youth, and how about you? Firm in his rationalist version of Christianity, he also lives in the shadow of nihilism. One absolute bruises another.

The most painful but also fruitful of Tolstoy's contradictions is that between the esthetic and the ethical. The writer who would dismiss *Anna Karenina* ("there is no good in it") weeps with emotion upon hearing a Beethoven sonata. Determined to shake off the trivialities of literary representation—yet another triangle, yet another sensitive hero!—he can also write in his 1903 diary: "It's time to die and I'm still thinking up things" for new stories. A year before his death, after producing all those doctrinal tracts (some very brilliant, by the way), he confides to his diary "the desire to do some literary work, but a real desire—not as before with a definite [moral] purpose, but without any purpose—or rather with an invisible purpose beyond my reach: to look into the human soul." The artistic side of Tolstoy may be subdued, it is never quite destroyed.

I love the old magician in the way, I like to imagine, that Chekhov and Gorky loved him: for his relentlessness of mind, his unquenchable desires. Of course he succumbs to moral crankiness, to demented attacks upon Shakespeare, to intemperate demands for temperance. But stubborn and even perverse, he remains faithful to the contradictions of his sensibility. In an astonishing 1903 entry he writes in his diary: "The truth is always accessible to man"—as if it hardly bears notice that for seventy-five years he has been stumbling in the "deserts of thought," imploring like his Father Sergius: "Lord, I believe. Help thou my unbelief!"

In person Tolstoy must often have been insufferable, except of course when he chose to charm the heart out of you. His "style of old age" brought neither calm nor resignation—only weariness. Little time is left to him, and the truth, "always accessible!," keeps slipping away, so that he continues wearily to grope and to search.

"The more infectious art is," he writes in 1899, "the better it is." But whether "this activity [art] is good or bad does not depend only on how far it satisfies the demands of art, i.e., on its infectiousness, but also on how far it satisfies the demands of religious awareness, i.e., morality, conscience." (A few decades later T. S. Eliot would say something fairly similar.) In 1897 Tolstoy speculates on the relations between art and morality: "The esthetic and the ethical are two arms of one lever: to the extent to which one side becomes longer and heavier, the other side becomes shorter and lighter. As soon as a man loses his moral sense, he becomes particularly responsive to the esthetic. . . ."

Tolstoy keeps groping—there is no end to it—for some stable position between the "two arms," a conciliation, if only in thought, between the esthetic and the ethical. He never quite finds it, perhaps because no one can, but in such major fictions as *Master and Man* and *Father Sergius*, as also in parts of his last novel, *Resurrection*, he can write as if indeed he had. The usual complaint that in old age Tolstoy became a scold—for example, the charge of the Tolstoyan scholar R. F. Christian that the late writings are spoiled by an "urge to point a moral"—is beside the point, at least with regard to the fictions. For what happens is not at all an abandonment of art, but a radical change in the esthetic that motivates his art. Nothing, to be sure, in the late Tolstoy reaches the "epic" largesse of *War and Peace* and *Anna Karenina*, but several of the late works are of a very high order. There is now less interest in the free flow of representation, the witnessing of life for its own pleasurable sake. There is now less likelihood of esthetic surprise such as we gain from reading about a character seen in spontaneous behavior. And while the passion for enclosing an entire way of life which informs much nineteenth-century fiction—a passion the earlier Tolstoy shares with Dickens and Balzac—is not wholly suppressed, it is frequently subordinated to a parabolic narrative openly stressing the interrelation between depicted event and thematic line. In a few instances Tolstoy's ethical imperiousness does overwhelm his esthetic pattern, but even in so notorious a story as *The Kreutzer Sonata*, with all of its revulsion from human sexuality and its tirades against both male desire and female coquetry, there are still keen Tolstoyan renderings and insights, bitter but accurate, into the miseries of marriage. What he would call "the tragedy of the bedroom" is strongly insinuated as a universal plight of *post coitum triste*, the affliction that manifests itself as hostility between the sexes after "the cessation of sexuality." This quoted phrase comes from the character Podznyshev, the *raisonneur* of *The Kreutzer Sonata*, and notwithstanding a few humanizing touches at the story's end, we must assume that he speaks as Tolstoy's mouthpiece, so unrelenting is his voice and so little resistance does the story, either through other characters or Tolstoy himself, offer to his outpouring of wrath.

Excessive, even brutal, *The Kreutzer Sonata* is far from Tolstoy at his best. Yet only hopeless romantics would deny that even in this dour story Tolstoy seizes upon portions of truth.

The relationship in the late Tolstoy between the esthetic and the ethical is always unsettled—it is not the monolithic dogmatism that many readers suppose. In a very fine story like *Master and Man* the ethical thrust emerges clearly even before its climax, but in this sort of quasi-allegorical piece it hardly matters. So gratifying is the narrative itself and so elegantly does the ethical suffuse the action of the story that we become quite content to be guided to a foreseeable conclusion. The merchant Brekhunov and his servant Nikita get lost on a journey during a snowstorm; their sled provides slight refuge; the merchant, snug in his fur coat, throws himself upon the freezing body of the servant:

> He no longer heard the horse's movements or the whistlings of the wind, but only Nikita's breathing. At first and for a long time Nikita lay motionless, then he sighed deeply and moved. "There, and you say you are dying! Lie still and get warm, that's our way . . ." began [Brekhunov].

In part *Master and Man* is a fable of fraternity, in which signs of status and power are brushed aside, clearly following Tolstoy's fixed design more than any realized sense of verisimilitude; but Tolstoy's design—some would say, his will—is so commanding that we grant him a fusion of image and idea, esthetic and ethical. Especially touching, one of those fine Tolstoyan details, is Brekhunov's remark "that's our way"—the "way" of all God-fearing Russians, the noblesse oblige of the gentry, the democracy of mankind, or what? It hardly matters; what suffices is the story's openness of possibility.

Another of Tolstoy's late stories, *Father Sergius*, centers on a figure of such fierce moral passion that it becomes tempting to see him as Tolstoy's surrogate. Upon learning that his fiancée had been a mistress of the emperor, Prince Kasatsky forsakes the ugliness of the world to become a monk. But he continues to be captive to his "passion for distinguishing himself," a passion not exactly unknown to Tolstoy himself. In his new life as Father Sergius, the prince still wishes "to be [morally] above those who considered themselves his superiors." He undergoes a series of tests, the first of these with a society beauty who schemes to lure him into a sexual encounter—and he can resist only by the desperate act of chopping off a finger. While actually a sign of weakness, at least in the eyes of Tolstoy and his character, this wins him fame as a holy man, bringing with it a sequence of tragicomic confusions in which he is beset by pilgrims begging for miracle cures. Father Sergius tries to resist but again the drives of his character, what might be called his "true self," push him into acts of vanity which, to everyone but him, seem saintly. At the end, in a last reaching toward humility, Father Sergius is glimpsed as a hired hand in Siberia, but Tolstoy refrains from telling us whether the monk has indeed managed to rein in his desires and subdue his will.

Life itself, the story suggests, is the temptation—life and the world in which it must be endured. About *Father Sergius* Tolstoy said, "The old man wrote it well," and he was right: here surface and implication are almost completely joined. Almost: for when Father Sergius turns toward an old peasant woman, Pashenka, for guidance out of his self-torments and finds it in her unassuming ethical goodness, we feel the uneasiness which Tolstoy's resort to the saintliness of the simple usually produces.

The dominating masterpiece among Tolstoy's later works is *Hadji Murad*, often praised as an instance of how the old Tolstoy, for once abandoning his tiresome moralizing, returns to the purity of art. But that is a misreading—the purity of art is for Tolstoy (perhaps for all serious writers) achievable only through the impurity of moral substance. This supposedly unmarred narrative actually advances all of the old Tolstoy's sentiments and ideas: the rejection of worldly authority, in this instance both Russian and Tatar, which underlies his "Christian anarchism" (the great Russian critic Boris Eichenbaum calls it "social anarchism"); the disdain for all bureaucratic modes of behavior, whether in public affairs or private relations; the sympathy for "the outsider," here the Tatar chieftain Hadji Murad, who can find a place among neither his own people nor the Russian conquerors. Seamless, even blithe as the prose surface may appear, the story is full of dramatized thought and inducements to persuasion. John Bayley has put this so well, I cede the floor to him:

> . . . the parabolic conception of art which he had come to hold had the unexpected effect of making his artistry seem more . . . and not less evident—the smell of art is also the smell of a moral. [*Hadji Murad*] can be seen as a marvelous esthetic object from which the perishable matter of assertion and dogma have been drained off. . . . But in fact . . . the story is as full of

tendentious Tolstoyan matter as any other of his works, and as impregnated with the . . . assertiveness of his personality. If it were not so, it would be less remarkable than it is.

Of all the major literary texts in Tolstoy's late years the most problematic is *Resurrection*, a novel we can neither live with easily nor abandon with good conscience. It is a novel little read, condemned by the received opinion that again the old scold brushes aside the pleasures of creativity for the aridity of dogma. Even more tempered judgments suggest that while there are indeed some fine portions, especially the idyllic flashbacks to the youth of its protagonist Prince Nekhlyudov (these might almost have been written by the young Tolstoy), most of the book resembles a tract. But *Resurrection* is much richer in felt life, far less monochromatic than *The Kreutzer Sonata*, if only because the novel form virtually mandates that the artist in Tolstoy reveal himself.

Still, the usual disparagement of *Resurrection* has some truth. We no longer encounter many of those seemingly spontaneous touches of incident and characterization—the surprises of recognition—which light up the earlier novels. We no longer enjoy the free interaction between mind and mind, with Tolstoy maintaining the optimal distance of a serene narrator. Something has happened, a shift from the depiction of life to a stringent interpretation—but that puts the matter too simply, for there is of course plenty of interpretation in the earlier Tolstoy and a quantity of depiction in the later. Say, rather, that in *Resurrection* we are always aware that his artistry is driven by "a definite purpose," certainly more doctrinal than the purpose of "looking into the human soul."

The story itself is apparently familiar even to many people who have not read it. Prince Nekhlyudov, well-born and pleasing in manner, seduces the young maid Katusha, and more through thoughtlessness than malice, abandons her. Years later, serving as a juror in a sordid trial, he recognizes a defendant, a worn-out woman of the streets, as the once lovely girl he had seduced. Again through that carelessness which Tolstoy saw as a privilege of the powerful, Nekhlyudov acquiesces in her conviction, though in fact she is innocent. But then, through a severe examination of his own past, he undergoes a change of mind (more than of heart) and recognizes that he is responsible for Katusha's plight. As an act of contrition he accompanies the wronged woman to Siberia and, in the same rational spirit, offers to marry her; but sensing the abstractness of his decision, she refuses him. Finally, Nekhlyudov begins "an entirely new life," though what it will be like and whether the effort will succeed Tolstoy, as at the end of *Father Sergius*, shrewdly avoids saying. And perhaps it is just as well.

There is a sense in which *Resurrection* is the most Dostoevskian of Tolstoy's novels, dealing as it does with themes of guilt, self-accusation, and renewal. While this has of course its strong interest, it does not account for what I take to be the power of the book. The modern reader, perhaps because such a reader is likely to be closer in sensibility to the rationalist Tolstoy than to the visionary Dostoevsky, may find Nekhlyudov's self-transformation less persuasive, certainly less exciting, than that of, say, Raskolnikov in *Crime and Punishment*. A Tolstoyan in style of thought if not in explicit ideas, Nekhlyudov goes through his conversion largely as an exercise in rational self-scrutiny; he makes a considered moral judgment, so that his "purging of the soul," in Tolstoy's phrase, seems to lack the psychic vitality and high rapture of a Dostoevskian spiritual conversion. There is a certain dryness to Nekhlyudov's experience, especially if it is momentarily detached from its encasing Tolstoyan reflections. ("Life only requires us to do what is right," says Nekhlyudov to his sister, and "with a sigh"—that sigh is one of Tolstoy's sharp details—she replies, "I don't understand.")

Tolstoy, then, is not really the master of reincarnation that Dostoevsky is. We are told by Tolstoy that the youthful Nekhlyudov enters "a state of exaltation" upon discovering "all the beauty and significance of life. . . . That year he had read [Herbert] Spencer's *Social Statics*. . . ." Perhaps serious people in the late nineteenth century felt otherwise, but by now the linkage of Spencer and "exaltation" seems faintly comic.

The spiritual wanderings of Pierre Bezukhov in *War and Peace* are not only relieved by Tolstoy's affectionate smile—and, still more, by Pierre's self-mockery—but also climaxed by the portrayal of Pierre at the close of the book as a seriously reflective man though deeply troubled and uncertain, perhaps soon to become a Decembrist. Even by the last page, we cannot quite fix Pierre: he slips out of our descriptions. By contrast, Nekhlyudov's conversion, though rendered with much earnestness, seems something settled in advance, as to both its direction and its magnitude. In fairness to the old magician, it should be added, however, that he focuses several times upon the moments of smugness that mark Nekhlyudov's ponderings, quite as he had recognized the pride behind Father Sergius's plunges into humiliation.

When Nekhlyudov decides to tell Katusha that it is he who

had wronged her, Tolstoy remarks: "The idea that, on moral grounds, he was ready to sacrifice everything and marry her made him feel very warm and tender toward himself. . . ." But Katusha—this forms another fine moment—will not let Nekhlyudov "make use of her spiritually as he had done physically, nor would she allow herself to be an object for magnanimity on his part." In her rejection of Nekhlyudov, the battered Katusha achieves a pitch of eloquence:

> "Go away from me! I am a convict and you are a prince, and you've no business here," she cried, her whole face distorted with anger. . . . "You want to save yourself through me. . . . You had your pleasure from me in this world, and now you want to get your salvation through me in the world to come! You disgust me—with your spectacles and your fat ugly mug!"

That this woman, in her anger against Nekhlyudov, should notice his "fat ugly mug" is the kind of enhancing detail we expect from Tolstoy—Tolstoy at any age. The old master could still command the resources of his art when he chose to, but the argument I want to make for *Resurrection* depends mainly on another and riskier mode of perception.

If, as I believe, a case can be made for the greatness of *Resurrection*, it is not of the kind we are likely to provide with regard to most novels. The greatness of this book resides not primarily in the narrative of Nekhlyudov's journey from betrayal to contrition, nor in the finely (if faintly) drawn figure of Katusha as innocent maiden and exploited woman. It resides in what happens near and about these figures, in the events for which they serve mainly as literary auxiliaries or catalysts; in the thickly brushed depictions of what the world calls justice, the sadism it calls punishment, the heartlessness of what it declares to be civilization, and the humiliations of those forgotten and obscure souls upon whom it turns its back. Here Tolstoy's "Christian anarchism" comes into full play, not merely as a theoretical option or ideological position but as a great upswell of moral fury, an outpouring of rage and shame.

John Bayley, though certainly responsive to these aspects of Tolstoy's late writings, makes the criticism that the rejection of "worldliness" which he rightly sees as a central motif in *Resurrection* leads Tolstoy to "close his eyes to the kind of justice which [worldliness] may be capable of administering, even in a corrupt society." A standard rebuttal might be that what Bayley says does not really engage Tolstoy's book, since he is making a political argument for moderate liberalism while Tolstoy is writing a work of the literary imagination—that is, the two move along different planes of discourse. But with regard to *Resurrection* such a rebuttal would be too easy, for this is explicitly and by design a tendentious novel and therefore critics ought to have the right to make, at least in part, tendentious criticisms.

In *Resurrection* Tolstoy writes as both artist and rhetorician. He wants to create a work of art and also to convert readers to a moral position. And he does this through a prophetic stance, so that his moral condemnations must be as sweeping as those of prophets customarily are. He cannot stop to notice, let alone accept, the reasonable view that a measure of justice may be possible even in a "corrupt" society. And this for at least two reasons. First, he offers the tacit but strong argument that the conditions prevailing in czarist Russia, a society that enforces the social gap between Nekhlyudov and

Katusha, makes the unjust trial at the center of the book entirely typical (if not inevitable). Second, he writes out of a deep persuasion that the very presence of organized government entails injustice—and at this point his prophetic stance and his Christian anarchism come together. In every prophetic posture there is likely to be an anarchist strain—a total rejection of society as it exists, an unqualified assault upon the prevailing morality, all declared with impatience and righteousness. That is one reason prophetic utterances can be tremendously powerful while still usually being taken more as incitements to conscience than guides to action. The prophet's cry is not reasonable in the way John Bayley's critical point is; that cry cannot be met by declaring the prophet's case to be extreme, since he has made it precisely in order to be extreme. The old Tolstoy has no interest in compromise.

The central thrust of *Resurrection* is Tolstoy's moral passion as it becomes, so to say, an autonomous presence, almost a "character" in the novel, released at times through direct authorial statement and at other times rendered through brilliant scenes such as those which show the sufferings of prisoners on the way to Siberia. If you start with a strict Flaubertian conception of the novel, all this will seem superfluous and unintegrated; but Tolstoy rejected such a conception of the novel. He looms before us, the old man grand in his dishevelment, refusing to make peace with the world, ferocious in his monomania. He looms *within* the novel, his voice filling its every space, speaking as the godlike judge who will not heed moderate cautions but keeps asking the one question before which even the most humane liberalism must tremble: Why should these things be?

The shackled prisoners march through the city, and a little boy

> knew without any doubt—he was quite sure, for he had the knowledge straight from God, that these people were just the same as he and everyone else was, and therefore something wicked had been done to them, something that ought not to be done and he was sorry for them, and horrified not only at the people who were shaved and fettered but at the people who had fettered and shaved them.

I do not suppose anyone but the old Tolstoy could get away with saying about the little boy's knowledge that "he had [it] straight from God." And then the scene in which the prisoners lie about in the Siberian muck and Nekhlyudov sees that

> all the vices which developed among the convicts . . . were neither accidents nor signs of mental and physical degeneration (as certain obtuse scientists have declared, to the satisfaction of the government) but that they were the inevitable result of the delusion that one group of human beings has the right to punish another.

I wish to be clear. The case I am proposing—it can be validated, if at all, only by a full reading of the book—is not, as a sympathetic reader has put it, that in *Resurrection* Tolstoy "stepped outside the framework of pure art." No; it is that he has himself stepped *into* the framework of the novel, so that the force of his moral passion becomes, as it were, transformed into something very like the matter of art—of art and also of his truth, which, like the little boy watching the prisoners, he has had "straight from God." For if God vouchsafed it to anyone, who else could it be but the old magician?

The Famous Details

Tolstoy's contemporaries were quick to respond to the striking—we can by now say, the famous—details that are strewn through *War and Peace* and that have since given pleasure to generations of readers. They were not, however, as enchanted by these details as we are likely to be. Some felt that they were gratuitous, mannered, even pretentious. A good friend, P. Annenkov, is quoted in Boris Eichenbaum's study of Tolstoy as having written in 1865 that the novel "is amazing for its perception of infinitely small details . . . and even more for the fact that nothing comes of this." Turgenev, in whom it seems reasonable to suspect some jealousy, wrote in the same year: "All these little items cunningly marked off and artificially expressed, petty psychological observations which, on the pretext of offering 'the truth,' [Tolstoy] plucks from his heroes' sleeves . . . —how wretched all this is on the broad canvas of the historical novel."

But perhaps Turgenev did not really grasp what Tolstoy was trying to do, that is, to bring together, in a fresh way, the panoramic sweep of the historical novel with those domestic "little items cunningly marked off." For a novelist like Turgenev, in whose work psychological insights are not usually marked off but seem to emerge "naturally" as part of a lyrical flow, Tolstoy's annotations had to seem an alien irritant. And then too Turgenev may have been anticipating the Flaubertian distaste for authorial "intrusions"—a criticism Tolstoy would have dismissed out of hand.

As many later readers have seen, Tolstoy's "little items" form an integral part of *War and Peace*, simultaneously set off from and, as it were, also set within the narrative. They fall into several groups: remarks made by the characters; tiny bits of action, dumb show, revealing Tolstoy's unspoken attitudes; and direct statements, *aperçus* delivered by Tolstoy the narrator (nor is there any reason plausibly to concoct a fictional persona here; it is really Tolstoy himself whose voice we hear). Putting aside such all-too-famous incidents as Prince Andrei's reflections on the battlefield, I will cite a few from each group.

The Characters Speak:

Pierre encounters a number of soldiers who are discussing the prospects of death; the larger action of the novel is suspended for a time as they reflect upon fear, courage, fatalism. Comprising a sort of chorus introduced as an interval, they seem to distribute among themselves the range of Tolstoyan opinions. (I, 2)

Nikolai Rostov, bewildered during battle, sees some French soldiers rushing toward him. "Can they be running at me?" he asks himself. "And why? To kill me? *Me* whom everyone is so fond of?" Fear releases an innocence of egoism which in ordinary circumstances would be held in check. (I, 2)

Prince Andrei, projecting onto a great oak tree his feelings of disillusion, imagines that the tree speaks back to him: "Spring, and love, and happiness! . . . the same stupid, meaningless tale . . ." Immediately afterward, he overhears the two young girls, Natasha and Sonya, talking in the silence of night, ecstatic about the beauty of the moon. Lost within himself, Prince Andrei can only think, as if Natasha's pleasure has no independent existence, that "for her I might as well not exist." (II, 3)

Speaking through Gesture:

Natasha, watching the "half-naked" society women at the opera, feels "an impulse to give a tap of her fan to an old gentleman sitting not far from her, or lean over to Hélène and tickle her." To tickle that marble-cold, imperturbable beauty: Will she jump? laugh? Can her surface calm be broken? (II, 5)

During an interval in the war Prince Andrei encounters a group of soldiers bathing in a lake. " 'Flesh, bodies, *chair à canon*,' he reflected, looking at his own naked body and shuddering, not so much with cold as with aversion and horror, incomprehensible even to himself, aroused by the sight of that immense multitude of bodies splashing about in the dirty lake." The horror, we may infer, is caused by Andrei's anticipation of what will soon be happening to that "multitude of bodies." (III, 2)

Natasha, married and deep into domesticity, reads a letter from "a certain Prince Fiodr" inviting Pierre to a public discussion—and then a telling parenthesis from Tolstoy: "(she read all her husband's letters)." Of course; their state of bliss is not without sloth. (Epilogue, 1)

In *Anna Karenina*, as the relationship between Anna and Vronsky grows increasingly strained, there occurs an incident (easy enough for the casual reader to pass by) that is full of a terrible significance. The two have quarreled, Vronsky feels Anna's jealousy has become unbearable, and he decides to leave the house.

> Then she heard the sound of the carriage, and the door open, and he went out again. But now he was back in the hall, and someone ran upstairs. It was his valet who had run back for the gloves his master had forgotten. [Anna] went to the window and saw him take the gloves without looking up, tap the coachman on the back and say something to him. Then, without a glance at the window, he settled himself in the carriage, crossing one leg over the other in his usual fashion, and, pulling on a glove, disappeared round the corner.

The aplomb with which Vronsky pulls on his glove "in his usual fashion" tells Anna all she needs to know of his readiness to return to his old way of life, thereby dismissing her despair and anger. The gloves come to signify the virtual breakdown not of their love but of their relationship, which cannot rest on love alone. Without saying a word to her, he has declared himself.

Tolstoy's Voice:

His comparison of the full-bosomed Hélène with the as-yet-undeveloped Natasha, begun as a visual contrast, takes on moral point through a concluding remark: "Hélène seemed, as it were, covered with the hard polish left by the thousands of eyes that had scanned her person. . . ." (II, 3)

Nikolai Rostov, a major character who for a time has been treated with a certain respect, is placed by an anticipatory sentence that prepares us for the conventional landowner he will finally become: "He possessed the common sense of the mediocre man which showed him what he ought to do." (II, 4)

There are scores of such details scattered through *War and Peace* and *Anna Karenina*, and we may well ask: What are they doing there? What is their function? Clever and charming, sometimes even profound in their own right, what relation do they bear to each novel as a whole? D. S. Mirsky in his *History of Russian Literature* shrewdly calls these "elusive details" an "accompaniment," something that enters, as a subsidiary harmonic element, the larger historical sweep of the narrative. But more is at stake. The details serve as a counterforce or counter presence to that historical sweep which dominates Tolstoy's novels; nor does Tolstoy hesitate to signal this meaning, pointing to the values of daily existence:

> Meanwhile life—actual everyday life with its essential concerns of health and sickness, work and recreation, and its intellectual preoccupations with philosophy, science, poetry, music, love, friendship, hatred, passion—ran its regular course, independent and heedless of political alliance or enmity with Napoleon Bonaparte. . . .

As Boris Eichenbaum writes: "A densely detailed and principled domesticity has been released upon literature to counterbalance social and political themes." The little details perform this function within "the broad canvas of the historical novel."

Tone in Fiction

WHEN EMPLOYED IN literary discussion, the word "tone" reminds one of what Dr. Johnson said about light: everyone knows what it is but no one can describe it. Tone has some kinship to style, yet is rather different. Perhaps it helps to say that tone is an emanation of style, that the arrangement of words in a fiction can shape its stresses. Most critics, whether or not they use the word, resort to some equivalent of tone: there is really no escaping it. Some critics even find it a supreme test of their acuity to be able to describe or evoke the tone of a work of fiction.

Nor is this easy to do. It requires that the critic have what Hazlitt has called "the power of that trembling sensibility which is awake to every change and every modification of its ever-varying impressions." These words of a great critic lead to the writings of a great novelist. In the novels of Stendhal, especially *The Red and the Black*, there is so rapid and frequent a change of tone, from abrasive irony to lucid statement and back again, that it becomes very difficult to account for its tone. Stendhal is too shifty for our ears. The best we can do is probably a rough approximation of Stendhal's dominant tone, with the hope that it allows for some awareness of the many modulations that occur from page to page.

With other writers we may succeed somewhat more, since few are as tricky or agile as Stendhal. But even in the work of glum, tone-deaf naturalists like Theodore Dreiser and James T. Farrell, you can find—it takes a bit of listening—some modulations of tone, usually in the form of slight variations upon a single note.

When we speak of the tone of a novel, we are implying that we hear a "voice." That voice speaks to us, whether through an omniscient narrator or an interplay of dialogue or whatever. But there is of course a crucial difference between the "voice" of a written work and the voice of a person engaged in conversation. Listening to a person who talks to us, we can usually tell with fair accuracy which tone is being employed: whether deadly serious or lightly ironic or wistfully elegiac. Even in speech, mistakes and confusions occur, but usually we trust our ears, if only because most speakers want their tone to register (unless they are in circumstances where precision of tone might be dangerous). Oral delivery entails a range of nonverbal devices—bodily gestures, facial expressions—that indicate or complicate tone. With written prose, however, things become more difficult, since in "hearing" prose we often have to supply the tone ourselves, inferring through attention to lexical and rhetorical cues which tone is intended. This is a notoriously unreliable procedure, accounting in part for the different interpretations a literary work can receive.

Some novelists, usually the more traditional ones, try to defeat this problem by providing what might be called stage directions: "Mary spoke in a voice of rising anger," "John replied with a touch of derisive irony." But modern novelists have largely abandoned such devices, either because they find them crude or because they wish to confer upon their readers the blessings of ambiguity. (Which tone do you hear in that last clause?) And even when descriptive nouns and adjectives are employed, they are likely to be helpful only in making out local passages. There remains the problem of the novel's tone as a whole or even whether it is possible to describe a novel's tone as a whole.

In an essay written some years ago about the fiction of Isaac Babel, John Berryman said that Babel's tone is "jaunty and dubious." That is a good description, though the word "dubious" in this context may be a little dubious. I would myself prefer to say about Babel's stories that they are "aggressive and melancholy," but without much confidence that my description is any better than Berryman's. For there is a subjective element in "hearing" a piece of prose, and what matters about the two descriptions of Babel's tone is that both recognize the tension of inner conflict—as if there were two Babels jarring one another. Still, to recognize the subjective aspect in the reception of tone is not to suggest that all our responses are equally valid. Some are just wrong.

A famous confusion of tone deliberately created by the writer is to be found in Daniel Defoe's *The Shortest Way with Dissenters* (1702). This brilliant piece of mimicry is written as the supposed rant of a High Churchman excoriating the Dissenters. ("If the Gallows instead of the Counter, and the Gallies instead of the Fines, were the Reward of going to a Conventicle, to preach or hear, there wou'd not be so many sufferers.") Composed in a tone of mock gravity, this polemical satire was so sharp a piece of counterfeit that it took in friend and foe. It earned for Defoe a heavy fine and three trips to the pillory—people do not like to be fooled, not even by clever writers.

The same gift for deceptive mimicry is to be found in Defoe's novels. At least with *The Shortest Way* we know by now what his intentions were, but with *Moll Flanders*, his pioneering novel, we cannot say with any assurance whether he was echoing a drab mercantilist view of life or was engaging in a sly takeoff. Nor does the presence of a few passages clearly ironic in tone settle the matter. So it seems as if the critical debate about *Moll Flanders* could go on forever.

A writer especially sensitive to tone is Marcel Proust. Here is a suggestive passage from *Cities on the Plain*:

> There are times when, to paint a complete portrait of someone, we should have to add a phonetic imitation [that is, of tone] to our verbal description, and our portrait of the figure that M. Charlus presented is liable to remain incomplete in the absence of that little laugh, so delicate, so light, just as certain works of Bach are never accurately rendered because our orchestras lack those small, high trumpets, with a sound so entirely their own, for which the composer wrote this or that part.

Not even a linguist could improve on this passage about the way behavioral context helps to determine the "voice" of a novel. In the same volume Proust engages the problem of tone through a number of examples:

> Mme de Cambremer loved to tease other people in a way that was often highly impertinent. As soon as she began to attack me, or anyone else, in this fashion, M. de Cambremer would start watching her victim with a laugh. As the Marquis had a squint—a blemish which gives the impression of intended wit to the mirth even of imbeciles—the effect of this laughter was to bring a segment of pupil into the otherwise complete whiteness of his eye. Thus does a sudden rift bring a patch of blue into an otherwise clouded sky. His monocle moreover protected, like the glass over a valuable picture, this delicate operation. As for the actual intention of his laughter, it was hard to say whether it was friendly: "Ah! you rascal, you're a lucky man and no mistake! You've won the favor of a woman with a very pretty wit." Or vicious: "Well then, I hope you'll learn your lesson when you've swallowed all those insults." Or obliging: "I'm here, you know. I take it with a laugh because it's all pure fun, but I shan't let you be ill-treated." Or cruelly conniving: "I don't need to add my little pinch of salt, but you can be sure I'm enjoying all the snubs she's handing out to you."

Proust offers a number of possibilities, all the more tantalizing because these refer to a minor character about whose intentions we can hardly be certain. So we had better let it go at that, quite as, in ordinary experience, we also have to.

In the course of reading we seldom think of tone as if it were something separable from the rest of a work of fiction. Our apprehension of tone comes to us through an integral grasp of the work as a whole. Intuitively, we try to determine the tone of a novel by focusing on one or another of its crucial elements—the writer's "intrusive" comments, if there are any, or the interplay of the voices of the characters, or the gradual emergence of the narrative's main themes or concerns. Sometimes this apprehension of tone through our grasp of the novel as a whole can occur very quickly—we sense that our writer will probably stick to one dominant note; sometimes it takes some sustained reflection after we have finished the last page.

Let us now turn to a few novels.

The Bostonians

About the tone of Henry James's *The Bostonians* there can be little doubt. It is a tone of sustained coldness, directed against both the milieu it depicts—late-nineteenth-century Boston—which James sees as marking a decline in New England culture, and the characters in the novel, all of whom are treated not quite with enmity, which might after all entail a certain closeness of feeling, but with something like disdain, a distancing response. There is a virtually complete withdrawal of affect with regard to the characters, something rare in fiction since in most novels there are one or two characters who elicit a certain tenderness from the author. The coldness of tone in *The Bostonians*—neither violent nor even impassioned—is a rarity, as if the writer were fastidiously examining a minor species.

On first meeting the central female character, Olive Chancellor, we are told that a smile played about her lips that "might have been likened to a thin ray of moonlight resting upon the walls of a prison." We are invited to see the central male character, the reactionary Southerner Basil Ransom, as an opinionated provincial: "he had read Comte, he had read everything," and we are further told that he considered women to be "essentially inferior to men and infinitely tiresome when they refused to accept the lot which men had made for them." Selah Tarrant, the mesmerist father of the pliant young heroine, Verena, "looked like the priest of a religion that was passing through the stage of miracles." Matthias Pardon, a venomous reporter, "regarded the mission of mankind upon earth as a perpetual evolution of telegrams." The ancient Abolitionist Miss Birdseye has "no more outline than a bundle of hay."

The coldness of tone which runs through *The Bostonians* is neither fortuitous nor a mere sign of personal eccentricity; it expresses a radical dissociation on James's part from a cultural milieu which he sees as the locale of moral disorder and pretension. His dismissal of the ideological obsessions controlling his major characters is pitiless, unrelenting, perhaps even shocking to an admirer of his other novels, since there is nothing here of his characteristic hovering over "the poor shabby gentlemen" and misguided young women "affronting" their destiny. The Bostonians who disliked James's novel were, from their point of view, justified—they saw it as a cultural attack, which indeed it was.

Perhaps most remarkable about the tone of *The Bostonians* is the steadiness with which James maintains it, a cold glare from start to finish. It is all, in this brilliant novel, like the coldness of a clear winter day when it can seem that the line of our vision is endless.

Remembrance of Things Past

It would be absurd to claim that there is a single dominating tone in a work as complex and lengthy as Proust's great novel. Each of the seven volumes has its own distinctive tone: the sweet lyricism of childhood remembered in *Swann's Way*, the often sardonic representations of French society in the middle volumes, the nervous inwardness of *The Captive*, the sad preparation for death in *The Past Recaptured*. Within each volume there are also numerous shifts of tone, some abrupt and startling. Yet I want to assert that coursing through the entire work, like a half-suppressed motif, is a recognizable undertone or subtone which shapes the meaning and holds together the work's component narratives. It is a subtone of lament that bears a certain resemblance to a ground bass in music, that repeated phrase which lies beneath the stronger melody of the moment. This subtone of lament, struck only lightly and occasionally in the opening volume, grows more frequent in later pages, and by *The Past Recaptured*—all this survives translation—it swells to a sustained expression. It keeps repeating that Time is merciless, nothing can keep it from going about its task of destruction.

In Proust's second volume, *Within a Budding Grove*, he inserts a description of this lament that seems exactly right. He speaks of "murmurings of a long-drawn melancholy." These "murmurings" are clearly Proust's, though faintly disguised as those of the narrator, Marcel. They are further described in the same volume as reflecting "the long, desperate, daily resistance to the fragmentary and continuous death that insinuates itself throughout the whole course of our life." This ground bass, as I have called it, brings death ever closer to our consciousness and sees it as present even when apparently stored beneath our consciousness. It speaks of Time lost— also, for a moment, of Time regained, though that too will soon be lost. A silent implacable enemy, Time hovers over us even in those rare "privileged moments" which, through involuntary memory, bring an ecstasy of transcendence that, in turn, creates a brief comfort of timelessness.

In *The Guermantes Way* a remarkable passage likens the individual to an actor in a play who, once the curtain drops, must suffer "dissolution which . . . causes one to doubt the reality of the self and to meditate on the mystery of death." This death serves as an accomplice of memory, not least at the very end when Marcel feels that he has won a victory over death, if but for a moment, by entering a state of joy that links present sensation with an event lost to the past. For death creates a sharpened awareness, that "impression," writes Proust, "at once so particular and so spontaneous which the sudden revelation of death, striking like a thunderbolt, had carved within me."

What begins as a subdued note of anxiety becomes in Proust's final pages an onrushing music of death. It had earlier reached a moment of eloquence in *The Captive* when Proust apostrophized Bergotte's death: "They buried him, but all through that night of mourning, in the lighted shop-windows, his books, arranged three by three, kept vigil like angels with outspread wings and seemed, for him who was no more, the symbol of his resurrection." In this great passage we find an anticipation of the concluding theme that art can serve as a triumph over the blackness of extinction, the terror of nothingness, yet a few pages later, writing about the death of Swann, Proust takes a grimmer view:

> For we talk of "Death" for convenience, but there are almost as many different deaths as there are people. . . . Often they are deaths that will not be entirely relieved of their duties until two or, even three years later. They come in haste to plant a tumour in the side of a Swann, then depart to attend to other tasks, returning only when, the surgeons having performed their operations, it is necessary to plant the tumour there afresh.

A little further along Marcel connects the "secrets of death" with the beloved "little phrase" in Vinteuil's music, the phrase that has haunted him all his life and is now revealed to be a preparation for "the secrets of death." The tone of the prose keeps darkening as if in obedience to "the general law of oblivion," and for only a moment can Marcel's memories of Combray and Venice "suffice, without any further proof, to make death a matter of indifference to me." What had begun as the ground note of the entire work tends increasingly to subdue the various tones of each volume.

Arriving finally at the party of the Princess de Guermantes, Marcel encounters a roomful of bent, white-haired people and thinks at first that some masquerade is in progress. But he soon realizes that the drawing room was "like a peaceful cemetery," a cemetery that contains his life. Waiting in an anteroom for a musical performance to be finished, he experiences some of his "privileged moments," those gifts of memory that yield a rare happiness. They do not last.

What Marcel gains in these moments might be called a glimpse of the Absolute. One critic has written about Proust that "in man's long struggle with Time, it is man, thanks to the . . . charms of art, who remains the victor." So we might conclude from the final paragraphs of *The Past Recaptured*, that peal of triumph with which the novel ends. But by now the tone that I have called the ground bass has risen to a crescendo, holding at the very least an equal place with the note of victory.

> The idea of death took up permanent residence within me in the way that love sometimes does. Not that I loved death, I abhorred it . . . its image adhered now to the most profound layer of my mind, so completely that I could not give my attention to anything without that thing first traversing the idea of death. . . .

(Shortly before Proust's death, he reportedly cried out to his housekeeper, Celeste, that "she [death] is huge and all in black. I'm afraid of her. Don't touch me, Celeste, she is implacable, and she gets more and more horrible.")

The "victory" of art, echoing through Time and perhaps holding off its destruction, is certainly there in the concluding pages of the novel, but so too is the ground bass, the swelling tone of the prose:

> No doubt my books too, like my fleshly being, [says Marcel], would in the end one day die. But death is a thing that we must resign ourselves to. We accept the thought that in ten years we ourselves, in a hundred years our books, will have ceased to exist. Eternal duration is promised no more to men's works than to men.

Art decays like life, and in the end there is only the dust of centuries.

Tender Is the Night

In the mature novels of F. Scott Fitzgerald—*The Great Gatsby, Tender Is the Night, The Last Tycoon*—there are frequent passages of direct authorial comment that are striking for their powers of moral and psychological generalization. If Fitzgerald was in many respects faithful to the Flaubertian idea of the art novel, his use of such passages—often epigrammatic and "poetic" in tone—marked a break from the master. Like Stendhal and George Eliot (the comparison goes no further), Fitzgerald did not hesitate to place himself as a commanding presence or voice in his novels, and often with high eloquence. When successful, such "intrusions" of authorial comment add richness to the work and help to propel and deepen its story. But such a method can be very risky, and in some instances, as with a great writer like Faulkner, the results may turn out to be dismaying.

With Fitzgerald, the inclusion of such reflective passages comes to seem an integral part of the narrative, a kind of moral ligature binding segments of the work. Bringing together personal charm and reflective gravity, such passages work especially well in *The Great Gatsby*. Having apparently learned from Henry James, Fitzgerald introduces a character, Nick Carraway, who serves as commentator-observer of the action, often, it seems clear, speaking for the author himself: "I was within and without, simultaneously enchanted and repelled by the inexhaustible variety of life." When an author speaks in his own right within a novel, possible dangers include excessive subjectivity and ponderousness of tone, but if his surrogate character, someone like Nick Carraway, becomes an interesting figure with his own distinctive qualities, then the recurrent commentary can flow into the narrative. So I would contend that the tone of *The Great Gatsby*—a kind of wry reflectiveness—draws heavily upon the passages of comment.

No such semidetached observer as Nick Carraway appears in *Tender Is the Night*, and while it remains a deeply moving work, it seems deficient for lack of such a character, especially since Fitzgerald is tempted into damaging alliances with some of the figures in his book.

The passages of direct statement—a Fitzgerald aficionado can quote them as if they were lines in Shakespeare's sonnets —endow the novel with a strong emotional vibration, sometimes in excess of what the narrative can sustain. At their best, such passages, providing Fitzgerald's unmistakable signature, shape the tone of this novel, a tone of mature reflectiveness or sadness, deeper than that of *The Great Gatsby*, though not as uniformly successful. But in my own reading, the strong emotions elicited by such passages have less to do with the events or characters of the novel than with the novelist's voice, hovering in the background and speaking with the tones of exquisite courtesy that form Fitzgerald's distinctive mark.

The passages I have in mind are well known, but let me cite just a few. About halfway through the novel, in Section XI, Dick Diver has been trying to keep his emotions about Nicole his wife separate from his emotions about Nicole his patient. The text continues:

This made it difficult now to distinguish between his self-protective professional detachment and some new coldness in his heart. As an indifference cherished, or left to atrophy, becomes an emptiness, to this extent he had learned to become empty of Nicole, serving her against his will with negations and emotional neglect. One writes of scars healed, a loose parallel to the pathology of the skin, but there is no such thing in the life of an individual. There are open wounds, shrunk sometimes to the size of a pin-prick but wounds still. The marks of suffering are more comparable to the loss of a finger, or the sight of an eye. We may not miss them, either, for one minute in a year, but if we should there is nothing to be done about it.

It is hard to imagine that any reader would fail to be moved by a passage like this. But sensing perhaps that his narrative suffers from a number of serious flaws, Fitzgerald found himself relying on a good number—indeed, too many—of such golden sentences to carry his story. And so there were times when he strained too hard. Here, for example, Dick has just kissed the young actress Rosemary:

> She clung nearer desperately and once more he kissed her and was chilled by the innocence of her kiss, by the glance that at the moment of contact looked beyond him out into the darkness of night, the darkness of the world. She did not know yet that splendor is something in the heart: at the moment when she realized that and melted into the passion of the universe he could take her without question or regret.

Where the first passage seems an instance of profound seriousness in a prose of pure eloquence, this one is marred by a forced rhetoric, at some points embarrassing in its closeness to the language of popular fiction. ("Melted into the passion of the universe"—grandiose, almost grand.) Another over-strained passage occurs somewhat later in the novel, when Dick sees Rosemary in her hotel room:

> She saw him as something fixed and Godlike as he had always been, as older people are to younger, rigid and unmalleable. . . . It took him a moment to respond to the unguarded sweetness of her smile, her body calculated to a millimeter to suggest a bud yet guarantee a flower.

In each of these last two passages, the first more than the second, a wonderful writer is pressing too hard in the hope of "lifting" his story.

The unevenness of these reflective passages may account for the insecurities of tone—ranging from the sublime to the embarrassing—that recur throughout the novel. And beneath these insecurities of tone there are large troubles of conception, most of all, a greater quantity of released emotion than Fitz-gerald could control.

A Note on George Gissing

Of flaws and faults there is no lack in George Gissing's novels. A twentieth-century novice who has attended a "writers' work-shop" is likely to be more technically adept than Gissing. Ex-cept for his masterpiece *New Grub Street*, most of Gissing's novels are drawn out intolerably in order to fill the Victorian three-decker. His prose style is wooden, flavorless. He tends to argue his themes rather than realizing them through actions.

And yet, as we read Gissing, we come to wait for and take a subdued pleasure in his dominant tone. Sometimes it slips into a self-pitying querulousness, and that is irritating; but almost always this is redeemed by his awareness of "the injustice which triumphs so flagrantly in the destinies of men." Gissing's greatest gift lies in depicting the life of partly educated persons who are unhappy precisely to the extent that they have approached yet cannot enter the precincts of cultivation. He is always aware of how hard it is for men and women simply to get by. He is sensitive to the perplexities (in *The Odd Women*) of intelligent women caught between traditional roles and the programs of feminism.

What we hear in Gissing's novels is a voice of sustained moral seriousness. The tone is troubled, uneasy, utterly plain. Even in his numerous failures, that tone merits respect.

Is this enough to make for a successful fiction? No, I think not. And yet, relieved at having escaped facile virtuosity, we return to those Gissing novels, half-forgotten, so dispirited in their honesty of tone, as if obeying some command of one's soul.

Lolita

Lolita is a comic novel but the comedy turns out to be streaked with sadness, even despair. For about three-quarters of the text, Nabokov's tone is a mixture of jauntiness (larks!) and a taunting derisiveness, as if he took pleasure (I suspect he did) in befuddling his readers, not with modernist obscurities but with his own puzzles of intent and meaning. Every sentence of Nabokov is clear, so too every paragraph; what is hard to make out is the work as a whole. He keeps varying his tone, and part of the pleasure in reading him is the effort to keep up with him. The shifting elements of Nabokov's tone reflect Humbert Humbert's elaborate dissimulations, but also, and harder to pin down, Nabokov's distancing views of those dissimulations. There is Humbert Humbert's cultural persiflage, a European's disdain for American coarseness; his self-pity, the whining of someone who is not really sure he is "above" ordinary moral norms; and his sexuality, which leads him to both lyrical adulation and physical possession of a twelve-year-old girl, his "nymphet."

Of all the "unreliable narrators" in the history of the novel, Humbert Humbert is surely one of the most unreliable. Everything in this novel reaches us through his perceptions, and with a linguistic virtuosity that comes to seem indistinguishable from that of Nabokov himself. Humbert Humbert is "unreliable" in the common ways of most first-person narrators who color everything with subjective bias, and then he is unreliable in ways special to him. To indulge in a bit of Nabokovian hyperbole, he proves unreliable even as an "unreliable narrator." Still, the language Nabokov grants him is so brilliant and funny, and, above all, so enticing in its charm that it lures us into a virtual suspension of moral judgment, deflecting attention from the blunt fact that Humbert Humbert is a murderer as well as a violator of Lolita's youth. We are drawn into the state of "esthetic bliss" which Nabokov declares to be the prime objective of literature—only, that "bliss" brings with it an entrapment in Humbert Humbert's rancid consciousness. For some readers—we do not after all want to be thought of as square—the whole thing may come to seem a delightful romp.

The last part of the novel, especially the powerful chapter 29, in which Humbert Humbert visits Coaltown to find once more his beloved nymphet, evokes urgently his pain at discovering that she is now worn-out at seventeen, married, pregnant, and poor. Still, he loves her. Yet the sense of the damage done by Humbert Humbert becomes clear even to himself: "In her washed-out gray eyes, strangely spectacled, our poor romance was for a moment reflected, pondered upon and dismissed like . . . a bit of dry mud caking her childhood. . . ." And a few pages later: "It had become gradually clear to my conventional Lolita during our singular and bestial cohabitation that even the most miserable of family lives was better than the parody of incest, which, in the long run, was the best I could offer the waif." Repentance—something hardly in Humbert Humbert's line anyway—is by now too late.

In Chapter 29 Nabokov drops his mask of prickly cleverness; the prose is now free of allusions and puns; and the tone assumes a grave severity. But even as Humbert Humbert keeps declaring his love for Lolita, or at least his memory of that love, he goes off to murder the devilish Quilty for having taken his nymphet away. Though no admirer of Dostoevsky, Nabokov seems here to be subscribing to the Dostoevskian notion that each transgressor finds his double.

In a novel told by an "unreliable narrator," the problem of tone is likely to become the problem of interpretation. With superficial pleasure, we can read *Lolita* as a wild caper through the jungles of American popular culture, a journey making few demands for moral severity or even judgment and in which Humbert Humbert's final confession of guilt may well be seen as an exercise in irony, no more to be taken seriously than, say, the concluding pieties of Moll Flanders. Or we may concur with Lionel Trilling's celebration of *Lolita* as a love story of sorts, exalting through the perverse those romantic passions that have slipped away from us in an age more attracted to sex than to love. As Trilling remarks: "We find ourselves the more shocked when we realize that, in the course of reading *Lolita*, we have come virtually to condone the violation it presents."

Until the concluding section of the novel we are likely to find it difficult to decide how Nabokov wants us to feel about Humbert Humbert's obsessional love, if love it is, and what in fact we do feel. To give ourselves to the liveliness of Humbert Humbert's quest and to the brilliance of his language, is probably the easiest way to read this novel, with a suspicion at the end that his statements of repentance are to be taken as the dodges of a man who realizes his time has run out.

But I believe, even if I cannot quite prove, that Nabokov intends us to take seriously Humbert Humbert's several statements of guilt. While unpleasant, Humbert Humbert is certainly intelligent (Nabokov helps him), and there is no reason to call his self-awareness into question. The essential narrative line—the narrative stripped of verbal elaboration—comes then to resemble a morality play. And it is here that we approach the main difficulty with this brilliant work: that mostly its tone stands in conflict, even contradiction to the flow of narrative. Why so self-aware a writer as Nabokov failed to see this, or whether in fact he so intended it, I cannot say.

At the end Humbert Humbert remarks that "Lolita has been deprived of her childhood by a maniac," or in Hawthornesque terms, that he has violated the integrity of her person. Nabokov has said that he believes he has done everything possible to make this clear. But as Wayne Booth remarks in his book *The Rhetoric of Fiction*:

> . . . the laws of art are against [Nabokov]. . . . One of the major delights of this delightful, profound book is that of watching Humbert *almost* make a case for himself. But Nabokov has insured that many, perhaps most, of his readers . . . will identify Humbert with the author more than Nabokov intends. And for them, no amount of final recantation will cancel out the vividness of the earlier scenes.

Perhaps stung by such readers, who were troubled by the moral economy of *Lolita*, Nabokov said in a 1971 interview: "I believe that one day a reappraiser will come and declare that, far from being a frivolous firebird, I was a rigid moralist kicking sin, cuffing stupidity, ridiculing the vulgar and the cruel—and assigning power to tenderness, talent and pride."

We can honor this statement without hesitation, while still remarking upon the distance between the teller and the tone, yet another instance of the treacherous character of art, which, long ago, Plato had already noticed.

Tone

—echoes the writer's inner voice, the voice behind his voice;

—approximates what the reader has "heard," so that it comes to represent an unstable alliance between author and reader; it is the trembling wavelength where the two meet;

—tells us how to take what the words tell us.

Acknowledgments

I OWE A great debt to Ilana Wiener Howe for her assistance and encouragement during the preparation of *A Critic's Notebook*. She has been a wonderful collaborator, and I thank her. I owe much as well to Drenka Willen for her careful and devoted editing of this book. For help of various sorts, I want also to thank David Bromwich, William Bukowski, Paula Fox, Martin Greenberg, John Hollander, Nina Howe, Audrey Jaffe, Georgina Kleege, Nicolaus Mills, Brian Morton, and Leon Wieseltier.

Some of the pieces included in *A Critic's Notebook* were first published, sometimes in slightly different form, in *The New Republic, Pequod, Salmagundi*, and *The Threepenny Review*. I thank their editors for permission to reprint them here. "The Self in Literature" is reprinted with permission of the University of Utah Press from the Tanner Lectures on Human Values, Volume 12, 1991.

Nicholas Howe

Index

Books by Irving Howe
available from Harcourt Brace & Company
in Harvest paperback editions

A Critic's Notebook

A Margin of Hope

Selected Writings, 1950–1990

Socialism and America